Knowing Enough.

A CONVERSATION ABOUT MONEY AND LIFE

—AND FIGURING OUT WHAT TO DO WITH YOURS

John C. Bogle
William J. Bernstein

Foreword by William Jefferson Clinton

Prologue by Tom Peters, *In Search of Excellence*

WILEY

Published by John Wiley & Sons, Inc., Hoboken, New Jersey.
Published simultaneously in Canada.

The manufacturer's authorized representative according to the EU General Product Safety Regulation is Wiley-VCH GmbH, Boschstr. 12, 69469 Weinheim, Germany, e-mail: Product_Safety@wiley.com.

Trademarks: Wiley and the Wiley logo are trademarks or registered trademarks of John Wiley & Sons, Inc. and/or its affiliates in the United States and other countries and may not be used without written permission. All other trademarks are the property of their respective owners. John Wiley & Sons, Inc. is not associated with any product or vendor mentioned in this book.

Limit of Liability/Disclaimer of Warranty: While the publisher and author have used their best efforts in preparing this book, they make no representations or warranties with respect to the accuracy or completeness of the contents of this book and specifically disclaim any implied warranties of merchantability or fitness for a particular purpose. No warranty may be created or extended by sales representatives or written sales materials. The advice and strategies contained herein may not be suitable for your situation. You should consult with a professional where appropriate. Further, readers should be aware that websites listed in this work may have changed or disappeared between when this work was written and when it is read. Neither the publisher nor authors shall be liable for any loss of profit or any other commercial damages, including but not limited to special, incidental, consequential, or other damages.

For general information on our other products and services or for technical support, please contact our Customer Care Department within the United States at (800) 762-2974, outside the United States at (317) 572-3993 or fax (317) 572-4002.

Wiley also publishes its books in a variety of electronic formats. Some content that appears in print may not be available in electronic formats. For more information about Wiley products, visit our web site at www.wiley.com.

Library of Congress Cataloging-in-Publication Data is Available:

ISBN 9781394278039 (Paperback)
ISBN 9781394278046 (ePub)
ISBN 9781394278053 (ePDF)

Cover Design: Paul McCarthy
Printed and bound by CPI Group (UK) Ltd, Croydon, CR0 4YY

C9781394278039_260325

Contents

Contents

Preface to
Knowing Enough

N o one, and I mean no one, did more for investors than Jack Bogle. My fellow Boglehead Taylor Larimore likes to say that he lives in "the house that Jack built." Count me, and many thousands more, in that happy group.

And millions more, whether they know it or not, sleep well at night without money worries because of the at-cost mutual funds that Jack invented at the Vanguard Group.

A quarter of a century ago, a few dozen people met at Taylor's "house that Jack built" (actually, a condominium overlooking Biscayne Bay) to chat with Jack. He was in town for the *Miami Herald*'s March 2000 Making Money Seminar, which wouldn't make time for the group to talk to Jack. It seems that the *Herald* did not let Muhammad come to the mountain, so the mountain came to Muhammad; Jack went to Taylor's place for a meetup with this little group. (The *Herald*, realizing their mistake, sent a reporter and photographer to Taylor's place and splashed out a front-page story in the following Sunday Business section.)

The attendees by that point had already been cyber-buddies on the Morningstar forum devoted to Vanguard funds. Every year thereafter, save during Covid, the Bogleheads have gathered for an annual fall meeting. As one attendee at the 2001 meeting in Chicago put it, "I told my kids, 'I'm going off to spend the weekend with 50 people I don't know, and I met them on the Internet.'" When journalist Jason Zweig asked the other attendees what their friends and family thought about that, most replied. "They think I'm nuts." I attended my first meeting in 2002, and, to be honest, as I flew out for it the following year I recall asking myself, "Exactly why am I doing this?" As soon as I arrived, I got reminded of the answer: The Bogleheads are the sweetest, best-informed bunch of folks you'd ever want to hang out with.

As educational and enjoyable the annual meetings are, the conference facilities allow for only a few hundred attendees. The bogleheads.com forum, in contrast, has 120,000 registered users, and many more visitors. (Morningstar graciously hosted it initially, after which it became an independent organization.) For my money, it's the single best source of both general and personalized financial advice on the web.

Early on, one contributor to another Morningstar forum posted that he had a rapidly progressive cancer with a fatal prognosis and needed financial advice for his wife and young children. Within days, the Bogleheads offered solid direction about how to handle Social Security, probate, and 401(k) rollovers. As I'm typing this, a fast look at the bogleheads.org home page features posts about how to handle a teenager's first investment account, student loan forgiveness, paying off a mortgage, and more than a dozen threads about asset allocation, as well as one on the choice between a ¼-inch and a ⅜-inch socket wrench set.

Most famously, the Bogleheads epitomize Jack's focus on what he calls "The Majesty of Simplicity," which they formulated as their patented "three-fund portfolio": stone-simple mixes of total U.S. stock market, total international stock market, and total bond market, a portfolio that can now be put together at a cost of just a few one-hundredths of a percent per year.

Jack's great rival in the fund business, Fidelity's Edward C. Johnson III, once derided Vanguard's index funds, opining, "I can't believe that the great mass of investors are going to be satisfied with just receiving average returns." The joke was on him; it turned out that investors increasingly cottoned to the simple arithmetic of mutual fund investing: Because of their low expenses, index funds routinely waxed actively managed ones.

Johnson couldn't have been more wrong: Investors *were* happy with "average" returns. As Vanguard's assets swelled, the resultant increase in economy of scale increased that advantage even more, a "flywheel" that lost Fidelity so much business that it had to bring out its own index funds, and eventually, wait for it, a family of *zero*-cost funds. (There's no free lunch here, of course; once you purchase Fidelity's zero-cost funds, their shares cannot be transferred out of their platform.)

★★★

In 2007 Jack asked me to join him on the conference stage for what became a high point on my personal calendar, a nearly hour-long "fireside chat" during which I'd fire questions at him and, on occasion, educate him about Yiddish expressions. The last of these was in October 2018, shortly before he passed away.

In 2023, Bill Falloon of John Wiley & Sons approached me about a "last fireside chat" memorial volume that combined two books, Jack's *Enough* and my *If You Can*, with all royalties going to the Boglehead charitable arm, the John C. Bogle for Financial Literacy. The two books dovetail nicely: *Enough* is a meditation on the meaning of money and on the ethics of the money management, both of which matter a great deal to the individual investor.

The book's title derives from a conversation between novelists Joseph Heller and Kurt Vonnegut at a soiree thrown by a wealthy financier. Vonnegut remarks that their host undoubtedly made more in a day than Heller had made from his runaway bestseller *Catch 22*. "Yes," replies Heller, "but I have something he will never have . . . enough."

Enough's other central passage recounts a mythical dialogue between a preacher and a recently retired greyhound racing dog:

> *Are you still racing?*
>
> *No.*
>
> *Well, what was the matter? Did you get too old to race?"*
>
> *No, I still had some race in me.*
>
> *Well, what then? Did you not win?*
>
> *I won over a million dollars for my owner.*
>
> *Well, what was it, bad treatment?*
>
> *Oh no. The treated us royally when we were racing.*
>
> *Did you get crippled?*
>
> *No.*
>
> *Then why? Why?*
>
> *I quit.*
>
> *You quit?*
>
> *Yes, I quit.*
>
> *Why did you quit?*
>
> *I just quit because after all that running and running and running, I found out that the rabbit I was chasing wasn't even real.*

If You Can came from the same place. In 2014, in the spirit of the Bogleheads, I decided to make it available as a free download (just google "if you can" and my name). Nearly all of my financial writing is aimed at older individuals, most of whom are, or soon will be, fairly prosperous. Both writing about and practicing finance have been good to me; *If You Can* seemed a good way to pay forward some of that to young people just starting out on that journey.

The two books fit together; Jack's describes the zen of personal finance, while mine is the Boglehead three-fund nuts and bolts version. Wiley first published *Enough* in 2009; both books are now more than a decade old, and upon rereading them I'm pleased at how well the two have held up.

The one part of *Enough* that needs only the slightest revision is the few pages on exchange traded funds (ETFs). Because they're so easy to speculate with, Jack didn't like them, and their champion at Vanguard, Gus Sauter, nearly had to step over Jack's metaphorical dead body to debut Vanguard's.

Jack's criticisms of ETFs are even more valid now than they were then: It seems not a day goes by that an investment company doesn't bring out one bit of speculative toxic sludge or another packaged in an ETF wrapper—leveraged funds, inverse leveraged funds, hyper-narrow sector funds, and the like.

But there's also no denying that because anyone's ETFs can be bought on anyone else's brokerage platform—even on those of the bad old "full-service" wirehouses—they've greatly expanded the investing public's access to low-cost vehicles.

Mr. Sauter also realized before Jack did that ETFs treated investors more fairly than the traditional open-end mutual funds, which penalize long-term buy and hold investors with the trading costs of short-term speculators. Mutual funds trade enormous dollar amounts of stocks and bonds when investors purchase or redeem their shares, and these large trading volumes can incur considerable "transactional costs." By "externalizing" those trading costs with the small bid/ask spreads incurred when individuals buy and sell ETFs, this shifts the high costs of rapid trading to ETF speculators, leaving the buy-and-hold investors nearly untouched.

The improvements in ETFs, as well as the increased ease of trading them, also have also negated one of the major recommendations in *If You Can*, which was its emphasis on dealing, wherever possible, with the Vanguard Group. Since then, two things have rendered that recommendation obsolete. First, in 2013, the online platform

Robinhood fired the brokerage shot heard round the world when it debuted its commission-free trading phone app for stocks and ETFs. Over the next several years, the big discount brokerage houses—Fidelity, Schwab, TD Ameritrade, and E★Trade—followed suit. So it's possible to buy Vanguard ETFs at any of these brokerage houses commission free; this is even possible, though I don't recommend it, at some of the old wirehouses. Moreover, over the past decade both open-end funds and ETFs from both Schwab and Fidelity have matched Vanguard's low-cost structure, so investors can even purchase, for example, a Schwab ETF on the Vanguard platform.

Second, and sad to say, since Jack's passing customer service at Vanguard has deteriorated, with long hold times, an outdated website, and often clueless offshore phone support. That said, Vanguard still possesses two advantages over other brokerage firms. First, because its money market funds have lower expenses than those of other firms, your cash balances there earn a higher return than elsewhere. Second, because Vanguard is owned by its customers, its incentive structure and corporate culture will always be more customer-oriented than those of its competitors. These two reasons are, in my opinion, enough to stick with Vanguard, despite their recent customer service problems. (The low cash balance interest rate at Schwab is a problem that requires constant attention from their customers, who must be on the lookout for accumulated cash needing to be manually swept into Treasury bills or money market/short-term bond funds. This gets old fast.)

★★★

Any other founder of a large investment company would have used his or her great good fortune to make billions by shaving off just a few basis points of the firm's managed assets. That Jack didn't spend his life chasing after the mechanical rabbit of wealth is testament to both his intelligence and character. My hope is that this small volume will help you on your own voyage to Enough.

Original Foreword to *Enough*

My professor of ancient civilizations at Georgetown taught us that the United States became the greatest nation in history because our people had always believed in the two main pillars of Western civilization: that tomorrow can be better than today, and that we all have a personal moral obligation to make it so. He called it "future preference."

In recent years, some American finance leaders have strayed from these beliefs, making vast wealth in the moment without regard to its consequences for the future. In the United States and around the globe, we are still living with the repercussions of this business conduct, some of it illegal, all of it fruitless. We cannot continue on the same road we followed before the recent financial crises—not if we want to build a better tomorrow.

In *Enough.*, John C. Bogle offers a compelling account of what went wrong and some clear advice on how we can restore our financial system and create a more prosperous and equitable world. His book is an important call to action, to bring moral principles and integrity back into our financial affairs in a way that will support, not undermine, long-term economic growth.

With his own impeccable credentials in finance, Bogle reminds us that the United States was built upon a tradition of hard work, temperance, and duty, and shows why sacrificing these values in the pursuit of success sooner or later breeds destruction that harms many innocent people. In this meditation on ambition and society, Bogle argues that we cannot measure the meaning of our lives by quick profits. Instead, real worth comes in making long-term contributions to the larger communities of which even the most powerful financiers are simply facilitators, with a duty to help others build their dreams.

In our fast-moving digital age, with more than $2 trillion crossing borders every day before the current crisis, Bogle's analysis and argument seem, at first glance, strikingly old-fashioned. But our pervasive interdependence makes *Enough.* more relevant than ever. Our actions have profound consequences both within and beyond our borders. It is wrong to ignore them in pursuit of purely personal advantage. Future preference still matters. We have to get it back.

John Bogle is a brilliant and good man, and every concerned citizen can learn and benefit from the important lessons he shares in *Enough.* It is a reminder that what Alexis de Tocqueville said about our nation so long ago remains true: America is great because America is good, and if she ever ceases to be good, she will no longer be great. *Enough.* is about reclaiming both.

WILLIAM JEFFERSON CLINTON
March 2010

Original Prologue to *Enough*

I n the late 1970s, I began a journey with Bob Waterman examining how good companies were managed that led to the publication of *In Search of Excellence*. Along the way we met an extraordinary cast of characters. There was Jim Burke, CEO of Johnson & Johnson, who when beset with the infamous Tylenol crisis in 1982 turned to J&J's quasi-religious "Credo." With the guidance of core values, the company handled the crisis with integrity and transparency that stands to this day as a memorial to the power of values-based organizations.

And then there was Delta Airlines, mired in crisis courtesy of the recession of the early 1980s—the company's balance sheet was helped enormously by the decision of Delta employees to buy their employer an airplane! There was McDonald's, living with rigor in the early 1980s on the bedrock established by founder Ray Kroc called QSC&V, or quality, service, cleanliness, and value. And then there was John Young of Hewlett-Packard, who managed by wandering around (MBWA), engaging with line employees on project specifics.

The key concept of our book was captured in six words: "Hard is soft. Soft is hard." As engineers, MBAs, and McKinsey consultants, we were firmly rooted in the virtues of measurement and metrics—but we also damn well knew how easy the numbers are to fudge! Purportedly hard numbers turn out again and again to be soft. Enron, circa 2000, masterminded by a Harvard Business School–McKinsey grad, and the derivatives, super-derivatives, and credit default swaps of the 2000s, masterminded by PhDs, came about by numbers that were so soft they deflated.

What matters? What is really "hard"? Integrity. Trust. Values that last (like J&J's Credo). Deep-rooted relationships. Good corporate citizenship. Listening—to the customer and to the front-line employee—and acting on what they tell us. Matchless quality, the bugbear of those early 1980s. And, yes, excellence. Those are the things they mostly didn't and don't teach in business schools, but which are the bedrock of effective enterprise.

It was memories of that startling journey that explained why, in the middle of the Great Recession of 2007++, I picked up, for no particular reason, Jack Bogle's book, *Enough*. I quickly found, while standing in the bookstore in fact, that I couldn't put it down. It explains why I have now read it through four times; why I have bent some 57 pages to return to again and again; why I have given away over 50 copies to friends and associates; and why, I'm almost embarrassed to admit, I carry it with me as I travel from Angola to Abu Dhabi to China to Chicago—*Enough.* has taken on totemic significance. As I prepare a seminar in, say, Novosibirsk, Siberia, I thumb through the book and check myself as to whether I may have gone soaring off into some obscure theoretical corner and forgotten the lesson of the likes of Bill Hewlett's supposedly old-fashioned MBWA as practiced by John Young.

The Australian writer Peter Temple's thriller *The Broken Shore* won a bushel of prestigious global awards. Several prominent reviewers struck the same chord. In effect, "This is not a great thriller—this is a great *novel.*" That's precisely what I feel about *Enough.* It is not a great finance book. It is not a great business book. It is a great *book.* Period.

Jack Bogle writes in plain English, and his reasoning is straightforward and based on a staggering sum of observations. Though he is a finance guy, not a single equation is unfurled as he takes us through finance, business, and life itself. It is not hyperbole to say, with some certainty at age 67, that this *is* clearly the best business book I've ever read, and as good a primer on life as I've read as well, save perhaps the works of Bogle's fellow Philadelphian, wise old Ben Franklin!

Jack Bogle and the organization he founded in 1974, The Vanguard Group, have been recognized far and wide and again and again for the sort of excellence that lit so bright and true a lamp for Bob Waterman and me in the 1980s. Jack Bogle is one the great financiers of our times and perhaps all times. He and Vanguard have contributed to the financial well-being and security of millions upon millions of people. His secret is a carefully formed belief that you will not, over the long haul, beat the market, and a belief that the best performance will therefore come from index funds that return their enhanced value, virtually in full, to investor-owners. His life and his life's work are built on a bedrock of integrity, transparency, simplicity, and value.

Interestingly, I've never met Jack, and, alas, have not invested with Vanguard, which is to say that I have no vested interest whatsoever in making these remarks— and singling this book out as the matchless, perhaps life-changing gem that I think it unequivocally is. I have devoted my adult life to trying to help people manage organizations as effectively as possible, and have discovered, as Jack Bogle has, that being straightforward is best and that character and integrity and common sense and decency are the keys to running enterprises of all sorts— not to mention the life well lived in service to others.

I will not reprise the best of the book in this Prologue. I tried to do so in a first draft, but was flummoxed by those 57 bent pages—each of abiding personal importance. Jack's straight talk is offered in spare and lucid prose that puts me to shame. However, I can give you a flavor of what is to follow by simply offering up the chapter titles (I was totally hooked on the book by the time I'd perused the Contents page):

"Too Much Cost, Not Enough Value"

"Too Much Speculation, Not Enough Investment"

"Too Much Complexity, Not Enough Simplicity"

"Too Much Counting, Not Enough Trust"

"Too Much Business Conduct, Not Enough Professional Conduct"

"Too Much Salesmanship, Not Enough Stewardship"

"Too Much Management, Not Enough Leadership"

"Too Much Focus on Things, Not Enough Focus on Commitment"

"Too Many Twenty-First Century Values, Not Enough Eighteenth-Century Values"

"Too Much 'Success,' Not Enough Character"

I'm inclined to hijack these chapter titles and make them my Ten Commandments. The concerns encapsulate, better than anything I've come across before, the life I hope I lead, the life I would surely like to lead—and the sorts of things I'd pray people might say about my endeavors when I check out.

★★★

I begin my lectures these days with two PowerPoint slides. The first recalls a celebration honoring the peerless hotelier Conrad Hilton. After a roast of sorts, Mr. Hilton was called to the podium and asked to share the secrets of his magnificent career. He faced the crowd, as the story is told, paused, and said, "Don't forget to tuck the shower curtain into the bathtub."

And with that he returned to his seat.

The second slide recalls a conference near Monterey, California, perhaps 20 years ago, during which I was chatting with the president of a very successful Midwestern community bank. As the financial crisis of 2007 engulfed us, I recalled his words clearly: "Tom, let me describe to you a successful lending officer. On Sunday after church, driving his family home, he takes a little detour to drive past a factory or distribution center he's lent money to. He doesn't go in or any such thing, just drives by, eyeballs the place, and continues home."

The shower curtain.

The simple drive by a business.

Enough.

Tom Peters
Golden Bay, New Zealand
April 2010

John C. Bogle's
Author's Note to *Enough*

A Crisis of Ethic Proportions

I n early September 2008, just as the manuscript for *Enough.* was completed, the federal government decided against bailing out the investment banking firm of Lehman Brothers Holdings. The firm, whether it knew it or not, was bankrupt. Then–Treasury Secretary Henry Paulson later described a group of Lehman's toxic investments as being carried at $52 billion, but with an estimated value of (as little as) $27 billion, part of a huge capital hole that led inevitably to the firm's demise.

Powerful echoes from the government's decision to let Lehman fail quickly resounded. The stock market decline that began in mid-2007, when the Dow Jones Industrial Average had reached a high of 14,160, accelerated, with the Dow dropping 510 points to 10,910 when the market reopened after the Lehman collapse. That was only the beginning. Over the next six weeks, the Dow fell to 7,550. After a few months of consolidation, it tumbled again to a low of 6,550 in March 2009—a shocking decline of 54 percent from the high, equivalent to a \$9 *trillion* drop in stock values, the largest drop since the 1930s.

The stock market, of course, was simply anticipating and then reflecting the reality of the economic crisis that followed. Banks wrote off trillions of dollars in the values at which they carried the toxic assets on their balance sheets. Business activity declined sharply, and our nation's economic production slumped. Unemployment soared; credit became scarce and often unattainable; and we entered into the deepest economic abyss since the Great Depression.

Causes of the Collapse

The causes of this collapse are no secret. While it is often claimed that "victory has a thousand fathers, but defeat is an orphan," the defeat suffered by investors in our devastating financial crisis seems to have, figuratively speaking, a thousand fathers. The Federal Reserve kept interest rates too low for too long after the 2000–2002 stock market crash and failed to impose discipline on mortgage bankers. Not only did our deposit banks and investment banks design and sell trillions of dollars' worth of incredibly complex and risky mortgage-backed bonds and tens of trillions of dollars' worth of derivatives (largely credit default swaps) based on those bonds, but they were also left holding the bag, with many of these toxic derivatives held on balance sheets that were highly leveraged—sometimes by as much as 33 to 1 (or more). Just do the math; a mere 3 percent decline in asset value wipes out 100 percent of shareholders' equity.

These institutions also brought us securitization, selling off loans as the backing for untested financial instruments, and severing the traditional link between borrower and lender. With that change, the incentive to demand creditworthiness on the part of those who borrow almost vanished as banks lent the money, only to sell the loans to the creators of these new financial instruments. In banking, we've come a long, long way from community lending built on financial probity and the character of the borrower, the kind of thing that we saw in *It's a Wonderful Life*. (Remember Jimmy Stewart as George Bailey and Lionel Barrymore's crusty Mr. Potter?)

Our market regulators, too, have a lot to answer for: The Securities and Exchange Commission was almost apathetic in its failure to recognize what was happening in the capital markets. The Commodity Futures Trading Commission (CFTC) allowed the trading and valuation of derivatives to proceed opaquely, without demanding the sunlight of full disclosure, and without concern for the ability of the counterparties to meet their financial obligations if their bets went sour.

And let's not forget Congress, which passed responsibility for regulation of the derivatives market to the CFTC almost as an afterthought. Congress also allowed—indeed encouraged—risk taking by our government-sponsored (now essentially government-owned) enterprises—Fannie Mae and Freddie Mac—enabling them to expand far beyond the capacity of their capital, and pushing them to lower their lending standards. Congress also gutted the Glass-Steagall Act of 1933, which had separated traditional deposit banking from the riskier business of investment banking, a separation that for more than 60 years well served our national interest.

Our professional security analysts also have much to answer for, especially in their almost universal failure to recognize the huge credit risks assumed by a new breed of bankers and investment bankers, far more interested in earnings growth for their institutions than in the sanctity of their balance sheets. So do our credit rating agencies, for bestowing AAA ratings on securitized loans in return for enormous fees—handsomely paid in return by the very issuers who demanded those ratings, allowing what proved to be largely junk bonds to be marketed as high-quality securities. (Yes, it's called conflict of interest.)

"A Failure of Capitalism"

But there was also something more fundamental taking place—a failure of capitalism. Capitalism simply hasn't worked the way it is supposed to. We've trusted in Adam Smith's "invisible hand," in which pursuing our own self-interest ultimately leads to the good of society. But this free-market-based philosophy has failed. In an age of giant global corporations and giant (and independent) financial institutions, principles that applied in a world of smaller enterprises and more intimate communities simply lost their effectiveness.

This is not just my view. It is also the view of some of the most intelligent and respected minds in the nation. For example, Judge Richard Posner of Chicago (and leader of the conservative "Chicago School" of economists) entitled his post-crisis book *A Failure of Capitalism*. Even more poignantly, the same view is held by former Federal Reserve Chairman Alan Greenspan, who was central to the development of the financial bubble and the burst that inevitably followed. He successfully urged his fellow Fed governors to continue to make easy credit available—even though the time to tighten credit had long since arrived—and to ignore the perils created by the growth of securitization, which severed the essential link between borrowers and lenders. Greenspan's intellectual analysis and his market-moving power, it turns out, had been based on a false premise.

To his credit, in his testimony before Congress in October 2008, Greenspan admitted his mistake. Hear the *New Yorker*'s John Lanchester on the topic:

> *Greenspan acknowledged that the crisis was prompted by "a once-in-a-century credit tsunami," which had arisen from the collapse of a "whole intellectual edifice." "Those of us who have looked to the self-interest of lending institutions to protect shareholders' equity— myself especially—are in a state of shocked disbelief," he said. This failure of self-interest to provide self-regulation was, he said, "a flaw in the model that I perceived as the critical functioning structure that defines how the world works."*
>
> *It's worth dwelling on that phrase:* "the critical functioning structure that defines how the world works." *That's a hell of a big thing to find a flaw in. Here's another way of describing that flaw: the people in power thought they knew more than they did. The bankers evidently knew too much math and not enough history—or maybe they didn't know enough of either.*

To which I would add, enough indeed!

The Story of *Enough.*

Many of these happenings were foreshadowed in the pages of *Enough.*, which in retrospect seems weirdly prescient, even predictive. I first expressed the basic idea behind *Enough.* in a May 2007 commencement speech before MBA graduates at Georgetown University. You'll read more about that talk later in the book, but it's important to consider some of the context of my remarks:

> *"Money" has become increasingly important in our bottom-line society, the Great God of prestige, the Great Measure of the Man (and Woman). So this morning I have the temerity to ask you soon-to-be-minted MBA graduates, most of whom will enter the world of commerce, to consider with me the role of* enough *in business and entrepreneurship in our society,* enough *in the dominant role of the financial system in our economy, and* enough *in the values you will bring to the fields you choose for your careers.*
>
> *Once a profession in which business was subservient, the field of money management— "Wall Street"—has become a business in which the profession is subservient. Harvard Business School Professor Rakesh Khurana was right when he defined the conduct of a true professional with these words: "I will create value for society, rather than extract it." And yet money management, by*

definition, extracts value from the returns earned by our business enterprises.

If you enter the field of money management, do so with your eyes wide open, recognizing that any endeavor that extracts value from its clients may, in times more troubled than these, find that it has been hoist by its own petard. It is said on Wall Street, correctly, that "money has no conscience," but don't allow that truism to let you ignore your own conscience, nor to alter your own conduct and character.

Now, three years after that commencement speech, the financial sector indeed has been "hoist by its own petard," a Shakespearean phrase meaning "blown up by its own dynamite." The economy has followed suit. Earnings of financial companies in 2006, cited in my Georgetown speech at $215 billion, plummeted to *losses* of $233 billion in 2008, a difference of almost a mere half-*trillion* dollars. (By 2009, profits had returned to the sector, but only to a measly $29 billion.)

So What's to Be Done?

We need to not only resolve the specific issues that have been brought into focus in the financial crisis, but take steps to preclude future crises, some of which could be the same, some inevitably different. Here is a summary of my ideas:

- Deal with "too big to fail" by returning *moral hazard* to its rightful place in the banking system. Yes, a federal agency that monitors financial risk should happen, but the first step may well be "Let the bank fail!"
- Lift the veil of secrecy surrounding derivatives by requiring open and transparent markets.
- Raise bank capital requirements substantially (i.e., reduce leverage) and raise the quality of the investments on the balance sheet (i.e., reduce risk).
- Establish an independent consumer protection agency.
- Bring back the Glass-Steagall Act of 1933, separating commercial banking (deposit taking) and investment banking (underwriting, bridge loans, etc.).
- Develop market-based incentives to reduce leverage among our financial institutions, corporations, and households, gradually phasing out interest as a tax-deductible expense.
- Establish a federal standard of fiduciary duty for institutional money managers, who today control 70 percent of all shares of U.S. public corporations. By requiring those agents to serve solely the interests of their principals, they would come to act with due diligence in the selection of securities, and would assume the rights and responsibilities of participating in the governance of the corporations whose shares they hold.

An Ethical Crisis

But there is yet another factor underlying this crisis that is the broadest of all, pervasive throughout our society today. It was well expressed in a letter I received from a Vanguard shareholder who described the global financial crisis as "a crisis of *ethic* proportions." Substituting *ethic* for *epic* is a fine turn of phrase, and it accurately places a heavy responsibility for the meltdown on a broad deterioration in our society's traditional ethical standards.

Commerce, business, and finance have hardly been exempt from this trend. Relying on Adam Smith's invisible hand, we have depended on the marketplace and competition to create prosperity and well-being. But self-interest got out of hand. It created a "bottom-line" society in which success is measured solely in monetary terms. Dollars became the coin of the new realm. Unchecked market forces overwhelmed traditional standards of professional conduct, developed over centuries.

The result has been a shift from moral absolutism to moral relativism. Repeating what you will read on page 139, we've moved from a society in which "there are some things that one simply doesn't do" to one in which "everyone else is doing it, so I can do it, too." Business ethics and professional standards have been lost in the shuffle. The driving force of any profession includes not only the special knowledge, skills, and standards that it demands, but also the duty to serve responsibly, selflessly, and wisely, and to establish an inherently ethical relationship between professionals and society. The old notion of trusting and being trusted—which once was not only the accepted standard of business conduct, but the key to success—came to be seen as a quaint relic of an era long gone. Somehow, our society must be spurred into action to return to that standard.

Public Acceptance

Since the initial publication of *Enough.*, happily, I've seen a few early signs of an awakening understanding of the factors underlying the crisis. Many respected and totally independent voices have joined in echoing the multiple themes in the book. Listen to Thomas L. Friedman, best-selling author and *New York Times* columnist, writing in early 2010: "Our financial crisis was the result of a broad national breakdown in ethics." General Electric's chief executive, Jeffrey Immelt, expressed a similar view, as quoted in the *Financial Times*: "At the end of a difficult generation of business leadership . . . tough-mindedness—a good trait—was replaced by meanness and greed—both terrible traits . . . rewards became perverted," and "the richest people made the most mistakes with the least accountability." Immelt, the article concluded, "noted that it was wrong for the U.S. economy to have 'tilted toward the quicker profits of financial services' at the expense of the manufacturing industry and research and technology investments."

Writing in the *New York Times*, journalist and economist Edward Hadas expanded on that theme:

A distressingly large portion of activity in the financial world is little more than gambling. When shares and bonds, or derivatives based on them, are bought and sold, the gains and losses almost cancel each other out. Such trading may be fun—portfolio management is a common hobby—but it does almost nothing for the nonfinancial economy.

As in organized gambling, the losses in financial trading are actually a bit greater than the gains because the house takes its share. In recent years, the financial house—brokers, exchanges, fund managers—has augmented its gains by playing from the inside. Until the crisis came along, such trading often paid off handsomely.

There is a psychological, even a moral, problem with finance. A country gets rich by making stuff, not by seeming to make money from money. But when people see huge financial profits—on Wall Street or just from owning a house—they tend to want more of them. The economically illusory gains of finance distract people from more valuable tasks.

So will the United States, and the world, decide that it has had too much of this not particularly good thing? Not necessarily, since a four-decade trend has the momentum of a speeding train. But the current hurricane of financial destruction might just be strong enough to derail it.

There's more than money involved. For at least a generation, finance has been taken up as a career by a disproportionately large proportion of the world's most talented people. If more of the best and the brightest were to take up careers in industry, education or the arts, everyone would be better off.

And these words from "Buttonwood," writing in *The Economist*: "If anyone suffers from the short-termism of fund managers, it is the clients. Funds with the highest costs produce the lowest returns, as client money is absorbed in charges and bid-offer spreads. . . . If governments really want a scandal to attack, it is the way the finance sector enriches itself at the expense of retail investors."

Of course the fact that these prominent experts are echoing the many themes of *Enough.* delights me. But perhaps the most rewarding comment of all appeared in a *New York Times* review of a new book by gifted British journalist John Lanchester, whose *New Yorker* piece was cited earlier. "'So: a huge, unregulated boom in which almost all the upside went directly into private hands, followed by a gigantic bust in which the losses were socialized. That is literally nobody's idea of how the world is supposed to work.' . . . These reforms include personal ones, aimed at me and at you. Do we need so much stuff in our lives?, [Lanchester] asks. 'In a world running out of resources, the most important ethical, political and ecological idea can be summed up in one simple word: "*enough*."'"

And, that's, well, "enough," for now. So enjoy former President Clinton's Foreword to this new edition, enjoy management guru Tom Peters's Prologue, and then enjoy the book itself.

Enjoy. Learn. Teach. And join the parade.

JOHN C. BOGLE
April 2010

The Great Seduction

The people who created this country built a moral structure around money. The Puritan legacy inhibited luxury and self-indulgence. Benjamin Franklin spread a practical gospel that emphasized hard work, temperance, and frugality. Millions of parents, preachers, newspaper editors, and teachers expounded the message. The result was quite remarkable.

The United States has been an affluent nation since its founding. But the country was, by and large, not corrupted by wealth. For centuries, it remained industrious, ambitious, and frugal.

Over the past 30 years, much of that has been shredded. The social norms and institutions that encouraged frugality and spending what you earn have been undermined. The institutions that encourage debt and living for the moment have been strengthened. The country's moral guardians are forever looking for decadence out of Hollywood and reality TV. But the most rampant decadence today is financial decadence, the trampling of decent norms about how to use and harness money.

DAVID BROOKS
THE NEW YORK TIMES
June 10, 2008

Original Introduction to *Enough*

A t a party given by a billionaire on Shelter Island, Kurt Vonnegut informs his pal, Joseph Heller, that their host, a hedge fund manager, had made more money in a single day than Heller had earned from his wildly popular novel *Catch-22* over its whole history. Heller responds, "Yes, but I have something he will never have ... enough."

Enough. I was stunned by the simple eloquence of that word—stunned for two reasons: first, because I have been given so much in my own life and, second, because Joseph Heller couldn't have been more accurate. For a critical element of our society, including many of the wealthiest and most powerful among us, there seems to be no limit today on what *enough* entails.

We live in wonderful and sad times—wonderful in that the blessings of democratic capitalism have never been more broadly distributed around the globe, sad in that the

1

excesses of that same democratic capitalism have rarely been more on display. We see the excesses most starkly in the continuing crisis (that is not an extreme description*) in our overleveraged, overly speculative banking and investment banking industries, and even in our two enormous government-sponsored (but publicly owned) mortgage lenders, Fannie Mae and Freddie Mac, to say nothing of the billion-dollar-plus annual paychecks that top hedge fund managers draw and in the obscene (there is no other word for it) compensation paid to the chief executive officers of our nation's publicly held corporations—including failed CEOs, often even as they are being pushed out the door.

But the rampant greed that threatens to overwhelm our financial system and corporate world runs deeper than money. Not knowing what *enough* is subverts our professional values. It makes salespersons of those who should be fiduciaries of the investments entrusted to them. It turns a system that should be built on trust into one with counting as its foundation. Worse, this confusion about *enough* leads us astray in our larger lives. We chase the false rabbits of success; we too often bow down at the altar of the transitory and finally meaningless and fail to cherish what is beyond calculation, indeed eternal.

---

*According to the International Monetary Fund, it is "the biggest financial crisis in the United States since the Great Depression."

That message, I think, is what Joseph Heller captured in that powerful single word *enough*—not only our worship of wealth and the growing corruption of our professional ethics but ultimately the subversion of our character and values. And so that's where I want to start, with what I know best: how my own life has shaped my character and values, and how my character and values have shaped my life. As you will see, I've been given enough in countless ways.

Growing Up

Perhaps the best place to begin is with my heritage: heavily Scottish, which may be enough to explain my apparently legendary thriftiness. The Armstrongs—ancestors of my grandmother on my mother's side—came to America from Scotland in the early 1700s to farm here (a wonderful reminder that nearly all of us are descendants of immigrants). I've always thought of my great-grandfather—Philander Banister Armstrong—as my spiritual progenitor. He was an industry leader, but did his best to reform first the fire insurance industry (in an 1868 speech in St. Louis, he implored, "Gentlemen, cut your costs"), and then the life insurance industry. His spirited 1917 diatribe—258 pages long—was entitled *A License to Steal: How the Life Insurance Industry Robs Our Own People of Billions.* The final sentence: "The patient [the insurance industry] has a cancer. The virus is in the blood. He is not only sick unto death, but he is dangerous to the community. Call in the undertaker."

The Hipkins family—my mother's family—were Virginians who also came to America early in the eighteenth century; some of their progeny would serve in the Confederate States Army. My Hipkins grandparents, John Clifton Hipkins ("The Skipper") and Effie Armstrong Hipkins ("Chick"), were colorful characters who expected their three children and six grandchildren to be good citizens and to make the most of themselves.

William Brooks Bogle and his wife Elizabeth also arrived here from Scotland, but much later, during the early 1870s. Although Ellis Island was not yet the port of entry, their names are on a plaque there. Their son (and my grandfather) William Yates Bogle was a successful merchant in Montclair, New Jersey, highly respected in the community, and the founder of a company that became part of the American Can Company (which in turn became Primerica Corporation in 1987), large enough to be among the 30 stocks in the Dow Jones Industrial Average for 75 years.

His son, William Yates Bogle Jr., was my father. At the start of World War I—before the United States declared war—he volunteered to serve in the Royal Flying Corps and flew a Sopwith Camel. This dashing pilot, handsome to a fault, was said to resemble the then Prince of Wales, who became king of England in 1936 (before abdicating to marry "the woman I love"). My father was injured when his plane crashed, and he returned home, marrying my mother, Josephine Hipkins Bogle, in 1920.

Life was easy for the well-to-do young couple, but sadly, their first two children (twins, Josephine and Lorraine) died at birth. Their first son was my brother William Yates Bogle III, born in 1927, shortly followed by another set of twins on May 8, 1929, David Caldwell Bogle and me, John Clifton Bogle.

No Idle Hands

We were born some years after my Bogle grandfather had provided a handsome new home for the growing family in Verona, New Jersey (abutting Montclair). But the Great Crash came, and soon both my home and my father's inheritance were gone. We moved into my mother's parents' house, the first of the frequent moves that were to send the struggling family up and down the Jersey coast.

So while my family began with enough—in fact, much more than enough—we soon were in difficult financial straits. (My father, having grown up surrounded by the good things of the era, lacked the determination of his father, and struggled to hold a job.) From an early age, all three boys had to earn what they got. How well I remember the constant refrain, "Idle hands are the tools of the devil" (pronounced, in the Scots way, *divil*).

I've often thought that we three brothers had the perfect growing-up environment: a family with community standing and never a concern about being inferior or disrespected, yet with the need to take responsibility for our own spending money (and even to help fund the family exchequer), the initiative to get jobs, and the discipline of working for others. While we had wonderful friends—still friends today—who had more than enough and who played while we worked, we learned early on the joy of accepting responsibility, of using our wits, and of engagement with the people (rich and far from rich alike) whom we served in our various jobs, winter, summer, spring, and fall.

Blair Academy: "Come, Study, Learn"

In seventh and eighth grades, we twins attended a small grammar school in Spring Lake, New Jersey; we then moved on to nearby Manasquan High School. But my mother, ambitious for her sons and deeply concerned that we weren't getting the best of schooling, sought something much better. Through her persistence and determination, all three Bogle boys became boarding students at

Blair Academy in northwestern New Jersey—an incredible opportunity to begin a fine education. It was my mother's drive for her boys' education that overcame our lack of money, and Blair provided us with scholarships and jobs. In my first year, I waited on tables and, as a senior, rose to the demanding job of captain of the waiters.

Blair's motto (translated from the Latin) is "Come, Study, Learn," and so I did. Pushed by demanding old-school masters who seemed to sense that I could, with great effort, excel—although the classwork was far more demanding than any I'd ever before encountered—I gradually managed to overcome my early lag in studies. At graduation, I was class salutatorian, and was voted "Best Student" and "Most Likely to Succeed," accolades that may hint at both the determination that I still can't seem to shake and, perhaps, the entrepreneurial spirit that would later shape my career. I'll never forget the inspiration that I received when in my junior year I read this sentence in Thomas Macaulay's essay on Samuel Johnson: "The force of his mind overcame his every impediment."

So my attitude to what's enough in this life, I think, has been largely shaped by my heritage and the experiences of my youth, not least among them being blessed by a strong family: proud grandparents, loving parents, and a marvelous brotherhood of three who fought with each other but were united when others wanted to take us on.

That combination might well have led nowhere; after all, the Bogle boys were hardly worse off than countless numbers of other American youths. But as I reached toward maturity and ever after, I have been blessed with infinite good fortune in my life, often of miraculous dimension. Surely my first major break was when Blair Academy accepted the responsibility for my education. Without these breaks, who knows where I'd be (indeed, as you'll soon learn, even *if* I'd be) today? I have come to refer to each turn of good fortune as akin to discovering a diamond. Over the course of my life, as it has turned out, I would discover "acres of diamonds."

Acres of Diamonds

In ancient Persia, a wealthy farmer leaves his home to seek even greater wealth, and spends his life in a fruitless search for a perhaps mythical diamond mine. Finally, as age and years of frustration take their toll, he throws himself into the sea and dies, an unhappy pauper far from home. Meanwhile, back at his estate, the new owner, surveying his vast acreage, sees something in a stream, something bright, glistening in the sunlight. It is a large diamond, and turns out to rest atop the fabulous Golconda mine.

This story was a special favorite of Dr. Russell Conwell, who founded Philadelphia's Temple University in 1884. The story inspired his classic lecture, "Acres of Diamonds," which he delivered more than 6,000 times, all the world over. The moral of the story: "Your diamonds are not in far distant mountains or in yonder seas; they are in your own backyard, if you but dig for them."

The very first student at what would become Temple was so inspired by the speech that he came to Dr. Conwell, eager for an education but unable to pay for one. Accepted on the spot for tutelage, the man went on to rise to a position of eminence and public service. I have no trouble believing that story because when, as a young man, I first read Dr. Conwell's lecture, its message also inspired me, even as it continues to inspire me today. And all of those fortunate discoveries of one diamond after another took place right in my own backyard, in a city in which I'd never before set my foot.

Coming to Philadelphia

It was just before Thanksgiving of 1945, shortly after the end of World War II, when this young resident of New Jersey first arrived in Philadelphia. My late twin brother, David, bless his soul, was with me; we were two 16-year-old boys getting off a bus from Blair Academy, coming

to the City of Brotherly Love for the first time to cele-
brate the holiday with our mother and father. Our parents
(my older brother, William, then 18, was serving in the
U.S. Marine Corps) had recently moved into two rooms
on the third floor of a modest home in suburban Ardmore,
but the tiny space was enough for all of us—at least for
the holidays. We ate our dinners at the small Horn &
Hardart's restaurant around the corner. Later, when I was
on vacation, I worked the graveyard shift at the Ardmore
Post Office.

I found my first diamond, if not quite in
Philadelphia, nearby. Through the extraordinary prepa-
ration for college that Blair Academy had given me,
I gained admission to Princeton University. To make
it financially possible for me to attend, the university
offered me both a full scholarship and a job waiting on
tables in Commons. (A waiter yet again—I must have
been good at it!) In later years, I worked at the Athletic
Association ticket office, managing one of its departments
during my junior and senior years.

With a series of summer jobs (one as a runner in a
local brokerage firm; another as a reporter on the police
beat for the *Philadelphia Evening Bulletin*), I was able to
earn the remaining money I needed. I worked very hard,
and the hours were long. But I loved hard work then—
I still do—and I grew up with the priceless advantage

of having to work for what I got. But in my long career I don't ever recall thinking of work as work, with one exception: a stint as a pinsetter in a bowling alley (now there's a truly Sysiphean job!).

At Princeton, a Discovery

While I was studying at Princeton, my parents' marriage fell apart. My father moved to New York, and my beloved mother, terminally ill, remained in Philadelphia. I wanted to return there to be with her after my graduation in 1951, and fate intervened to make it possible. (Sadly, her life ended in 1952.)

At Princeton, this callow, idealistic young kid with a crew cut had determined to write his economics department senior thesis on a subject on which no earlier thesis had been written. Not John Maynard Keynes, not Adam Smith, not Karl Marx, but a subject fresh and new. What but fate can account for the fact that in December 1949, searching for my topic, I opened *Fortune* magazine to page 116 and read an article ("Big Money in Boston") about a financial instrument that I had never heard of before: the mutual fund. When the article described the industry as "tiny but contentious," I knew that I had found my topic and, though I couldn't know it at the time, another diamond as well.

After a year of intense study of the mutual fund industry, I completed my thesis and sent it to several industry leaders. One was Walter L. Morgan, mutual fund pioneer, the founder of the Philadelphia-based Wellington Fund and member of Princeton's class of 1920. He read my thesis and liked it sufficiently that he would soon write: "A pretty good piece of work for a fellow in college without any practical experience in business life. Largely as a result of this thesis, we have added Mr. Bogle to our Wellington organization." I started right after my 1951 graduation (magna cum laude, thanks largely to my thesis) and never looked back. I have worked there—one way or another, as you will soon see—ever since.

I have no way of knowing whether it is true, as some of his closest associates told me after his death, that Walter Morgan thought of me as the son he never had. But he was like a father to me. He became my loyal and trusted mentor, the man who gave me the first break of my long career. More, Mr. Morgan was my rock, the man who had confidence in me when I had little confidence in myself, the man who gave me the strength to carry on through each triumph and tragedy that would follow.

When I joined Wellington Management Company in 1951, it was an important company in a tiny industry, and managed a single mutual fund (Wellington Fund) with but $150 million in assets. But we were growing rapidly.

By the early 1960s, I was deeply involved in all aspects of the business and soon became Walter Morgan's heir apparent. Early in 1965, when I was just 35 years old, he told me I would be his successor as the leader of the firm. Yet another diamond! Although many other diamonds still lay hidden in the earth beneath me, undiscovered, the company was in troubled straits, and Mr. Morgan told me to "do whatever it takes" to solve our investment management problems.

A Door Slams; a Window Opens

Headstrong, impulsive, and naive, I found a merger partner—in Boston, of all places—that I hoped would help me do exactly that. The merger agreement was signed on June 6, 1966. With an ebullient bull market in stocks on our side, the marriage worked beautifully through early 1973. But when the bear market came and the stock market tumbled (a decline that would ultimately slash stock prices by 50 percent), both the aggressive young investment managers who were my new partners and I let our fund shareholders down. (The asset value of one of our funds plummeted by 75 percent!)

By late 1974, as the bear market took its toll and large numbers of our shareholders took flight, the assets under our management had plunged from $3 billion to \$1.3 billion. Not surprisingly, my partners and I had a falling out. But my adversaries had more votes on the company board than I did, and it was they who fired me from what I had considered my company. What's more, they intended to move all of Wellington to Boston. I wasn't about to let that happen.

I loved Philadelphia, my adopted city that had been so good to me. I had established my roots there, finding even more unimaginable diamonds. In 1956, I had married my beloved wife, Eve, who was born and grew up in Philadelphia, and by 1971, we had been blessed with six wonderful children (followed eventually by 12 terrific grandchildren). We intended to stay where we were, and I had a plan to do just that. For when the door slammed on my career at Wellington, a window opened just wide enough to allow me to remain in Philadelphia.

Pulling off this trick was not easy, and in fact I might not have tried doing so if I hadn't had the two characteristics that someone once attributed to me: "the stubbornness of an idealist and the soul of a street fighter." After a long and bitter struggle, I was able to parlay a slight difference in the governance structure of the Wellington funds (owned by their own shareholders) and Wellington Management Company (owned by public shareholders but now largely controlled by the former partners who had just fired me) into a new career—and with it more diamonds than I ever could have imagined.

Complications

A majority of the directors of the board of the funds themselves were independent of Wellington Management Company, and I proposed that they adopt an unprecedented, unique structure, one in which the funds would govern themselves. The idea was simple. Why should our mutual funds retain an outside company to manage their affairs—the modus operandi of our industry then and now—when they could manage themselves and save a small fortune in fees? They could be truly *mutual* mutual funds. The battle was hard fought over a period of eight busy, hectic, and contentious months, with the fund board almost evenly divided. But this new structure finally carried the day.*

I named our new company after *HMS Vanguard*, Lord Horatio Nelson's flagship at the great British victory

---

*This favorable outcome would never have been possible without the unflinching support of the chairman of the Wellington funds' independent director group, the late Charles D. Root, Jr. Thanks, Chuck, for without you Vanguard would likely not have come into existence.

over Napoleon's fleet at the Battle of the Nile in 1798.
I wanted to send a message that our battle-hardened
Vanguard Group would be victorious in the mutual fund
wars, and that our Vanguard would be, as the dictionary
says, "the leader in a new trend." However, my idea suffered a setback when the fund directors allowed Vanguard
(now owned by the funds) to handle only the administration side of the firm's activities, responsible for the funds'
operating, legal, and financial affairs. When we began in
May 1975, we were barred from assuming responsibility for investment management and marketing, the other
two—and far more critical—sides of the triangle of
essential mutual fund services. To my chagrin, these key
services would continue to be provided by my rivals at
Wellington Management Company.

A Complete Firm Emerges

I knew that we would have to expand our narrow mandate and take responsibility for the full range of admin-
istrative, investment, and marketing services that all
fund complexes require if Vanguard were to have even a
fighting chance to succeed. So we had to seek yet more
diamonds. We quickly found one to rival the fabled
Kohinoor diamond in size. The fact that investment management was outside of Vanguard's mandate led me within
months to develop a great idea that I had toyed with for

years, which had even been suggested by the research I had done for my senior thesis, and in which I had written, mutual funds "can make no claim to superiority over the market averages." Before 1975 had ended, we had formed the world's first index mutual fund.

The idea was the essence of simplicity: The portfolio would simply hold all of the stocks in the Standard & Poor's (S&P) 500 Stock Index, based on their market weight, and would closely track its returns. Our index fund was derided for years, and was not copied until nearly a full decade had passed. The new fund, originally named First Index Investment Trust (now Vanguard 500 Index Fund), began with just $11 million of assets, and was dubbed "Bogle's Folly." But it proved its point. The first index fund gradually earned compound returns that were substantially higher than the returns earned by traditional equity funds, and would become the largest mutual fund in the world. Today Vanguard 500 is one of 82 index and virtual index mutual funds that constitute nearly $1 trillion of Vanguard's now-$1.3 trillion asset base.*

---

*We actually operate 45 "true" index funds, narrowly defined. Although they're soundly managed by excellent investment professionals, I consider another 37 funds to be "virtual" index funds— largely bond and money market funds administered at nominal cost under rigorous maturity and quality standards, and closely tracking appropriate measures of the fixed-income markets.

Thus, in the words of Psalm 118, "the stone that the builders rejected . . . became the chief cornerstone" of our new firm. But its birth was a mighty fragile thing. The argument that we were not overstepping our narrow initial mandate just squeaked past approval by the board of directors. The trick of the index fund, I contended, was that it didn't need to be "managed"; it would simply buy all of the stocks in the S&P 500 Index. But with this quasi-management step, we had edged into the second side—the investment side—of the triangle of essential fund services.

How to again expand our mandate to control the third and final side—the marketing function? Why, just find another diamond! And so we did. The idea was to eliminate the very need for distribution, abandoning the network of stockbrokers that had distributed Wellington shares for nearly a half-century, and instead relying not on sellers to sell fund shares, but on buyers to buy them. The risks of such a sea change were enormous, but so were the opportunities.

On February 7, 1977, after yet another divisive battle and another board decision that was closely won, we made an unprecedented overnight conversion to a no-load, sales-charge-free marketing system. Once again, we've never looked back. We've never had to. With the extraordinarily low operating expenses that became our hallmark—a product of our mutual structure and our cost discipline—offering our shares without sales commissions proved a logical and timely step into a world that would be increasingly driven by consumer choice and the search for value. The motto of our marketing strategy: "If you build it, they will come" (a now-familiar phrase that inspired the creation of a baseball diamond, of all things, in Iowa, immortalized in the film *Field of Dreams*). And, though what we had built took years to reach full fruition, come the investors did, first by thousands, and then by the millions.

A Stunning Endorsement from the Court of Last Resort

The diamonds Vanguard had accumulated during those struggles, however, were not yet quite in our possession. We held them only on loan. For the Securities and Exchange Commission (SEC) had given us only a temporary order allowing us to take some of these crucial steps. Believe it or not, after a tedious weeklong regulatory hearing, the SEC staff ruled *against* our unprecedented plan. Aghast, for I knew that what we were doing was right for investors, we mounted a vigorous appeal and—after a struggle that lasted four long years—triumphed at last in 1981, when the SEC did an about-face and at last approved our plan. The Commission did so with a rhetorical flourish that concluded with these words:

> *The Vanguard plan . . . actually furthers the [1940 Investment Company] Act's objectives, . . . fosters improved disclosure to shareholders, . . . clearly enhances the Funds' independence, [and] promotes a healthy and viable mutual fund complex within which each fund can better prosper.*

In every respect, the Commission's parting salute was to prove prescient.

So the diamonds weren't going to Boston. They were at last permanently in our hands—or, far more accurately, in the hands of our shareholders, remaining where they belonged, in Greater Philadelphia, birthplace of Wellington in 1928 and of Vanguard in 1974. You might think that the store of diamonds in my Golconda was at last exhausted. But miraculously, there proved to be yet another diamond awaiting my discovery.

A Change of Heart

Paradoxically, the next diamond I was to discover, also right in my own backyard, was in the form of a new heart. (As we all know, in card games a heart beats a diamond every time. It's true in life, too!) I had been struggling with a failing heart since my first attack, of dozens, in 1960. By 1995, time had almost run out; only half my heart was still pumping. That fall, I entered Philadelphia's Hahnemann Hospital, and on February 21, 1996, I at last received my new heart, only months, or perhaps weeks or even days, before my own tired heart would have expired. I had waited in the hospital for 128 days, connected around the clock to an intravenous line feeding me heart-stimulating drugs.

Strangely, despite the traumatic circumstances, I never thought I would die. I never thought I would live, either. It just didn't seem sensible to think about the outcome either way. But live I did, and with the heart that now beats in my body—the gift of life from an anonymous donor—and through the care of the doctors and nurses who have been my guardian angels, I have enjoyed superb health for what has now been more than a dozen years, one more reason why I am convinced that I have received more blessings—more "acres of diamonds in my own backyard"—than any other human being on the face of this earth. You were right, Dr. Conwell!

Treasures False and True

I take special joy in telling you about the diamonds in my life and career, for I'm confident that each of you readers has also been blessed with diamonds, maybe many of them, if only you would stop and take a moment to count them. But too often, like the wealthy farmer in Dr. Conwell's parable, we search for illusory treasures and ignore the real ones that lie right beneath our feet. (Note the *we*—I'm as guilty as the next person!)

So I have indeed been given enough—enough diamonds (and hearts) to live a wonderful life, one that I hope has been useful to a family, a firm, an industry, even a society. But during these early years of the twenty-first century, I've developed a profound concern that our society is moving in the wrong direction, a concern so beautifully expressed in David Brooks's epigraph that begins this book. I'm guessing that Kurt Vonnegut and Joe Heller would share that view. While on Shelter Island they were talking about "enough" in the context of money and investments, their work held up a mirror to our entire society that reflected some of the absurdities and inequities that we've come to accept and take for granted.

In our financial system, we focus our expectations on the returns that the financial markets may deliver, ignoring the exorbitant costs extracted by our financial system, the excessive taxes engendered by record levels of speculative trading, and inflation borne of a government that spends (our) money beyond its means, grossly devastating these returns. We engage in the folly of short-term speculation and eschew the wisdom of long-term investing. We ignore the real diamonds of simplicity, seeking instead the illusory rhinestones of complexity.

In business, we place too much emphasis on what can be counted and not nearly enough on trusting and being trusted. When we should be doing exactly the opposite, we allow—indeed we almost force—our professions to behave more like businesses. Rather, we ought to be encouraging companies and corporations (the enterprises that create products and services) to regain the professional values that so many of them have cast aside. We have more than enough of the fool's gold of marketing and salesmanship and not enough of the real gold of trusteeship and stewardship. And we think more like managers, whose task is to do things right, than as leaders, whose task is to do the right thing.

In life, we too often allow the illusory to triumph over the real. We focus too much on *things* and not enough on the *intangibles* that make things worthwhile; too much on *success* (a word I've never liked) and not enough on *character*, without which success is meaningless. Amidst the twenty-first-century pressures for immediate satisfaction and amassing information on demand, we've forgotten the enlightened values of the eighteenth century. We let false notions of personal satisfaction blind us to the real sense of calling that gives work meaning for ourselves, our communities, and our society.

Socrates' Challenge

When I make these points in forums around the country, I sometimes feel like one of those sign-wielding *New Yorker* cartoon prophets ("Repent, for the end is near!"). While my message is hardly in the mainstream—and generally ill received by those in charge of our corporate and our financial institutions—the message is nothing new. Consider that 2,500 years ago, Socrates had much the same message to deliver in his challenge to the citizens of Athens.

> *I honor and love you: but why do you who are citizens of this great and mighty nation care so much about laying up the greatest amount of money and honor and reputation, and so little about wisdom and truth and the greatest improvement of the soul? Are you not ashamed of this? . . . I do nothing but go about persuading you all, not to take thought for your persons and your properties, but first and chiefly to care about the greatest improvement of the soul. I tell you that virtue is not given by money, but that from virtue comes money and every other good of man.*

I hardly have the standing to compete with Socrates. But over the course of these remarkably blessed 79 years of life that I have enjoyed to the fullest, I have, like Socrates, arrived at some strong opinions on money, on what we should be proud of and ashamed of in our business and professional callings, and on what are the false and true treasures in our lives. I offer those opinions here in the hope that, to borrow one of Kurt Vonnegut's favorite lines, I might poison your minds, dear readers, with a little humanity.

MONEY

Chapter 1

Too Much Cost, Not Enough Value

L et me begin with this wonderful old epigram from nineteenth-century Great Britain:

Some men wrest a living from nature and with their hands; this is called work.

Some men wrest a living from those who wrest a living from nature and with their hands; this is called trade.

Some men wrest a living from those who wrest a living from those who wrest a living from nature and with their hands; this is called finance.

Even today, these strong words continue to describe the realities of the relationship between the financial system in which I've spent my entire career and the economy at large.

The rules under which our system works—which I call, after Justice Louis Brandeis, "The Relentless Rules of Humble Arithmetic"—are ironclad:

- The gross return generated in the financial markets, minus the costs of the financial system, equals the net return actually delivered to investors.
- Thus, as long as our financial system delivers to our investors in the aggregate whatever returns our stock and bond markets are generous enough to deliver, but only *after* the costs of financial intermediation are deducted (i.e., forever), the ability of our citizens to accumulate savings for retirement will continue to be seriously undermined by the enormous costs of the system itself.
- The more the financial system takes, the less the investor makes.
- The investor feeds at the bottom of what is today the tremendously costly food chain of investing.

The essential truth, then, that sums up each of these inarguable points: On balance, the financial system subtracts value from our society.

Those are the modern realities of our financial system, but they have been building for a long time, just as the financial sector itself has been building for many decades into the largest single element of the American economy.

We have moved to a world where far too many of us seemingly no longer make anything; we're merely trading pieces of paper, swapping stocks and bonds back and forth with one another, and paying our financial croupiers a veritable fortune. In the process, we have inevitably added even more costs by creating ever more complex financial derivatives in which huge and unfathomable risks have been built into the financial system.

Warren Buffett's wise partner Charlie Munger lays it on the line:

> *Most money-making activity contains profoundly antisocial effects. . . . As high-cost modalities become ever more popular . . . the activity exacerbates the current harmful trend in which ever more of the nation's ethical young brain-power is attracted into lucrative money-management and its attendant modern frictions, as distinguished from work providing much more value to others.*

I share Mr. Munger's concern about the flood of young talent into a field that inevitably subtracts so much value from society. When I speak to college students, I often say exactly that. But I never advise them directly not to go into the field of managing money. Words alone aren't going to discourage anyone from entering a field so highly profitable. Rather, I ask young graduates to consider three caveats before doing so. And I would ask you, whatever your calling, to consider these same caveats and how they might apply to your own life and your own understanding of how, in our own transitory lives, we go beyond what is "enough" in the search for satisfaction and happiness, and strive to do much more than enough good for our fellow human beings.

A Prophetic Forecast

At the very peak of the boom in the financial sector, in a commencement speech at Georgetown University in May 2007, here's what I had to say on this subject:

- One, if you enter the financial field, do so with your eyes wide open, recognizing that any endeavor that extracts value from its clients may, in times more troubled than these, find that it has been hoist by its own petard. It is said on Wall Street, correctly, that "money has no conscience," but don't allow that truism to let you ignore your own conscience, nor to alter your own conduct and character.
- Two, when you begin to invest so that you will have enough for your own retirement many decades hence, do so in a way that minimizes the extraction by the financial community of the returns generated by business. This is,

yes, a sort of self-serving recommendation to invest in low-cost U.S. and global stock market index funds (the Vanguard model), but doing so is the only way to guarantee your fair share of whatever returns our financial markets are generous enough to provide.

- Three, no matter what career you choose, do your best to hold high its traditional professional values, now swiftly eroding, in which serving the client is always the highest priority. And don't ignore the greater good of your community, your nation, and your world. As William Penn pointed out, "We pass through this world but once, so do now any good you can do, and show now any kindness you can show, for we shall not pass this way again."

As it turns out, the warning I set forth in that speech—the need to recognize "that any endeavor that extracts value from its clients may, in times more troubled than these, find that it has been hoist by its own petard"—proved not only eerily prophetic, but surprisingly timely. The industry has been blown up by its own dynamite.

Sure enough, in July 2007, just two months after my speech, the financial sector—led, as it were, by Citigroup and investment banks Merrill Lynch and Bear Stearns—began to crumble, as the risky, reckless, complex, and costly debt instruments that its firms created began to come home to roost. Enormous write-downs in balance sheet valuations followed. By mid-2008, those write-downs in the aggregate totaled an astonishing $975 billion, with more to come.

Wresting a Living from Finance

In my speech at Georgetown, I noted that during 2006 the financial sector alone accounted for $215 billion of the $711 billion in earnings of the 500 companies that make up the S&P 500 Stock Index—30 percent of the total (and perhaps 35 percent, or more, if we included the earnings of the financial affiliates of large industrial companies, such as General Electric). The domination of financial companies in our economy and our stock market has been extraordinary. The earnings of these financial firms *alone* totaled more than the earnings of our highly profitable energy and technology companies *combined*, and about *three times* the earnings both of our booming health care sector and of our giant industrial firms.

By the time 2007 had ended, financial sector earnings had plummeted by almost half, to $123 billion for the year. Not only had financial sector earnings shrunk from 30 percent to 17 percent of the $600 billion earnings total of the S&P 500 companies; the sector also accounted for fully 90 percent of the S&P 500 decline in earnings for the year. The carnage has continued during 2008. Call it poetic justice.

But is it? The clients of the banking firms have lost hundreds of billions of dollars in the risky debt obligations that the banks created, and layoffs of employees are rife—more than 200,000 financial sector workers have already lost their jobs—yet most investment banking executives continue to be paid at astonishingly high levels.

I'm reminded of a story, perhaps apocryphal, I recently read about an investment banker addressing his colleagues after the collapse in the mortgage-backed bond market. "I have bad news and good news. The bad news is that we lost a ton of money. The good news is that none of it was ours." This story provides yet one more reminder that, for the most part, what is good for the financial industry is bad for you.*

---

*It is at least possible that not all financial firms put their own interests ahead of the interests of their clients. When John Thain, a former top executive at Goldman Sachs, became the CEO of Merrill Lynch in late 2007, he was asked how the firms differed. His answer: "Merrill does truly put clients first." You'll have to decide for yourself about the validity of the claim.

Fortunes from Failure

Consider the compensation of three well-publicized financial sector CEOs who failed their clients and their shareholders alike during the recent turbulence.

- Charles Prince, CEO of Citigroup, took office in October 2003, with Citigroup stock selling at $47 per share. While the bank did well for a few more years, it created a highly risky investment portfolio that fell to pieces within five years, with write-offs (so far) of some $21 billion. Citigroup's earnings fell from $4.25 in 2006 to $0.72 per share for 2007, and the stock, at this writing, is at about $20 per share. Mr. Prince was paid $138 million for his efforts when times were good, but incurred no penalty for the disaster that followed. (Prince resigned on November 4, 2007.)

- The experience of Stanley O'Neal, CEO of Merrill Lynch, was similar. The risks assumed by the firm in its risk-laden investment portfolio exploded late in 2007, with $19 billion of write-downs (with likely more to come). Merrill reported net losses for the year of $10.73 per share, and its stock price tumbled from $95 per share to less than $20 currently. Yet Mr. O'Neal's compensation of $161 million during 2002–2007 was not affected, and the retirement plan package that he received on his resignation in October 2007 was paid in full by the board (*another* $160 million, for a total of $321 million).

- Perhaps most egregiously, James E. Cayne, CEO of Bear Stearns, was paid some $232 million during 1993–2006 as the stock price of this investment banking powerhouse rose from $12 per share to $165. But the firm's risky and largely illiquid investment portfolio, along with its high leverage (assets of about 35 times capital), brought Bear to the edge of bankruptcy. The Federal Reserve was required to guarantee the value of much of the portfolio before JPMorgan Chase agreed to buy the company for a price of $2 per share (ultimately raised to $10)—measured from the high, a loss of some $25 billion of shareholder capital. But Mr. Cayne's millions of dollars of compensation had already been paid. (While his investment in Bear, once valued at $1 billion, had dropped to $60 million when he sold his shares in March 2008, probably most of us believe that $60 million is an awful lot of money, especially given the catastrophic loss of capital by other shareholders and the devastating loss of jobs by thousands of Bear employees who played no role in the firm's demise.)

To paraphrase Winston Churchill, "Never has so much been paid to so many for so little" in the way of accomplishment.

Heads I Win;
Tails You Lose

As rich as our financial kings have become over the past few decades—and as much unjustified cost as they have extracted from investors—their wealth pales in comparison with the wealth accumulated by our most successful hedge fund managers. In 2007 alone, the 50 highest-paid hedge fund managers together earned $29 billion (yes, *billion*). If you didn't make $360 million in that single year, you didn't even crack the top 25. Yes, for high-stakes gamblers, speculation—whether in Wall Street, at the race track, or in Las Vegas—can produce huge speculative rewards.

According to the *New York Times,* the highest-paid hedge fund manager for 2007 was John Paulson, who took down a cool $3.7 billion. It is said that his firm, Paulson & Company, made more than $20 billion for his clients by betting against certain mortgage-backed securities (more fully described later). Who's to begrudge Mr. Paulson a large share of the rewards that his firm earned for its clients by such a remarkably successful speculation?*

Not I! My problem with the incredible compensation earned by hedge fund managers is its asymmetry—its lack of fundamental equity. Managers on the winning side of speculation win big; but the losers don't lose big. For example, if the Paulson firm indeed *won* its gamble by betting that mortgage-backed securities or collateralized debt obligations would tumble (or being on the right side of the rank speculations known as credit default swaps), some other firm *lost* its gamble, betting that those debt obligations (or those swaps) would rise. The other side, it follows, would have *lost* $20 billion. But those managers, as far as anyone knows, didn't give $20 billion back to their clients. So the huge cost of our financial system rose, benefiting insiders even as their clients were impoverished (relatively speaking).

---

*I do begrudge hedge fund managers the maximum 15 percent tax rate that the federal government applies to so-called carried interest, an obfuscatory phrase referring to the share of profits paid to hedge fund managers. Such a low rate is an insult to those hardworking citizens whose far smaller earned incomes are often subject to standard federal tax rates that are twice as high or more. I also understand that clever tax planning enables this income to be deferred, free of any taxes and earning a return until drawn down later. Unsurprisingly, attempts at tax reform by Congress have been overwhelmed by the well-funded lobbyists hired by hedge fund managers.

A hypothetical example makes this point clear. Suppose you invested in a fund of hedge funds, with two managers running equal shares, one on each side of the trade described earlier. One earned 30 percent and one lost 30 percent, so your account was even ... so far. But you paid the winner, say, 20 percent of his 30 percent gain—or 6 percent—plus his 2 percent management fee, a total of 8 percent. You also paid the loser his base fee of 2 percent, bringing the fee on your entire account to an average of 5 percent. Then you paid the fund-of-funds manager another 2 percent. So, even though your portfolio had an investment return of zero (before costs), you lost 7 percent of your capital. Once again, industry wins; investor loses.

Brain Drain

Inevitably, the enormous incomes received by hedge fund managers in the recent era and the staggering salaries and bonuses paid to investment bankers have enflamed the imaginations of many of the nation's graduates of our business schools and made Wall Street the preferred destination for their careers. Despite the alarm sounded by the likes of Charlie Munger and others, the flood of young brainpower into the financial sector continued to pick up momentum even as the financial markets lost theirs. The number of Chartered Financial Analysts (CFAs) has reached a record high of 82,000, and *Barron's* recently reported that "no fewer than 140,000 new applicants—also a record high—from every corner of the earth are queued up to take the exams that will confer on the lucky ones the coveted [CFA] imprimatur."

Perhaps I should be cheered by such news. This is, after all, a calling to which I have devoted my entire career. I fear, though, that the motivation of too many of those rushing into finance is more aligned with what they can get from society than what they can give back to it; and it is a mathematical certainty that the cost of the services provided by their firms, as a group, will exceed the value that they create. That is the issue on which I want you to focus: *the disconnect between cost and value in our financial system*.

The Drain of Costs and Taxes

Let's start with the costs, where it is easiest to see through the haze. Over the past 50 years, the (nominal) *gross* return on stocks has averaged 11 percent per year, so $1,000 invested in stocks at the outset would today have a value of $184,600. Not bad, right? But it costs money for individuals to own stocks—brokerage commissions, management fees, sales loads, advisory fees, the costs of all that advertising, lawyers' fees, and so on. A good estimate of these costs is at least 2 percent per year. When we take out those assumed investment expenses, even at the rate of only 2 percent, the historic rate of *net* return would drop to 9 percent, and the final value would drop by more than one-half—to just $74,400.

If we assume that as little as 1.5 percent is paid by taxable investors to cover income taxes and capital gain taxes on that return, the after-tax rate of return would fall to 7.5 percent, and the final wealth accumulation would plummet by *another* one-half, to $37,000. Clearly, the wonderful magic of compounding *returns* has been overwhelmed by the powerful tyranny of compounding *costs*. *Some 80 percent of what we might have expected to earn has vanished into thin air.* (Caveat: In terms of *real* dollars, reduced by the 4.1 percent inflation rate over the past half-century, the final inflation-adjusted value of the initial $1,000 investment after costs and taxes would be—instead of $184,600 in nominal, precost, pretax dollars—a minuscule $5,300!)

The Wrong Kind of Wizardry

The costs of our financial system today are so high largely because we have abandoned the traditional (and successful) standards of investing, well described by the words of the legendary Benjamin Graham, as they appeared in the *Financial Analysts Journal* of May–June 1963:

It is my basic thesis—for the future as for the past—that an intelligent and well-trained financial analyst can do a useful job as portfolio adviser for many different kinds of people, and thus amply justify his existence. Also I claim he can do this by adhering to relatively simple principles of sound investment; e.g., a proper balance between bonds and stocks; proper diversification; selection of a representative list; discouragement of speculative operations not suited for the client's financial position or temperament—and for this he does not need to be a wizard in picking winners from the stock list or in foretelling market movements.

Anyone familiar with the ideas I've advocated during my long career would not be surprised to know that I passionately subscribe to these simple principles of balance, diversification, and focus on the long term—to say nothing of being skeptical that stock pickers and market-forecasting wizards can, on balance and over time, add value.

In fact, when I entered the mutual fund industry 57 long years ago, its money managers invested pretty much in the manner prescribed by Graham. Then, the portfolios of the major equity funds consisted largely of diversified lists of blue-chip stocks, and their portfolio managers invested for the long term. They eschewed speculation, operated their funds at costs that were (by today's standards) tiny, and delivered marketlike returns to their investors. However, as their long-term records clearly show, those fund managers were hardly "wizard[s] in picking winners."

Costs Rear Their Ugly Head

Today, if fund managers can claim to be wizards at anything, it is in extracting money from investors. In 2007, the direct costs of the mutual fund system (largely management fees and operating and marketing expenses) totaled more than $100 billion. In addition, funds are also paying tens of billions of dollars in transaction fees to brokerage firms and investment bankers and, indirectly, to their lawyers and all those other facilitators. Fund investors are also paying another estimated $10 billion of fees each year to financial advisers.

But in their defense, mutual funds represent just one part—actually a relatively *small* part—of the total costs that investors incur in our nation's system of financial intermediation. Add to that $100 billion in mutual fund costs a mere $380 billion in additional investment banking and brokerage costs, plus all those fees paid to the managers of hedge funds and pension funds, to bank trust departments and financial advisers and for legal and accounting fees, and the tab comes to roughly $620 billion annually. (No one knows the exact number. All that can be said for certain is that, one way or another, these billions are paid by the investors themselves.)

And don't forget that these costs recur year after year. If the present level holds—I'm guessing that it will grow—aggregate intermediation costs would come to a staggering $6 trillion for the next decade. Now think about these cumulative costs relative to the $15 trillion value of the U.S. stock market and the $30 trillion value of our bond market.

Investors Get Precisely What They *Don't* Pay For

The fact that investor returns lag market returns by the costs of the system is unarguable, yet it is often also argued that our financial system adds value to our society because of the other benefits it brings to investors. But such a claim belies the reality of our system, in that it does not operate under classical free market conditions. The system is fraught with information asymmetry (which favors sellers over buyers), imperfect competition, and irrational choices driven by emotions rather than reason.

This is not to say that our financial system creates only costs. It does create substantial value for our society. It facilitates the optimal allocation of capital among a variety of users; it enables buyers and sellers to meet efficiently; it provides remarkable liquidity; it enhances the ability of investors to capitalize on the discounted value of future cash flows, and other investors to acquire the right to those cash flows; it creates financial instruments (often including so-called derivatives, often of mind-boggling complexity, whose values are derived from still other financial instruments) that enable investors to assume additional risks, or to divest themselves of a variety of risks by transferring those risks to others.

No, it is not that the system fails to create benefits. The question is whether, on the whole, the costs of obtaining those benefits have reached a level that overwhelms those benefits. The answer, alas, seems obvious enough, at least to me: The financial industry is not only the largest sector of our economy; it is also the only industry in which customers don't come anywhere near getting what they pay for. Indeed, given those relentless rules of humble arithmetic, investors in the aggregate get precisely what they don't pay for. (Paradoxically, then, if they paid nothing, they would get everything!)

A Question So Important

Over the past two centuries, our nation has moved from being an agricultural economy, to a manufacturing economy, to a service economy, and now to a predominantly financial economy. But our financial economy, by definition, deducts from the value created by our productive businesses. Think about it: While the owners of business enjoy the dividend yields and earnings growth that our capitalistic system creates, those who play in the financial markets capture those investment gains only *after* the costs of financial intermediation are deducted. Thus, while investing in American business is a *winner's* game, beating the stock market before those costs is a *zero-sum* game. But after intermediation costs are deducted, beating the market—for all of us as a group—becomes a *loser's game*.

Yet despite the vast and, until very recently, rapidly growing dominance of the financial sector in our total economic life, I know of not one academic study that has systematically attempted to calculate the value extracted by our financial system from the returns earned by investors. Nor had a single article (except my own) on the subject ever appeared in the professional journals, neither the *Journal of Finance*, nor the *Journal of Financial Economics,* nor the *Journal of Portfolio Management*, nor the *Financial Analysts Journal.* The first article of which I am aware—Kenneth R. French's "The Cost of Active Investing" (in U.S. stocks)—is, in mid-2008, pending publication in the *Journal of Finance.*

That veil of ignorance must be lifted. We need to find ways to radically improve our nation's system of capital formation, through some combination of education, disclosure, regulation, and structural and legal reform.

If this book is a goad toward that goal, my writing it will have been time well spent. But the point is that the job must get done. Until it is, the financial economy will continue to subtract inordinately from the value created by our productive businesses, and in the challenging times that I see ahead, that is a loss we can no longer tolerate.

In June 2007, Princeton University valedictorian and economics major Glen Weyl (now Dr. Weyl, having earned his PhD in economics only a year later) described his passion for intellectual inquiry in this way: "There are questions so important that it is, or should be, hard to think about anything else." *There are questions so important that it is, or should be, hard to think about anything else.* The efficient functioning of our nation's flawed system of financial intermediation is just such a question.

It's high time not only to think about this question, but to study it in depth, to calculate its costs, and to relate those costs to the values that investors not only expect to earn, but are entitled to earn. Our financial system carries quite enough cost—in fact, far too much cost—and therefore (again, by definition) doesn't create nearly enough value for market participants. Finance indeed wrests its living from those who wrest their livings from nature, from commerce, and from trade. It is essential that we demand that the financial sector function far more effectively in the public interest and in the interest of investors than it does today.

Chapter 2

Too Much Speculation, Not Enough Investment

I nvesting is all about the long-term ownership of businesses. Business focuses on the gradual accumulation of intrinsic value, derived from the ability of our publicly owned corporations to produce the goods and services that our consumers and savers demand, to compete effectively, to thrive on entrepreneurship, and to capitalize on change. Business adds value to our society, and to the wealth of our investors.

Over more than a century, the rising value of our corporate wealth—the cumulative accretion of dividend yields and earnings growth—resembles a gently upward-sloping line with, at least during the past 75 years, precious few significant aberrations.

Speculation is precisely the opposite. It is all about the short-term *trading*, not long-term *holding*, of financial instruments—pieces of paper, not businesses—largely focused on the belief that their prices, as distinct from their intrinsic values, will rise; indeed, an expectation that the prices of the stocks that are selected will rise more than other stocks, as the expectations of other investors rise to match one's own. A line representing the path of stock prices over the same period is significantly more jagged and spasmodic than the line showing investment returns.

The sharp distinction between investment and speculation, however much it may have been forgotten today, is age-old. The best modern definition was set forth in 1936 by the great British economist John Maynard Keynes in his *General Theory of Employment, Interest and Money*. I first encountered his book at Princeton in 1950, and cited it in my undergraduate thesis on the mutual fund industry.

Keynes defined *investment*—he called it "enterprise" —as "forecasting the prospective yield of an asset over its entire life." He defined *speculation* as "the activity of forecasting the market." Keynes was greatly concerned by the likelihood that when professional money managers were unable to offset the uninformed opinion of the ignorant masses engaged in public speculation, they would move away from investment and toward speculation, becoming speculators themselves. So, fully 70 years ago, he warned us: "When enterprise becomes a mere bubble on a whirl-pool of speculation [and] the capital development of a country becomes a by-product of the activities of a casino, the job of capitalism is likely to be ill-done."

In the short run, investment returns are only tenuously linked with speculative returns. But in the long run, both returns must be—and will be—identical. Don't take my word for it. Listen to Warren Buffett, for no one has said it better: "The most that owners in the aggregate can earn between now and Judgment Day is what their business in the aggregate earns." Illustrating the point with Berkshire Hathaway, the publicly owned investment company he has run for more than 40 years, Buffett says, "When the stock temporarily over-performs or under-performs the busi-ness, a limited number of shareholders—either sellers or buyers—receive out-sized benefits at the expense of those they trade with. [*But*] *over time, the aggregate gains made by Berkshire shareholders must of necessity match the business gains of the company.*" [emphasis added]

Put another way, as Buffett's great mentor Benjamin Graham once pointed out, "In the short run the stock market is a *voting* machine . . . [but] in the long run it is a *weighing* machine." But we must take Buffett's obvious truism—and Mr. Graham's—one step further. For while "the aggregate gains made by Berkshire shareholders must of necessity match the business gains of the company," the aggregate gains or losses by the sellers and buyers—even though they are trading back and forth with one another in what is pretty much a closed circle—do not balance out evenly. As a group, investors capture Berkshire's return; as a group, speculators do not.

A Giant Distraction

When our market participants are largely *investors*, focused on the economics of business, the underlying power of our corporations to earn a solid return on the capital invested by their owners is what drives the stock market, and volatility is low. But when our markets are driven, as they are today, largely by *speculators*, by expectations, and by hope, greed, and fear, the inevitably counterproductive swings in the emotions of market participants—from the ebullience of optimism to the blackness of pessimism—produce high volatility, and the resultant turbulence that we are now witnessing became almost inevitable.

Is this speculation by mutual fund managers and by other market participants healthy for investors? For our financial markets? For our society? Of course not. In the very long run, all of the returns earned by stocks are created not by *speculation* but by *investment*—the productive power of the capital invested in our business enterprises. History tells us, for example, that from 1900 through 2007 the calculated annual total return on stocks averaged 9.5 percent, composed entirely of *investment* return, roughly 4.5 percent from the average dividend yield and 5.0 percent from earnings growth. (Dare I remind you that this return reflects neither the croupier costs of investing discussed in the previous chapter nor the erosion of inflation?)

What I call the *speculative* return—the annualized impact of any increase or decrease in the price-earnings (P/E) ratio or P/E multiple—happened to be zero during this period, with investors paying a little over $15 for each dollar of earnings (P/E = 15) at the beginning of the period, and about the same at the end. Of course, changes in the P/E can take place over long periods; but only rarely does the *long-term* speculative return add more than 0.5 percent to annual investment return, or subtract more than 0.5 percent from it.

The message is clear: In the long run, stock returns have depended almost entirely on the *reality* of the relatively predictable investment returns earned by *business*.

The totally unpredictable *perceptions* of market participants, reflected in momentary stock prices and in the changing multiples that drive speculative returns, essentially have counted for nothing. It is *economics* that controls long-term equity returns; the impact of *emotions*, so dominant in the short term, dissolves. Therefore, as I wrote in my *Little Book of Common Sense Investing* (John Wiley & Sons, 2007), "the stock market is a giant distraction from the business of investing."

A Loser's Game

The distinction between the *real* market and the *expectations* market was perhaps best expressed by Roger Martin, dean of the Rotman School of Business at the University of Toronto. In the real market of business, real companies spend real money and hire real people and invest in real capital equipment, to make real products and provide real services. If they compete with real skill, they earn real profits, out of which they pay real dividends. But to do so demands real strategy, real determination, and real capital expenditures, to say nothing of requiring real innovation and real foresight.

In the expectations market, by contrast, prices are set, not by the realities of business just described, but by the expectations of investors. Crucially, these expectations are set by numbers, numbers that are to an important extent the product of what our managements want them to be, too easily managed, manipulated, and defined in multiple ways. What is more, we not only allow but seemingly encourage chief executives, whose real job is to build real corporate value, to bet in the expectations market, where their stock options are priced and exercised. That practice should be explicitly illegal, just as it is illegal in most professional sports. Imagine, for example, what would happen if National Football League quarterbacks or National Basketball Association centers were allowed to bet on their own teams' pregame spreads. Yet CEOs do exactly that, which is one reason why stock-option compensation creates huge distortions in our financial system.

Which is the winner's game and which is the loser's game? Betting on real numbers and real returns, and buying and holding stocks for the long haul? (That is, *investing*.) Or betting on expected numbers and ginned-up returns, and in essence renting stocks rather than owning them? (That is, *speculating*.) If you understand how the odds in gambling diminish your chances of winning—whether in the lottery, in Las Vegas, at the racetrack, or on Wall Street—your decision as to whether to be a speculator or an investor isn't even a close one.

Speculation Is in the Driver's Seat

Despite the elementary mathematics that guarantee the superiority of investment over speculation, today we live in the most speculative age in history. When I first came into the financial field in 1951, the annual rate of turnover of stocks was running at about 25 percent.* It would remain in that low range for the better part of two decades, then gradually rise to above 100 percent in 1998, approaching the record 143 percent turnover rate of the late 1920s. Yet by last year, stock turnover had shot up another two times over. Turnover soared to 215 percent, and to 284 percent if we add in the staggering amount of speculation in exchange-traded funds (ETFs).

Consider a stark example of one of the new financial instruments that typifies the dramatic upsurge in speculation. In 1955, when the total market capitalization of the S&P 500 Index was $220 billion, neither futures nor options that would enable market participants to speculate on (or hedge against) the price of the index even existed. Then index futures and options were created—a marketing bonanza for the financial field. These new products made it easy not only to bet on the market, but to leverage

---

*We define "turnover" as the number of shares traded as a percentage of shares outstanding.

your bets as well. By the beginning of 2008, the value of these derivatives of the S&P 500 Index—these futures and options—totaled $29 trillion, more than *double* the $13 trillion market value of the S&P 500 Index itself. That expectations market, then, would be at least double the value of the real market, even if the high turnover activity in the S&P 500 Index stocks themselves were not dominated, as it is, by speculative trading.

A simple example demonstrates that speculation is a loser's game. Assume that one-half of the shares of each of the 500 S&P stocks are held by investors who don't trade at all, and the other half are held by speculators who trade solely with one another. By definition, the investors as a group will capture the gross return of the index; the speculators as a group will capture, because of their trading costs, only the (lower) net return. The obvious conclusion: *investors win; speculators lose.* There is no way around it. So the orgy of speculation we are witnessing today ill serves our market participants. It serves only Wall Street.

Black Swans and Market Returns

When the perception—interim stock prices—vastly departs from the reality—intrinsic corporate values—the gap can be reconciled *only* in favor of reality. It is simply impossible to raise reality to perception in any short time frame; the tough and demanding task of building corporate value in a competitive world is a long-term proposition. Still, whenever stock prices lose touch with corporate values and bubbles begin to form, too many market participants seem to anticipate that values will soon rise to justify prices, instead of the other way around.

That's what a speculative mind-set does to investors. It encourages them to ignore the inevitable even as they discount the probability of the improbable. And then along comes a trading day like October 19, 1987, and the eternal verities of the *real* market once again reassert themselves. On that single day, which came to be known as Black Monday, the Dow Jones Industrial Average dropped from 2,246 to 1,738, an astonishing one-day decline of 508 points or almost 25 percent. There had never been such a precipitous decline. Indeed, the drop was nearly twice the largest previous daily decline of 13 percent, which took place on October 24, 1929 (Black Thursday), a distant early warning that the Great Depression lay ahead.

From its earlier high until the stock market at last closed on that fateful Black Monday of 1987, some $1 trillion had been erased from the total value of U.S. stocks. The stunning decline seemed to shock nearly all market participants.

But why? In the stock market *anything* can happen—and I would argue the point even more strongly today.

Changes in the nature and structure of our financial markets—and a radical shift in its participants—are making shocking and unexpected market aberrations ever more probable. The amazing market swings we have witnessed in the past few years tend to confirm that likelihood. In the 1950s and 1960s, the daily changes in the level of stock prices typically exceeded 2 percent only three or four times per year. But in the year ended July 30, 2008, we've witnessed 35 such moves—14 were up, and 21 were down. Based on past experience, the probability of that scenario was . . . *zero.*

So not only is speculation a loser's game; it's a game whose outcome can't be predicted with any kind of confidence. The laws of probability don't apply to our financial markets. For in the speculation-driven financial markets there is no reason whatsoever to expect that just because an event has never happened before, it can't happen in the future. Metaphorically speaking, *the fact that the only swans we humans have ever observed are white doesn't mean that no black swans exist.* For evidence, look no further than the Black Monday I just mentioned. Not only was its occurrence utterly unpredictable and beyond all historical experience, but its consequences were, too.

Far from being an omen of dire days ahead, it proved to be a harbinger of the greatest bull market in recorded history. So one never knows.

Nassim Nicholas Taleb captures this idea with great insight in his book, *The Black Swan: The Impact of the Highly Improbable* (Random House, 2007).* But Taleb only confirms what we already know: In the financial markets, the improbable is, in fact, highly probable (or, as Taleb also notes, the highly probable is utterly improbable). Yet far too many of us, amateurs and professionals alike, investors and advisers and managers, continue to look ahead with apparent confidence that the past is prologue in the financial markets, based on our assumptions that the probabilities established by history will endure. Please, please, please: *Don't count on it.*

Black Swans and Investment Returns

Daily swings in market returns have *nothing* to do with the long-term accretion of investment values. In fact,

---

*Taleb defines a "black swan" as (1) an outlier beyond the realm of our regular expectations, (2) an event that carries an extreme impact, and (3) a happening that, after the fact, our human nature enables us to accept by concocting explanations that make it seem predictable. So there it is: events that are rare, extreme, and retrospectively predictable. Life is full of them, especially in the financial markets!

while there have been numerous black swans in our short-term-oriented and speculative financial markets, there have been *no* black swans in the long-term investment returns generated by U.S. stocks. Why? Because businesses—as a group—employ capital effectively, reacting to and often anticipating changes in the productive economy of manufactured goods and consumer services. Yes, for better or for worse, we are faced with cyclical swings in our economy, periodic recessions, and even rare depressions. But American capitalism has demonstrated remarkable resilience, plugging along steadily even as times change, driving growth in earnings and paying dividends that have risen apace over time, in step with our growing economy.

Nonetheless, there has always existed the serious risk that speculation in our flighty financial economy (emotions) might spread its contamination to our overproductive business economy (enterprise). The great U.S. economist Hyman Minsky dedicated much of his career to his financial instability hypothesis—"stability leads to instability"—which he summed up profoundly:

> *Financial markets will not only respond to profit-driven demands of business leaders and individual investors but also as a result of the profit-seeking entrepreneurialism of financial firms. Nowhere are evolution, change, and*

Schumpeterian entrepreneurship more evident than in
banking and finance, and nowhere is the drive for profits
more clearly the factor making for change.*

Long before the creation of the recent wave of complex financial products, Minsky observed that the financial system is particularly prone to innovation. He noted
the symbiotic relationship between finance and industrial
development, in which "financial evolution plays a crucial role in the dynamic patterns of the economy." When
money-manager capitalism became a reality during the
1980s and institutional investors became the largest repos-
itories of savings in the country, they began to exert their
influence on our financial markets and the conduct of our
business enterprises.

The crisis in our financial system that first became
painfully evident in mid-2007 was a stark warning of
Minsky's prescience. Among the few market participants
who seemed to see it coming was Jeremy Grantham,
one of the nation's most thoughtful professional investors. He entitled his brilliant year-end 2007 essay "The

---

*A reference to the work of the great economist Joseph
Schumpeter, whose analysis of the role of the entrepreneur as the
driving force in economic growth has now been accepted as part
of conventional wisdom.

Minsky Meltdown." With the collapse of the stocks of government-sponsored Fannie Mae and Freddie Mac and the U.S. Treasury formally assuming responsibility for their debt obligations barely six months later, there was little doubt that Grantham's prediction had come to pass. Only time will tell whether this Minsky meltdown will be merely cyclical or powerfully secular.

Tortoises Win

Yet the financial markets—as speculative as they are from time to time—provide the only liquid instruments that facilitate our ownership of business and enable us to invest our savings. So, what to do in an investment world fraught with speculation, rarity, extremeness, and retrospective predictability? Peter L. Bernstein, respected investment strategist, economist, best-selling author, and the recipient of a remarkable string of professional awards, provided sound advice in 2001 in an essay titled "The 60/40 Solution" (60 percent stocks, 40 percent bonds), a strategy focused on emulating investment tortoises rather than speculative hares:

> *In investing, tortoises tend to win far more often than hares over the turns of the market cycle. . . . Placing large bets*

on an unknown future is worse than gambling because at least in gambling you know the odds. Most of the decisions in life motivated by greed have unhappy outcomes.

Hares Win (But How Can That Be?)

Yet just a few years later, Bernstein changed his mind. Let me try to sum up in a few paragraphs the gist of his formidably influential article in the March 1, 2003, edition of his *Economics & Portfolio Strategy*.

We simply do not know about the future. There is no assurance that historical experience will replay itself in any shape, form, or sequence. The expected equity premium not only is low, but also doesn't take into account the abnormalities lurking in today's investment environment. We're living in unprecedented times.

So get rid of the extra freight of long-term optimization and let short-term forces play the dominant role. Rely on a bipolar portfolio, with one segment for good news and one for bad news, reaching for the most volatile asset classes to do the job. Build ramparts around equities, such as gold futures, venture capital, real estate, instruments denominated in foreign currencies, Treasury Inflation-Protected Securities (TIPS), and long-term bonds.

And the icing on the cake: Don't do any of these things permanently. Opportunities and risks will come and go. Change allocations frequently. Be flexible. Buy-and-hold investing is the past; market timing is the future.

I salute Peter Bernstein for marching, red cape and all, into an arena filled with bulls—and bears—and I admire him immensely for trying to reconcile the irreconcilable. And indeed there is much merit in what he recommends, however difficult it may be to implement. But what he is really recommending, in my judgment, is speculation. And it is a loser's game.

The Perils of Market Timing

Whether market timing is motivated by greed or fear or anything else, the inescapable fact is that, for investors as a group, *there is no market timing*. For better or worse, all of us investors together own the total market portfolio. When one investor borrows from Peter (no pun intended!) to pay Paul, another does the reverse, and the market portfolio neither knows nor cares. This transfer of holdings among the participants is speculation, pure and simple.

Individually, of course, any one of us has the opportunity to win by departing from the market portfolio. But on what rationale will we base our market timing? On our conviction about the prospective equity premium?* Concern about the *known* risks that are already presumably reflected in the level of market prices? Concern about the *unknown* risks? (It is no mean task to divine the unknowable.) Yes, as Bernstein says, "opportunities and risks will appear and disappear in short order." I agree with that proposition. But human emotions and behavioral flaws militate against our capitalizing on them. Count me as one who simply doesn't believe that market timing works.

Don't forget that *your* incredible success in consistently making each move at the *right* time in the market is but *my* pathetic failure in making each move at the *wrong* time. One of us, metaphorically speaking, must be on the opposite side of each and every trade. A lifetime of experience in this business makes me profoundly skeptical of all forms of speculation, market timing included. I don't know anyone who can do it successfully, nor anyone who has done so in the past. Heck, I don't even know anyone

---

*The equity premium is the amount by which the annual returns on stocks have exceeded—or are expected to exceed—the risk-free rate of return (usually U.S. Treasury bills or bonds).

who *knows* anyone who has timed the market with consistent, successful, replicable results.

It is difficult enough to make even one timing decision correctly. But you have to be right twice. For the act of, say, getting *out* of the market implies the act of getting *in* later, and at a more favorable level. But when, pray? You'll have to tell me. And if the odds of making the right decision are, because of costs, even less than 50–50, the odds of making two right decisions are even less than one out of four. And the odds of making, say, a dozen correct timing decisions—hardly excessive for a strategy that is *based* on market timing—seem doomed to failure. Over, say, 20 years, betting at those odds would give you just one chance out of 4,096 to win (even when we ignore the negative impact of the transaction costs entailed in the implementation of each of those decisions).

One chance out of 4,096? Are those good odds to bet on? Suffice it to say that Warren Buffett doesn't think so. In mid-2008 it was reported that he took the opposite side of a not totally-dissimilar wager. He laid on a $320,000 bet with Protégé Partners, a firm that manages funds of hedge funds, that over the 10 years ending in 2017, the returns from Vanguard's flagship 500 Index Fund would top the collective return from the five (inevitably) speculative, freewheeling, market-timing, trade-churning hedge funds selected by Protégé's supposed experts.

I'm partial, of course, but that's a bet I might even be glad to place with my own money. (Whoever wins, by the way, the prize money from both sides—$1 million, including interest earned—will go to charity.)

Striking a Balance

Of course, our markets need speculators—financial entrepreneurs, traders, and short-term traders, risk takers restlessly searching to exploit anomalies and imperfections in the market for profitable advantage. Equally certain, our markets need investors—financial conservatives, long-term owners of stocks who hold in high esteem the traditional values of prudence, stability, safety, and soundness. But a balance needs to be struck, and in my judgment, today's powerful and debilitating turbulence is one of the prices we pay for allowing that balance to get out of hand.

Most of the themes in the preceding paragraph appear in the brilliant 2001 memoir, *On Money and Markets,* by economist and investor Henry Kaufman, one of the wisest of all the wise men in Wall Street's long history. Clearly, Dr. Kaufman shares my concerns, as he expresses his own fears about the corporatization of Wall Street, the globalization of finance, the limits on the power of policy makers, and the transformation of our markets. In his final chapter, he summarizes his concerns:

Trust is the cornerstone of most relationships in life. Financial institutions and markets must rest on a foundation of trust as well. . . . Unfettered financial entrepreneurship can become excessive and damaging as well—leading to serious abuses and the trampling of the basic laws and morals of the financial system. Such abuses weaken a nation's financial structure and undermine public confidence in the financial community. . . . Only by improving the balance between entrepreneurial innovation and more traditional values can we improve the ratio of benefits to costs in our economic system. . . . Regulators and leaders of financial institutions must be the most diligent of all.

I couldn't agree more. Indeed it is our failure to deal earlier with these very issues that set the stage for today's financial crises. So every one of us must be concerned about the momentary triumph of short-term speculation in our financial markets, of which we have far too much, at the direct expense of long-term investment, of which we have not nearly enough. But it is up to today's market participants particularly, as well as academics and regulators, to work together to restore that balance and return financial conservatism to its rightful preeminence. Otherwise, to paraphrase the concern cited earlier in this chapter that was expressed by Lord Keynes all those years ago, "the hazards we face now that enterprise has become a mere bubble on a whirlpool of speculation means that the job of capitalism *is* being ill-done."

That is what has happened, and our society cannot afford to let it continue.

Chapter 3

Too Much Complexity, Not Enough Simplicity

F or me, simplicity has always been the key to successful investing, and the time-honored wisdom of Occam's razor, set forth by the fourteenth-century philosopher and friar William of Occam, has stood me in good stead: *When confronted with multiple solutions to a problem, choose the simplest one.*[*] My career has been a monument, not to brilliance or complexity, but to common sense and simplicity, "the uncanny ability," as one observer has said of me, "to recognize the obvious." (I'm not sure it was meant as a compliment!) So let's recognize some of the simple and

---

[*]Occam expressed the razor (or rule) in various ways in his writings. The most common version translates from the Latin as "Plurality ought never be posited without necessity."

obvious facts of our highly complex financial and investing life today, beginning with the role of innovation.

It is hard to argue against the value of innovation in general. Our laptop computers probably have enough calculating power to send a man to the moon. With tiny pocket versions, we can connect to Wi-Fi all over the world; keep in touch with our kids; and take, send, and store photographs. The Internet provides an infinite store of information available on demand. E-tailing has given consumers the benefit of previously unimaginable price competition. Medical technology (like my heart transplant) has enhanced and lengthened our life and its quality.

But in the financial sector innovation is different. Why? Because here there exists a sharp dichotomy between the value of innovation to the financial institution itself and the value of innovation to its clients. Financial institutions operate by a kind of *reverse* Occam's razor. They have a large incentive to favor the complex and costly over the simple and cheap, quite the opposite of what most investors need and ought to want.

Innovation in finance is designed largely to benefit those who create the complex new products, rather than those who own them. Consider, for example, the revenue production (and cost bloating) that occurs along the food chain of the creation of collateralized debt obligations (CDOs) backed by mortgages. The mortgage broker brings in the borrower and takes a commission from the bank.

The bank takes a commission when it secures the mortgage; the rating agency takes a fee (estimated at $400,000 a throw) for each security it rates (usually, of course, in return for the coveted AAA rating, without which it can't be sold). The stockbroker takes a commission when he sells the security to customers. These costs—however deeply hidden—end up being paid by some combination of the person who borrows the money to buy a home and the end-user investor who purchases the CDO for a portfolio. The multiple croupiers—all those middlemen—reap the rewards.

With the unfathomable complexity of these and other financial innovations and the endorsement—and, I would argue, the complicity—of our rating agencies, this financial legerdemain creates a modern version of alchemy. It begins with the *lead*, as it were—a package of, say, 5,000 B- or BB-rated mortgages, with maybe even a few A's thrown in. They are then miraculously turned into the *gold*, as it were, of a $500 million CDO with (in one typical case) 75 percent of its bonds rated AAA, 12 percent rated AA, 4 percent rated A, and only 9 percent rated BBB or below. (Hint: We now know that, despite the risk-reducing character of such broad diversification, lead is still lead.)*

---

*In mid-2008 *Grant's Interest Rate Observer* examined one such CDO. Its original principal value was $2 billion. Every series of bonds had been downgraded, with the AAA bonds now rated B1 ("speculative, high credit risk"). The estimated value of the entire portfolio had plummeted by more than 80 percent, to $362 million.

For banks, the lure of CDOs is elementary: They like getting paid large fees for lending money, and when they can quickly get the loans off their own books and into public hands (so-called securitization), it can hardly be surprising that they aren't much concerned about the creditworthiness of those families for whose homes they have provided mortgages.

Derivatives: Dancing to the Music

As rightly newsworthy as they have been, these complex CDOs and structured investment vehicles (SIVs) (essentially money market funds that borrow short and lend long, therefore lacking the security of true money market funds) are only the bleeding edge of an enormous growth in these complex financial instruments that has overwhelmed our financial markets and superseded the capitalization and trading volume of the investments themselves.

At the same time, the markets have been flooded by so-called derivatives, that is, instruments whose values are derived from yet other financial instruments. (Recall our earlier discussion of the futures and options on the S&P 500 Index.) Through interest rate swaps and credit default swaps (don't ask)—traded back and forth around the globe in nanoseconds—these derivatives are used to assume risk, to magnify risk, and (paradoxically) to hedge risk. Their trading volumes are staggering (though rarely disclosed), and their dimension is grotesquely disproportionate to the instruments from which their value is derived. (The credit obligations subject to default swaps are valued at $2 trillion; the swaps themselves total $62 trillion.) The notional principal value of all derivatives is almost beyond imagination—some $600 trillion, nearly 10 times the $66 trillion gross domestic product (GDP) of the entire world.

The innovation of derivatives has enriched the financial sector (and the rating agencies) with their enormous fees, even as the overrated, as it were, CDOs have wreaked havoc on the balance sheets of those who purchased them and have now been left holding the bag, surprisingly including the banks and brokers that created and sold them. Since virtually all of the main mutual fund managers also run pension money, their broad embrace of CDOs has in addition eroded the retirement plans of tens of millions of citizens.

Not to be outdone, SIVs have also created havoc. For it turns out that in order to sell these instruments to their customers, banks increasingly issued so-called liquidity puts to buyers, effectively guaranteeing to repurchase the SIVs on demand at face value. Citigroup, it turns out, was holding not only $55 billion of CDOs on its books, but also some $25 billion of SIV assets that could be (and later were) "put" back to the bank, a risk not publicly disclosed by Citigroup until November 4, 2007.

Astonishingly, Robert Rubin, chairman of Citigroup's executive committee (and a man, one might say, of not inconsiderable financial acumen), has stated that until the summer of 2007, *he had never even heard of a liquidity put.* That admission is not quite as embarrassing as former chairman Charles Prince's comment as the storm of the financial crisis was about to break: "As long as the music is playing, you have to keep dancing. We're still dancing." One can only wonder just when senior bankers stopped looking at their balance sheets.

In the months following the deterioration of the credit standing of our largest banks and investment banks (and many smaller banks), the crisis spread to two of our government-sponsored enterprises (GSEs), known as Fannie Mae and Freddie Mac. Together, they have provided some $5 trillion of mortgage loans to American families, an essential part of the nation's policy of encouraging home ownership. While their mortgage portfolios are of far higher quality than those alchemistic CDOs, these highly leveraged (say, $40 of borrowed money for each $1 of assets) shareholder-owned firms depend on regular borrowing in the money market.

Fears about their solvency (despite the implicit support of the federal government) have led to a collapse of about 80 percent in their stock prices. Faced with a credit crisis engendered in part by heavy mortgage foreclosures around the country, the U.S. Treasury had no choice but to formally affirm its backing for these GSEs.* This issue goes far beyond credit, however. It raises the profound policy question of whether it is sensible or desirable—or ultimately even possible—to privatize the substantial rewards earned in mortgage lending (their shareholders made billions; their executives received fortunes in compensation), at the same time as we socialize the risks (the taxpayers pick up the tab). More broadly, why should our government use taxpayer dollars to lift inefficient, indifferently managed firms to safety? Surely that is a long way from the kind of capitalism envisioned by the economist Joseph Schumpeter.

Marketers Win, Investors Lose

Since there's money to be made—lots of it—in the creation and marketing of inevitably complex innovations, the disease is contagious. CDOs and their by-now hundreds of

---

*Even this backing proved insufficient to relieve the great financial pressure on these two enterprises. So, in September 2008 the U.S. Treasury Department placed them in a federal conservatorship.

innovative kith and kin in banking are echoed in the flood of innovations among stock and bond mutual funds. Of late, these fund innovations that belie simplicity seem designed to respond more generally to the expectation that the returns on stock and bond funds over the coming decade will lag behind historic norms—and far behind the halcyon norms of the 1980s and 1990s, when annual stock returns averaged 17 percent and bond returns averaged 9 percent.

Who wouldn't want to recapture such days? We truly never had it so good before or since that time! But we know (within a reasonably narrow tolerance) what returns to expect from simple, broadly diversified portfolios of stocks and bonds over the next decade (likely 7 and 5 percent, respectively). So we have no choice but to rely on reasonable expectations, formed on the basis of the known sources of stock returns (the initial dividend yield plus the subsequent rate of earnings growth) and bond returns (the initial interest rate). What then explains our expectations (or our hopes) that we can outguess the markets and add additional returns by selecting complex strategies or managers that hold optimal subsets of the market portfolio? Dr. Samuel Johnson would answer: "It was the triumph of hope over experience."

Yet what comes from all this churn of fund innovation, other than a plethora of management and advisory and transaction fees? Inevitably, we are left with a certain melancholy about the objectives of those who provide these intermediation services. They must be well aware that most investors have been ill-served by innovation, and would be best served by the kind of simple, straightforward all-market index strategy that was pioneered at Vanguard. Indeed, as he relinquished the reins of the Magellan Fund in 1990, even Fidelity's remarkable Peter Lynch declared, *"Most investors would be better off in an index fund."* He was right!

"Don't Just Stand There. Do Something!"

But in finance, we have businesses to run. However unfortunately for our investors, there is great pressure both to shape and to respond to the short-term perceptions of our clients—a fact of life that, for better or worse, rules at least as strongly in the marketing of financial products as it does in consumer products such as automobiles, perfume, toothpaste, and jewelry. But of necessity, all of this shuffling of financial paper entails a cost that ill serves investors.

As Benjamin Graham pointed out way back in September 1976—coincidentally, only moments after the first index fund was launched—"the stock market resembles a huge laundry in which investors take in large blocks of each other's washing, nowadays to the tune of 30 *million* shares a day." (He could not have imagined today's speculation: more than three *billion* shares a day.) That's a lot of washing, a reflection of Wall Street's perennial advice to its clients: "Don't just stand there. Do something!"

Alas, the reverse proposition, "Don't do something. Just stand there," *while the inevitable strategy of all investors as a group*—think about that, please—not only is counterintuitive to the emotions that play on the minds of virtually all us individual investors, but also would be counterproductive to the wealth of those who market securities and who manage securities portfolios. While the industry, disingenuously, argues that investors should ignore indexing in favor of funds designed to serve their individual objectives and requirements, Ben Graham had an opinion on that, too: *"only a convenient cliché or alibi to justify the mediocre record of the past."*

Mutual Funds: Lowering the Bar

Sometimes the public interest demands introspection, so later I'll explore at greater length how the industry in which I have spent my life has failed in some of its most basic stewardship obligations—to its shareholders, to its owners, to itself, and to its own history—and how it can find the right path again. For now, let me just say that the industry has run its own mad rush to innovation—everything from the short-term global income funds and adjustable-rate mortgage funds of the 1980s to the "ultra short-term" high-yield bond funds of 2007 (which in the 2008 crisis became another one of the industry's abject failures).

Our creation of literally hundreds of technology funds, telecommunications funds, Internet funds, and the like to capitalize on the Information Age during the New Economy craze of 1998–2000 is but one more example of complex innovation run amok. As the market soared, fund investors poured hundreds of billions of dollars into these highly promoted funds, only to take a huge hit in the subsequent crash.

We actually can measure how much that wholesale embrace of fund innovation cost our investors. Let's compare the returns reported by the *funds themselves* (time-weighted returns) to the returns actually earned by *fund investors* (dollar-weighted returns) during the 25 years ended 2005. The average equity fund *reported* an annual rate of return of 10 percent for the period—trailing the 12.3 percent return on an S&P 500 Index fund. But the return *actually earned* by the investors in these funds was 7.3 percent, a lag of 2.7 percentage points per year below the return the funds themselves reported.

Cumulatively, then, fund investors on average experienced but a 482 percent increase in their capital over the period. Yet, simply by buying and holding the market portfolio through an index fund, they would have earned an increase in capital of 1718 percent, nearly four times as large! Thanks to the innovation and creativity of fund sponsors—and surely the greed (or perceived need) of fund investors—the return that mutual fund investors received on their hard-earned capital was less than a third of the return offered by the stock market itself. For the mainstream funds, the losses were much smaller; for their New Economy cousins, the losses were staggering. So much for the well-being of the investor!

As to the well-being of managers, we can conservatively estimate that the fees and sales loads paid to fund managers and distributors during this period totaled in the range of $500 billion. So yes, *someone* is earning enormous profits by jumping on the bandwagon of innovation, but unless you are a fund manager or distributor, that someone is not likely to be you.

Sometimes for Better, but Mostly for Worse

Amidst this wave of complexity, have we forgotten the fact that the most productive investing is the simplest investing, the most peaceable investing, the lowest-cost investing, the most tax-efficient investing—investing with the most consistent strategies and over the longest time horizon? Apparently so. And I'm afraid that the new jazzed-up iterations (largely exchange-traded funds) of the simple index fund that I spawned all those years ago are helping to lead the way. No wonder I wake up some mornings feeling like Dr. Frankenstein. *What have I created!?*

Let me be clear: I favor innovation when it serves fund investors. And I'm pleased that I've been lucky enough to have played a key role in a number of such innovations in the past: the stock index fund, the bond index fund, the defined-maturity bond fund, the tax-managed fund, and even the first fund of funds (and Vanguard is the only firm, I believe, that has never levied an additional layer of expense ratios on such funds).

In recent years, there have been other investor-friendly innovations, including target retirement funds and life strategy funds. Properly used (and properly costed!), these funds can easily serve as an investor's complete investment program for the long run. But in today's wave of fund innovation, I see little else that seems likely to serve investors effectively. Let me give a brief thumbnail sketch of the "products" (by my standards, the wrong way to think about mutual funds) that have been created of late, and offer my own perspectives.

Exchange-Traded Funds

Exchange-traded funds (ETFs) are clearly the most widely accepted innovation of this era. Of course I admire their endorsement of the index fund concept—and (more often than not) their low costs. And how could I not admire the use of broad market index ETFs that are held for the long term, and even broad market segment ETFs that are used in limited amounts to accomplish specific goals? But I have serious questions about the rampant trading of most ETFs, and the negative impact of those layers of brokerage commissions.

Further, I wonder why only 21 among today's 817 ETFs meet the classic requirement of the broadest possible diversification in U.S. or global stocks, with 739 of the remaining ETFs investing in equity market sectors that range from the reasonable to the absurd. (The remaining 57 are ETFs based on various bond indexes.) In this latter category I'd include sectors as narrow as "Emerging Cancer" and leveraged funds that promise to double the market's returns in either up or down markets. Not to be outdone, a few ETFs now offer the opportunity to triple those swings. Could quadruple be next?

Put another way, ETFs used for investment are perfectly sound, but using them for speculation is apt to end badly for investors. Back in 2005, in his 91st year, the Nobel laureate economist Paul Samuelson called the first index mutual fund the equivalent of the invention of the wheel and the alphabet. (Perhaps he was prejudiced: His holdings in that fund, the Vanguard 500 Index Fund, helped pay for the educations of Dr. Samuelson's six children and his 15 grandchildren.) He has never said anything comparable about ETFs, nor, I suspect, will anyone of equal stature do so.

Fundamental Indexing

While this so-called index method of value investing has been presented as some sort of Copernican revolution, the idea behind the methodology is many decades old. But offering such funds in ETF form suggests that they are useful for short-term trading—a dubious proposition on the face of it. And bringing them out only *after* the sharp upsurge in value-fund relative returns during the 2000–2002 stock market collapse suggests the marketing motivation that sponsors are so good at, even though it almost invariably leads to performance chasing that ill serves investors.

Of course, we've been assured by the sponsors of these dubiously dubbed index funds that "value investing wins" (not "has won in the past"), especially in troubled markets. But in the sharp market tumble of mid-2007 to mid-2008, the two leading fundamental index funds were down nearly 20 percent, a loss nearly half again larger than the 13 percent decline in a standard S&P 500 Index fund. As for the financial entrepreneurs who believe in weighting portfolios on the basis of book values, revenues, and earnings, and those who believe in weighting portfolios by dividends, I'm interested to read that they're now arguing with each other about which is the correct strategy, creating even more confusion for investors.

Absolute Return Funds

Given the truly remarkable successes of some of the nation's largest college endowment funds and some of our most speculative hedge funds, small wonder that fund sponsors are falling all over themselves to create fresh-faced new funds using purportedly similar strategies: hedging (funds that are long 130 percent in stocks and short 30 percent), market neutral (funds with no net equity exposure), commodities, purported private equity/venture capital equivalents, and so forth. Here are two pieces of advice: One, look before you leap. Two, don't leap until the fund has produced an actual 10-year track record. Above all, remember (again, courtesy of Warren Buffett), "What the wise man does in the beginning, the fool does in the end." Or, as the Oracle of Omaha sometimes expresses it, "There are three *i*'s in every cycle: first the innovator, then the imitator, and finally the idiot." No matter what fund managers may offer you, don't you be the idiot.

Commodity Funds

First principles: Commodities have no internal rate of return. Their prices are based entirely on supply and demand. That is why they are considered *speculations*, and rank speculations at that. Contrarily, the prices of stocks and bonds are ultimately justified only by their internal rate of return—composed, respectively, of dividends and earnings growth and by interest coupons. That is why stocks and bonds are considered *investments*. I freely concede that the growing worldwide demand that has helped drive the huge rise in the prices of most commodities in recent years may well continue. But it may not. I'm not at all sure that speculation on future price increases will be rewarded.*

Managed Payout Funds

The fund industry apparently only recently discovered that millions of investors are moving from the accumulation phase of investing to the distribution phase (even though that demographic handwriting has been on the wall for decades). So we have new funds that, in effect, guarantee the exhaustion of your assets in whatever time

*An interesting fact: From the time of the Great Fire in London in 1666 to the end of World War I in 1918, commodity prices in England were unchanged on balance. That's two and one-half centuries!

period you choose (something that has *always* been all too easy to accomplish!). We also have funds designed to distribute 3 percent, 5 percent, or 7 percent of your assets without necessarily invading principal. Only time will tell if that will happen, but what seems to have been ignored by the fund industry, for obvious reasons, is the alternative: serving retired investors by increasing fund *investment income*, the forgotten man of the fund industry. But the only sound way to provide more income per unit of risk is to slash fund expenses, so such client-focused innovation is unlikely to happen.

Brazil, Russia, India, and China (BRIC) Funds and International Funds

No doubt about it. With returns in Brazil, Russia, India, and China soaring in recent years, fund sponsors were quick to market them. My long experience warns that it's all too counterproductive for investors to jump on the bandwagon of superior past performance. Of course, the sharp declines (30 to 50 percent in the first half of 2008) that at least India and China have suffered will squash investor appetites for them.

History tells us that when U.S. stock returns lead the world, equity fund capital flows into international markets decline; and then they soar when non-U.S. issues lead. It's hardly surprising, then, that only 20 percent of equity fund cash flows were directed into non-U.S. funds in 1990–2000, when U.S. stocks vastly outpaced foreign issues. Nor is it surprising that since then, with foreign stocks outpacing U.S. issues, the tables have been turned. (Fully $220 billion flowed into foreign funds in 2007, and only about $11 billion into domestic equity funds. Now there's a red flag!) But in the hottest sectors of the international markets, risk is high, so be careful. (Also note that since 1990, the returns of non-U.S. stocks—even including their recent boom—have been dwarfed by the returns on U.S. equities: 6 percent annually versus 10 percent.)

The Innovation Blunderbuss

No objective industry veteran can look at this blunderbuss of innovation with other than a jaundiced eye. The problem is not only that future returns earned on untried and often costly strategies are unpredictable and rarely live up to their hyperbolic promises. The problem is that such a proliferation of idiosyncratic funds that ignore the value of simplicity inevitably results in a fund failure rate that, however rarely publicized, is little short of astonishing. In an earlier book, I wrote that of 355 funds that existed in 1970, only 132 made it through the next 35 years.

In the recent era, of the 6,126 mutual funds that existed at the start of 2001, 3,165 had already been consigned to the dustbin of history by mid-2008. Small wonder that even the portfolio managers who run the funds don't "eat their own cooking." Among 4,356 equity funds, 2,314 managers own no shares—*none*—in the funds they manage. How, I ask, can a less-informed member of the investing public successfully implement a long-term strategy involving mutual funds if only half of all funds can even make it through a period as short as seven years? And how can fund investors muster any faith whatsoever in the funds that now exist when more than half of their managers won't put their own money on the line?

In fact, it is clear that fund investors no longer muster much faith in their mutual funds. A survey of fund investors conducted for one prominent fund manager (not Vanguard) found that 71 percent of investors don't trust the fund industry. Some 66 percent said fund firms don't take responsibility for protecting their shareholders' well-being. And even in the deeply troubled financial sector, mutual funds are at the bottom of the list of trusted service providers.

Back to Basics

So mark me down as a believer in innovation that is based on clarity, consistency, predictability relative to the market, and low cost; innovation that will serve investors over the long term; innovation that provides an optimal opportunity that it will work tomorrow rather than innovation based on what worked yesterday; innovation that not only minimizes the risks of ownership but clearly explains the nature and extent of those risks.

Mark me down, too, as an adversary of complexity, complexity that obfuscates and confuses, complexity that comes hand in hand with costs that serve its creators and marketers even as those costs thwart the remote possibility that a rare sound idea will serve those investors who own it.

If it sounds like I'm reaffirming my belief in the index fund—in both its stock form and its bond form—and in ideas like tax-managed funds, defined-maturity bond funds, and target-date funds (all of which, at their best, have index funds at their core), well, you read me loud and clear. Like William of Occam, I believe that the simple way is the best way—almost always the shortest route to long-term investment success.

Mark me down, too, as an index fundamentalist (though not a fundamental index fundamentalist!), a passionate believer that the simplicity of the original index fund design—highly diversified portfolios of stocks weighted by their market capitalizations—continues to represent the gold standard for investors. If that is indeed true, then other complex fad products are debased by all that alchemy.

As we have seen earlier, many have tried, but no one has yet made lead out of gold. Indeed, all these years later, I still struggle to develop *any* methodology (other than relative costs) for identifying winning strategies or winning funds in advance, and for successfully predicting how long those winning strategies will persist or how long those portfolio managers will continue to manage the funds that have delivered those superior returns in the past.

An All-Too-Predictable Outcome

By now, I suppose, I've pretty much painted myself into a corner as an aging mutual fund Luddite who finds himself uninspired—and unimpressed—by the rise of complexity (and excess cost) at the expense of simplicity (and minimum cost). But it's a great corner!

Happily for my peace of mind, and my conscience, I find that nearly all of the positions I've set forth in this chapter have been endorsed by some of the most informed and respected academics of our time—among them, Nobel laureates William Sharpe and Paul Samuelson (soon to have 95 years of wisdom under his belt)—and by the most successful investors of the modern era, beginning with Warren Buffett himself. I'm happy to let David Swensen, the brilliant chief investment officer of the Yale

University Endowment, a man with an impeccable character and a peerless reputation for intellectual integrity, speak for these deservedly lauded intellects, and for me as well:

> *The fundamental market failure in the mutual-fund industry involves the interaction between sophisticated, profit-seeking providers of financial services and naïve, return-seeking consumers of investment products. The drive for profits by Wall Street and the mutual-fund industry overwhelms the concept of fiduciary responsibility, leading to an all too predictable outcome . . . The mutual fund industry consistently fails to meet the basic active management goal of providing market-beating returns . . . A well-constructed academic study conservatively puts the pre-tax failure rate at 78 to 95 percent for periods ranging from ten to twenty years [as measured against the Vanguard S&P 500 Index Fund]. . . .*
>
> *Investors fare best with funds managed by not-for-profit organizations because the management firm focuses exclusively on serving investor interests. No profit motive conflicts with the manager's fiduciary responsibility. No profit margin interferes with investor returns. No outside corporate interest clashes with portfolio management choices. Not-for-profit firms place*

investor interest front and center. Ultimately, a passive index fund managed by a not-for-profit investment management organization represents the combination most likely to satisfy investor aspirations . . . Out of the enormous breadth and complexity of the mutual-fund world, the preferred solution for investors stands alone in stark simplicity.

In a word, *amen.*

Swensen's apt tribute to an uncluttered, client-focused strategy combined with a simple client-focused structure serves as profound reaffirmation of the fact that our financial system today has quite enough complexity and innovation—with their grossly excessive costs—and not nearly enough simplicity, with its minimal dilution of investor earnings.

BUSINESS

Chapter 4

Too Much Counting, Not Enough Trust

A lbert Einstein was without peer as a theoretical physicist (save, perhaps, Sir Isaac Newton). Probably no human being in history did more to quantify the seemingly unfathomable mysteries of the universe. But he wasn't so much into mathematics, saying, "Do not worry about your difficulties in mathematics. I assure you mine are still greater."

Indeed, Einstein well understood the limits of quantification and the flaws inherent in thinking that counting alone could advance our understanding of how the world works. A sign that hung in his office at the Institute for Advanced Study in Princeton, New Jersey, is as applicable to all other human pursuits as it is to science:

*Not everything that counts can be counted, and not
everything that can be counted counts.*

That rule also applies to the conduct of business
affairs. Of course, as the father of relativity, Einstein
has to be taken in relative terms. No business can trust
everything and count nothing. Nor can any business
count everything and trust nothing. It's all a question of
balance, although my own instincts lead me toward far
less reliance on counting and far more reliance on trusting. Statistics—in charts, graphs, and tables—can be used
to prove almost anything in business, but unquantifiable
values have a way of holding steady as a rock.

During my sophomore year at Princeton University,
back in 1948, that lesson began to sink into my brain. It
was there that my interest in economics began with my
study of the first edition of Paul Samuelson's *Economics:
An Introductory Analysis.* In that ancient era, economics
was heavily conceptual and traditional. Our study covered
both economic theory and the worldly philosophers from
the eighteenth century on—Adam Smith, John Stuart
Mill, John Maynard Keynes, and the like. Quantitative
analysis was, by today's standards, conspicuous by its
absence. My recollection is that calculus was not even a
department prerequisite. ("Quants," of course—those
quantitative strategists who have flooded the financial

sector in recent decades and whose track record in the recent market downturn has been so erratic—had not yet entered the field.)

I don't know whether to credit or blame the original electronic calculator for inaugurating the sea change in the study of how economies and markets work. But with the coming of today's incredibly powerful personal computers and the onset of the Information Age, numeracy is in the saddle today and rides economics. Einstein's excellent advice seems to have been largely forgotten. If you can't count it, it seems, it doesn't matter.

I disagree with that syllogism. Indeed, I firmly believe that to presume that what cannot be measured is not very important is tantamount to blindness. But before I get to the pitfalls of measurement, to say nothing of trying to measure the immeasurable—things like trust, wisdom, character, ethical values, and the hearts and souls of the human beings who play the central role in all economic activity—I want to discuss the fallacies of some of the popular measurements of the day and the pitfalls created for investors and contemporary society by government, finance, and business.

Today, in our society, in economics, and in finance, we place far too much trust in numbers. *Numbers are not reality*. At best, they are a pale reflection of reality. At worst, they're a gross distortion of the truths we seek to measure. But the damage doesn't stop there. Not only do we rely too heavily on historic economic and market data; our optimistic bias also leads us to misinterpret the data and give them credence that they rarely merit. By worshipping at the altar of numbers and by discounting the immeasurable, we have in effect created a numeric economy that can easily undermine the real one.

Government: Making the Numbers Fit

Many of the numbers that we cannot count on, paradoxically, are produced by our federal government. As Kevin Phillips pointed out in his essay "Numbers Racket," published in the May 2008 issue of *Harper's* magazine, we're being grossly misled by government data, including the vital numbers that have become central to our national dialogue, such as our national output or gross domestic product (GDP), our unemployment rate, and our inflation rate.

- It turns out that our GDP includes so-called imputed income, such as the assumed value of income from living in our own homes, the benefits of free checking accounts, and the value of employer-paid insurance premiums. Such phantom income accounts for fully $1.8 trillion (!) of our $14 trillion GDP.
- The Bureau of Labor Statistics proudly reports that our mid-2008 unemployment rate is a relatively low

5.2 percent (albeit up from 5.0 percent earlier in the year). But the number of unemployed excludes workers too discouraged to look for a job, part-time workers looking for full-time jobs, those who want a job but aren't actively searching for one, and those who are living on Social Security disability benefits. If we include these unemployed souls, the unemployment rate nearly doubles, to 9.0 percent.

• The understatements in the consumer price index (CPI) are even more egregious. Years ago, the cost of living was changed to include "owner-equivalent rent," which sharply reduced the reported inflation rate during the recent housing boom. The concept of product substitution also was incorporated, meaning essentially that if top-grade hamburger gets too expensive, we substitute a cheaper grade. And (this is really true!) we don't count cost increases that are attributable to increased quality ("hedonic adjustments"). That is, if airfares double but air travel service is deemed twice as efficient, the calculated cost of air travel is unchanged.

Finance: Attributing Certitude to History

The counting we do in the investment field is also badly flawed. The notion that common stocks are acceptable as investments—rather than merely speculative instruments—can be said to have begun in 1925 with Edgar Lawrence Smith's *Common Stocks as Long-Term Investments*. Its most recent incarnation came in 1994, in Jeremy Siegel's *Stocks for the Long Run*. Both books unabashedly state the case for equities and, arguably, both helped fuel the great bull markets that ensued. Both, of course, were then followed, perhaps inevitably, by two of the worst bear markets of the past 100 years.

Both books, too, were replete with data, but the seemingly infinite data presented in the Siegel tome, a product of this age of computer-driven numeracy, puts its predecessor to shame. Siegel clearly established that, over two centuries of history, the real return on U.S. stocks has centered around 7 percent per year (about 10 percent in nominal terms, before the erosion of inflation, which has averaged about 3 percent).

But it's not the panoply of information imparted in *Stocks for the Long Run* that troubles me. Who can be against knowledge? As Sir Francis Bacon reminded us, "Knowledge is power." My concern is that too many of us make the implicit assumption that stock market history repeats itself when we know, deep down, that the only valid prism through which to view the market's future is the one that takes into account not *history*, but the *sources* of stock returns, discussed in Chapter 2.

The Experts Are Wrong . . . Again

That experts are so often wrong seems such a self-evident truth that you might well wonder who exactly would be so foolish as to project future returns at past historical rates. Yet the woods are full of expert investor advisers and analysts who do exactly that. Look at the modish popularity of so-called Monte Carlo simulations. The problem with these simulations—essentially calculating the monthly returns on stocks, tossing them into a blender, and casting the seemingly infinite series of permutations and combinations in the form of probabilities—is that by relying simply on historic total returns for their figures, they ignore the sources of those returns.

Yes, speculative returns, which are based on changes in the number of dollars investors are willing to pay for each dollar of corporate earnings—the price-earnings (P/E) ratio—tend to revert to the long-term norm of zero. Yes, corporate earnings growth tends to parallel the nominal growth rate of our economy. (No surprises there!) But *no*, the contribution of dividend yields to returns depends, not on historic norms, but on the dividend yield that *actually* exists at the time of the projection of future returns. With the dividend yield at 2.3 percent in July 2008, of what use are historical

statistics that reflect a dividend yield that averaged
5 percent—more than twice the present yield? (Answer:
None.) Reasonable expectations for future real returns
on stocks beginning mid-2008, then, should center
around 5 percent, not the historical norm of 7 percent.
What could be more elementary than that? But that's
often the trouble with complex calculations: They can't
be trusted to convey simple truths.

Even sophisticated corporate executives and their
pension consultants follow the same flawed course.
Indeed, one typical corporate annual report expressly
stated that "our asset return assumption is derived from
a detailed study conducted by our actuaries and our
asset management group, and *is based on long-term historical returns*." Astonishingly, but naturally, this policy leads
corporations to raise their future expectations with each
increase in past returns, precisely the opposite of what
reason correctly suggests.

At the outset of the bull market in the early 1980s,
for example, major corporations assumed a future return
on pension assets—bonds as well as stocks—of 7 percent.
At the market peak as 2000 began, nearly all firms had
sharply raised their assumptions, some to 10 percent
or even more. Since pension portfolios are balanced
between equities and bonds, they had implicitly raised the
expected annual return on the *stocks* in the portfolio to as

much as 15 percent, even as the bear market that followed would make that assumption seem like a bad joke.

If those corporate financial officers had only shut down their computers (and put aside their inherent self-interest in minimizing the contributions to those pension plans) and read John Maynard Keynes instead, they would have known what the numbers were never going to tell them: The bubble created by all the emotions that had fueled the boom—optimism, exuberance, greed, all wrapped in the excitement of the turn of the millennium, the fantastic promise of the Information Age and the New Economy—had to burst. And so, of course, it did, in late March 2000, at the very moment that those rosy 10 percent growth projections were being printed in glossy annual reports.

Clearly, investors would have been wise to set their expectations for future returns on the basis of the current sources of returns, rather than fall into the trap of looking to past returns to set their course. That the dividend yield as 2000 began was at an all-time low of just 1 percent and the P/E at a near record high of 32 times earnings together explain why the average return on stocks in the current decade is at present running at an annual rate of less than 1 percent. If the market remains where it is today at the close of 2009, the decade's return will be the second lowest of any full decade in history. (In the 1930s, the annual return on the S&P 500 averaged 0.0 percent.)

Business: The Bias toward Optimism

But it's not just our capital markets that have been corrupted by the perils of relying so heavily on the apparent certitude of numbers. Our businesses, too, have much to answer for, and indeed, the economic consequences of managing corporations by the numbers are both extensive and profound.

The terrible track record of CEOs in predicting growth for their own firms is a well-established fact, but their bias toward optimism—and their use (or, rather, abuse) of numbers to support optimistic assumptions—at least has the excuse of self-interest. Security analysts are supposed to bring a more objective eye to such numbers, but time and again, they too uncritically put on rose-colored glasses and go along for the ride.

With the earnings guidance from the corporations they cover, Wall Street security analysts have, over the past two decades, regularly estimated average future five-year earnings growth. On average, the projections were for growth at an annual rate of 11.5 percent. But as a group, these firms met their earnings targets in only three of the 20 rolling five-year periods that followed. And the actual earnings growth of these corporations has averaged only about one-half of the original projection—just 6 percent.

But how could we be surprised by this gap between guidance and delivery? The aggregate profits of our corporations are closely linked, indeed almost in lock-step, with the growth of our economy. It has been a rare year when corporate profits accounted for less than 4.5 percent of U.S. gross domestic product (GDP), and profits only rarely account for as much as 9 percent. Indeed, since 1929, after-tax profits have grown at an average rate of 5.6 percent annually, actually lagging the 6.6 percent growth rate of the GDP. In a dog-eat-dog capitalistic economy where the competition is vigorous and largely unfettered and where the consumer is king, how could the profits of corporate America *possibly* grow faster than our GDP?

Our optimistic bias has also led to another serious weakness. In a trend that has attracted too little notice, we have changed the very definition of earnings. While earnings reported to shareholders under generally accepted accounting principles (GAAP) had been the standard since Standard & Poor's first began to collect the data years ago, in recent years the standard has changed to *operating* earnings.

Operating earnings, essentially, are reported earnings bereft of all those messy charges like inventory revaluations and capital write-offs, often the result of unwise investments and mergers of earlier years. They are considered nonrecurring, though for corporations as a group they recur, year after year, with remarkable consistency. For the record, reported earnings for the S&P 500 Index over the past decade have averaged $51 per share, while operating earnings averaged $61 per share. The illusory number that we could so easily count was 20 percent higher than the real number that we could actually trust.

What's more, we now have pro forma earnings—a ghastly formulation that makes new use (or, again, abuse) of a once-respectable term—that report corporate results net of unpleasant developments. Such "no bad stuff" calculations are one more step in the wrong direction. Even auditor-certified earnings have come under doubt, as the number of corporate earnings restatements has soared nearly 18-fold—from 90 in 1997 to 1,577 in 2006. Does that sound like punctilious corporate financial reporting? Hardly. Indeed, it sounds like precisely its opposite.

Loose accounting standards (i.e., loose *counting*) have made it possible to create, out of thin air, what passes for earnings. One popular method is making an acquisition and then taking giant charges described as nonrecurring, only to be reversed in later years when needed to bolster sagging operating results. But the breakdown in our accounting standards goes far beyond that: cavalierly classifying large items as immaterial, hyping the assumed future returns of pension plans, counting as sales those made to customers who borrowed the money from the seller to make the purchases, making special deals to force extra sales at quarter's end, and so on. If you can't merge your way into meeting the numbers, in effect, just change the numbers. But what we loosely describe as *creative* accounting is only a small step removed from *dishonest* accounting.

The Real-World Consequences of Counting

When our government in effect cooks the books by which we weigh the economy, when our financial institutions attribute certitude to history, and when our businesses practice a willful and self-serving optimism, the ripples extend far beyond unfortunate numeric abstractions. These deeply ingrained flaws have societal implications, and most of them are negative.

For example, when investors accept stock market returns as being derived from a type of actuarial table, they won't be prepared for the risks that arise from the inevitable variability of investment returns and the inevitable uncertainty of speculative returns. As a result, they are apt to make unwise asset allocation decisions under the duress—or the exuberance—of the moment. Pension plans that make this mistake will have to step up their funding when reality intervenes. When investors base their retirement planning on actually achieving whatever returns the financial markets had provided in the past and then tacitly ignore the staggering toll taken by intermediation costs and taxes (to say nothing of inflation), they save a pathetically small portion of what they ought to be saving to assure a comfortable retirement.

Another example of the real-world consequences: Our financial system has, in substance, challenged our corporations to produce earnings growth that is, in truth, unsustainable. When corporations fail to meet their numeric targets the hard way—over the long term, by raising productivity; by improving old products and creating new ones; by providing services on a more friendly, more timely, and more efficient basis; and by challenging the people of the organization to work more effectively together (and those are the ways that our best corporations achieve success)—they are compelled to do it in other ways: ways that often subtract value from you, from me, and from society.

Finance Calls the Tune for Business

One of these ways, of course, is an aggressive mergers and acquisitions strategy. Even leaving aside the commonplace that most mergers fail to achieve their goals, the companies that followed these strategies were well described

in a 2002 *New York Times* op-ed essay as "serial acquirers [whose] dazzling number of deals makes an absence
of long-term management success easy to hide." Tyco
International, one of the most notorious examples of the
modern era, acquired 700 companies before the day of
reckoning came. But the final outcome of the strategy, as
the *Times* piece explained, was almost preordained: "Their
empires of [numbers] hype can be undone very quickly
by market discipline."

Much of this merger activity has reached the level of
absurdity. Michael Kinsley, writing in the *New York Times*
in May 2007, notes that in 1946, Warren Avis had an idea.
He founded Avis Airlines Rent-a-Car. Two years later Avis
sold the company to another businessman, who sold it to a
company called Amoskeag, which sold it to Lazard Freres,
which sold it to giant conglomerate ITT Corporation
(all this by 1965!). All told, Avis has gone through some
18 different ownerships, and each time, Kinsley notes,
"there have been fees for bankers and fees for lawyers,
bonuses for top executives [to pay them off for the past or
to sign them on for the future], and theories about why
this was exactly what the company needed."

Since then (it's a long story), Avis has been publicly
held again, then conglomerate-owned again (Norton
Simon, Esmark, Beatrice Foods); then sold to Wesray
Capital, which sold half of the business to PHH Group,

with the remainder sold to Avis employees, who sold it to a firm called HFS Corporation, which took it public, after which Avis bought, yes, PHH; the combined company was then bought by Cendant. Whew!

Kinsley sums it up well: "Modern capitalism has two parts: there's business, and there's finance. Business is renting you a car at the airport. Finance is something else." What we call business today is largely about finance. (Shades of Minsky, whom we met earlier.) I venture to suggest that the financiers who played all those trading games with Warren Avis's creation took far more money out of the business than the money that trickled down through that complex maze of transactions to the shareholders—who are, of course, the owners of the business.

"Rock, Scissors, Paper"

The saga of Avis is a compelling example of the fact that too many so-called industrial companies have become financial companies—companies that *count* rather than *make*. (Witness the fact that the senior aide to the CEO is almost invariably the chief financial officer, often viewed by the investment community as the éminence grise.) Such companies, again quoting Kinsley's *New York Times* article, "base their strategies not on understanding the businesses they go into, but assume that by scavenging about for good deals, they can better allocate their financial resources than can existing financial markets."

You may remember the children's game in which rock breaks scissors, scissors cut paper, and paper covers rock. In manias, as I noted in my book *The Battle for the Soul of Capitalism*, when prices lose touch with values, paper indeed covers rock. "Paper" companies that *count* have acquired "rock" companies that *make*, and the results have been devastating. When I mention the mergers of America Online (AOL) and Time Warner, of Qwest Communications and U.S. West, and of WorldCom and MCI, I don't have to tell you which was paper and which was rock. These are among the most poignant examples of a phenomenon in which many aggressive corporate acquisitions of companies that were once the rocks of their industries have fallen on perilous times, with hundreds of thousands of loyal long-term employees both losing their jobs and seeing their retirement savings slashed unmercifully.

Giving Judgment a Chance

Lest I be accused of innumeracy, please be clear that I'm not saying that numbers don't matter. Measurement standards—*counting*, if you will—are essential to the communication of financial goals and achievements. I know that. But for going on four decades, I've been engaged in building an enterprise—and a financial institution at that—based far more on the sound implementation of a few commonsense investment ideas, an enlightened sense of human values and ethical standards, and the bond of trust between our firm and its clients. We did our best to avoid measurement with quantitative goals and statistical achievements. Vanguard's market share, as I've said countless times, must be a *measure*, not an *objective*; it must be *earned*, not *bought*. Yet the fact is that our market share of fund industry assets has risen, without interruption, for the past 28 years.

Our strategy arose from a conviction that the best corporate growth comes from putting the horse of doing things for clients ahead of the cart of earnings targets. *Growth must be organic, rather than forced.* No company, of course—and certainly not one as huge as Vanguard is today—can ignore numbers altogether, but I've often noted the extremes in management style between companies that *trust* and companies that *count*, and I fervently hope that anyone who has ever worked for Vanguard includes our company among the former. For my part, I've tried to reinforce the point over the decades with an aphorism that I've seen posted at countless desks throughout our now seemingly countless buildings:

For God's sake, let's always keep Vanguard a place where judgment has at least a fighting chance to triumph over process.

The Spirit of Trust

My faith in trust goes back to the Golden Rule. We are, after all, implored in the Bible to love our neighbors, not to quantify their character; and to do unto them as we would have them do unto us, not to do unto them in exact equal measure what they have done to us. At Vanguard, our own patron saint the great British naval hero Lord Horatio Nelson, captain of the *HMS Vanguard* and an unparalleled molder of men, reaffirms this Golden Rule. Here's how Nelson was described in a sermon that my wife, Eve, and I heard in St. Paul's Cathedral in London on October 23, 2005, the 200th anniversary of his death at the Battle of Trafalgar:

It is true that Nelson was a consummate professional and a hard-working manager . . . but at times of decision, leaders need to make contact with foundational convictions and with a sense of calling which comes from going deep within oneself. This is the source of healthy self-confidence and the ability to master fear and to encourage people in the most extreme circumstances. Any education system which hopes to produce

*effective leaders and followers must take the formation
of these foundational convictions very seriously.*

*Yet we live at a strange time when the periodic table
and anything that can be quantified and reduced to a
mathematical truth is regarded as an accurate description of reality, but the Beatitudes and the teachings of
the world's wisdom traditions are seen as little more
than the debatable opinions of dead sages.*

*Nelson's sense of personal and individual call was
developed within a tradition which also understands
growth in the spiritual life as growth in love of neighbour. Nelson spared no pains to stand by and serve
his shipmates. He exhibited an infectious trust in
people which called out the best in them and engaged
them not only to Nelson's person but enrolled them
in the cause in which he believed . . . a faith that people are to be trusted in a way that helps them to be
trust-worthy.*

Measure First, Judge Later?

What, then, is to be done about this apparent triumph
of counting over trusting? For one good set of answers,
I turn to David Boyle, English social critic and author of
The Sum of Our Discontent.

We are . . . living at an age when life is completely overwhelmed by numbers and calculation, and we are all increasingly controlled by "targets." . . . The frightening thing is that, just because computers can *count and measure nearly everything, then we* do. *There was a time when we could trust our own judgment, common sense, and intuition to know if we were ill or not. Now we're in danger of being unable to do anything without it being measured first.*

Numbers and measurements are as vulnerable as the Emperor's New Clothes to the incisive, intuitive human question. The closer any of us get to measuring what's really important, the more it escapes us, yet we can recognize it, sometimes in an instant. Relying on that instant a bit more, and our ability to grasp it, is probably the best hope for us all.

But it is not just social critics who recognize that the role of counting must play second fiddle to the role of trusting. Hear exemplary business leader Bill George, former chief of medical technology pioneer Medtronic: "Trust is everything, because success depends upon customers' trust in the products they buy, employees' trust in their leaders, investors' trust in those who invest for them and the public's trust in capitalism. . . . If you do not have integrity, no one will trust you, nor should they."

An Empty Exercise

Please don't misunderstand me. I honor and respect counting. No one realizes better than I that business is demanding and competitive, and that many—indeed, most—business firms have lives that, in Thomas Hobbes's famous formulation, are "solitary, poor, nasty, brutish, and short." We must either compete or die. In such circumstances, we have no alternative but to construct objective and measurable goals and hold those responsible accountable for their achievement. But I recognize as well the deep wisdom that is required to understand that, without trust, counting is at best an empty exercise and at worst a dangerous one.

Agree with me or not, but at least I'm consistent. In 1972, nearly 40 years ago, I closed my annual message to the employees of Wellington Management Company (which I then headed) with this quotation from Daniel Yankelovich, about giving too much credence to counting numbers:*

> *The first step is to measure what can be easily measured. This is okay as far as it goes. The second step is to disregard that which cannot be measured, or*

---

*Having founded the premier marketing research firm of its day, the Harvard-educated Yankelovich knew better than most the uses and abuses of counting.

give it an arbitrary quantitative value. This is artificial and misleading. The third step is to presume that what cannot be measured really is not very important. This is blindness. The fourth step is to say that what cannot be measured does not really exist. This is suicide.

I'm convinced that this quotation is as true today as it was then, and more relevant than ever. Business organizations must learn that "not everything that can be counted counts." Yet today we rely too heavily on counting and not nearly enough on trusting. It is time—well past time, in fact—to strike a healthier balance between the two.

Chapter 5

Too Much Business Conduct, Not Enough Professional Conduct

Among the most obvious, and troubling, manifestations of the change from the stern traditional values of yore to the, well, flexible values of our modern age—with its myriad numeric measures and its largely missing moral measures—is the gradual mutation of our professional associations into business enterprises. Even as power corrupts, so money corrupts the sound functioning of our national agenda.

It was not ever thus. Only a bit more than 40 years ago, *Daedalus*—the venerable and prestigious journal of the American Academy of Arts and Sciences—proudly declared:

Everywhere in American life, the professions are triumphant.

But when *Daedalus* revisited the subject in its 2005 summer issue, the lead essay found that the triumph had been short-lived. "Our professions have gradually been subjected to a whole new set of pressures, from the growing reach of new technologies to the growing importance of making money." The idea of having a calling, the essay noted, was being undermined by "potent market forces [that] have made it increasingly difficult to delineate just how professionals differ from those non-professionals who have [most of] the power and resources in the society."

Let's begin by considering what we mean when we talk about professions and professionals. The article in *Daedalus* defined a profession as having these six common characteristics:

1. A commitment to the interest of clients in particular, and the welfare of society in general.
2. A body of theory or special knowledge.
3. A specialized set of professional skills, practices, and performances unique to the profession.
4. The developed capacity to render judgments with integrity under conditions of ethical uncertainty.
5. An organized approach to learning from experience, both individually and collectively, and thus of growing new knowledge from the context of practice.

6. The development of a professional community responsible for the oversight and monitoring of quality in both practice and professional educators.

Daedalus then added these wonderful words: "*The primary feature of any profession [is] to serve responsibly, selflessly, and wisely . . . and to establish [an] inherently ethical relationship between the professional and the general society*."

Times Have Changed

When we think of professionals, most of us would probably start with physicians, lawyers, teachers, engineers, architects, accountants, and clergymen. I think we could also find agreement that both journalists and trustees of other people's money are—at least in the ideal—professionals as well. And yet, profession by profession, the old values are clearly being undermined. The driving force in this instance, as in so many others, is our bottom-line society, focused on our ability to count with precision what doesn't count at all. Unchecked market forces not only constitute a strong challenge to society's traditional trust in our professions, but in some cases these forces have totally overwhelmed normative standards of professional conduct, developed over centuries.

Sad to say, the financial services industry—including the mutual fund industry to which I've devoted my entire career—seems to be leading the way in the development of these baneful forces, as in many other deteriorating values that do not bring credit on us. Once a profession in which business was subservient, the field of money management has become a business in which the idea of professional conduct is subservient.

Harvard Business School professor Rakesh Khurana was right on the mark when he defined the conduct of a true professional with these words: "I will create value for society, rather than extract it." Plenty of members of our economy do exactly that: create value. Value is created by those professions that I identified previously, as well as by the manufacturers of goods, the providers of services, engineers, builders, and on and on—but not by the financial sector.* As we learned earlier, money management extracts value from the returns earned by our

---

*Some economists argue that when excessive rewards go to those whose returns come from the redistribution of wealth rather than from the creation of wealth—they single out government, law, and financial services, including stock traders and money managers—the economy suffers. These redistributors of wealth contrast with wealth creators such as builders, manufacturers, and engineers. Paradoxically, however, the fastest growth among college engineering majors today is not in traditional engineering—aeronautical, electrical, mechanical, and the like—but in "financial engineering" for those seeking careers as hedge fund managers and Wall Street "quants."

business enterprises, and in the process of maximizing its own commercial interests, the industry seems to have lost its professional bearings.

Other examples of the harsh consequences of this move away from professional conduct are easy to come by. In public accounting, our once Big Eight (now Final Four) firms gradually came to provide hugely profitable consulting services to their audit clients, making them business partners of management rather than independent and professional evaluators of generally accepted (if loosely interpreted) accounting principles. The 2003 failure of Arthur Andersen, and the earlier bankruptcy of its client Enron, was but one dramatic example of the consequences of this conflict-riddled relationship.

This is hardly a new concern for me. I've written much about how the imbalance between business and professional values has invaded journalism, where we see the increasing dominance of "state" (publishing) over "church" (editorial). In recent years, scandals have reached the most respected echelons of the press—the *New York Times*, the *Los Angeles Times*, the *Washington Post*. The legal profession, too, has hardly been exempt from this trend. The imprisonment of two of the most prominent trial attorneys on criminal charges is but one example of how the once-high principles of the professional practice of law have deteriorated, and how the lure of money has overwhelmed the prestige of reputation.

A similar transition has taken place in the medical profession, where the human concerns of the caregiver and the human needs of the patient have been overwhelmed by the financial interests of commerce: our giant medical care complex of hospitals, insurance companies, drug manufacturers and marketers, and health maintenance organizations (HMOs).

Hammers and Nails

In all, professional relationships with clients have been increasingly recast as business relationships with customers. In a world where every user of services is seen as a customer, every provider of services becomes a seller. Put another way, when the provider becomes a hammer, the customer is seen as a nail. Please don't think me naive. I'm fully aware that every profession has elements of a business. Indeed, if revenues fail to exceed expenses, no organization—even the most noble of faith-based institutions—will long exist. But as so many of our nation's proudest professions gradually shift their traditional balance away from that of trusted professions serving the interests of their clients of the community and toward that of commercial enterprises seeking competitive advantage, the human beings who rely on those services are the losers.

A few years ago, the author Roger Lowenstein made a similar observation, bemoaning the loss of the "Calvinist rectitude" that had its roots in "the very Old World notions of integrity, ethics, and unyielding loyalty to the customer." "America's professions," he wrote, "have become crassly commercial . . . with accounting firms sponsoring golf tournaments," and, he might have added, mutual fund managers not only doing the same thing but buying naming rights to stadiums as well.* "The battle for [professional] independence," he concluded, "is never won."

Capitalism Changes Its Values

Our commercial enterprises, too, have moved a long way from the traditional values of capitalism. The origins of modern capitalism, beginning with the industrial revolution in Great Britain back in the late eighteenth century, had to do, yes, with entrepreneurship and risk taking, with raising capital, with vigorous competition, with free markets, and with the returns on capital going

---

*Bankers and investment bankers also have jumped on the bandwagon. In mid-2008, beleaguered Citigroup, even as it reported year-to-date losses of $17 *billion* (not to mention layoffs totaling 28,000), emphatically reaffirmed its plan to purchase the naming rights for the New York Mets' new baseball park, to be named Citi Field. Cost: $400 million.

to those who put up the capital. But central to the effective functioning of early capitalism was the fundamental principle of trusting and being trusted.

That is not to say that the long history of capitalism has not been punctuated by serious failings. Some were moral failings, such as the disgraceful treatment of laborers, often mere children, in the factories of an earlier era. Other failings included breaking the rules of fair and open competition, exemplified by the oil trusts and robber barons of yore. By the latter part of the twentieth century, yet another failure fell upon us: the erosion of the very structure of capitalism. Not only had trusting and being trusted come to play a diminishing role, but the owners of our businesses were relegated to a secondary role in the functioning of the system.

Owners, Not Agents

As I see it, there were two major forces behind this counterproductive development: First is the change that I've described as the pathological mutation from *owners'* capitalism to *managers'* capitalism. Our old ownership society—in which the shares of our corporations were held almost entirely by direct stockholders—gradually lost its heft and its effectiveness. Since 1950, direct ownership of U.S. stocks by individual investors has plummeted from 92 percent to 26 percent, while indirect ownership by institutional investors has soared from 8 percent to 74 percent—a virtual revolution in the ownership structure. Our old ownership society is now gone, and it is not going to return. In its place we have a new agency society in which our financial intermediaries now hold effective control of American business.

But these new *agents* haven't behaved as agents should. Our corporations, pension managers, and mutual fund managers have too often put their own financial interests ahead of the interests of the *principals* whom they are duty-bound to represent, those 100 million families who are the owners of our mutual funds and the beneficiaries of our pension plans.

While this mutation in the structure of ownership explains much of the change in our system of capitalism, a second force greatly accentuated the problem. Our newly empowered institutional agents also seemed to forget their traditional *principles* of trusteeship and prudent management, moving, as I have noted, from long-term investing to short-term speculation. When investors are focused, not on the intrinsic value of the corporation, but on the price of its stock, assuming some responsibility for corporate governance is the first casualty. Why be concerned with proxy voting, for example, if you may not even be holding the shares a year later?

The net result of this one-two punch was well described by Adam Smith, whose warning of 200-plus years ago seems to have been ignored:

Managers of other people's money [rarely] watch over it with the same anxious vigilance with which . . . they watch over their own . . . they very easily give themselves a dispensation. Negligence and profusion must always prevail.

And so in the recent era, negligence and profusion have prevailed among our corporate directors and our money managers, even to the point of an almost complete disregard of their duty and responsibility to the corporations' owners. Too few seem adequately aware of the lack of the "anxious vigilance" over other people's money that once defined professional conduct. To paraphrase Upton Sinclair: "It's amazing how difficult it is for a man to understand something if he's paid a small fortune *not* to understand it."

CEO Compensation: How Much Is Enough?

A "small fortune" may even be an inadequate description of what our corporations now pay their senior executives, driven in part by these two changes—from principal to agency ownership, and the short-term holding of corporate stocks by their new owners. One of the great differentiating factors between business and professional values is the role of money. In business, it seems that there is no such thing as "enough," while in the professions, money is, at least in the ideal, subservient to ethical standards and service to the general society.

Today, compensation of our business leaders has gone through the roof. Yet it's hard to see that the CEOs of our great corporations, as a group, have added much value to the natural growth of our economy. My own conclusion on the subject was also expressed in my book *The Battle for the Soul of Capitalism*:

> *In 1980, the compensation of the average chief executive officer was forty-two times that of the average worker; by the year 2004, the ratio had soared to 280 times that of the average worker (down from an astonishing 531 times at the peak in 2000). Over the past quarter-century, CEO compensation measured in current dollars rose nearly sixteen times over, while the compensation of the average worker slightly more than doubled. Measured in real (1980) dollars, however, the compensation of the average worker rose just 0.3 percent per year, barely enough to maintain his or her standard of living. Yet CEO compensation rose at a rate of 8.5 percent annually, increasing by more than seven*

times in real terms during the period. The rationale was that these executives had "created wealth" for their shareholders. But were CEOs actually creating value commensurate with this huge increase in compensation? Certainly the average CEO was not. In real terms, aggregate corporate profits grew at an annual rate of just 2.9 percent, compared to 3.1 percent for our nation's economy, as represented by the Gross Domestic Product. How that somewhat dispiriting lag can drive average CEO compensation to a cool $9.8 million in 2004 is one of the great anomalies of the age.

Even in the recent era when the returns on the stocks of many corporations have made little progress—and have often regressed—CEO compensation has remained at truly awesome levels, but with what justification? As noted earlier, the earnings of our corporations as a group have provided a relatively steady share of GDP over the years, not a growing share that might justify some rise in CEO compensation, to say nothing of the leap from 42 times the average worker's compensation to 280 times of a few years ago in 2004. Since then, that relationship has risen back to 520 times, and the average CEO compensation has risen to an even cooler $18.8 million, almost double the 2004 level.

If CEOs, as a group, are—and must be—average, what explains their soaring pay scales? One argument is that their pay is simply part of a trend in which the pay of the most talented and fortunate members of a variety of groups—for example, movie and television stars, and professional baseball, basketball, and football players—has increased by even more. Of course these star athletes and entertainment personalities are paid fortunes. But they are paid either directly or indirectly by their fans, and often by the owners of teams or networks out of their own pockets and out of their own self-interest. (The owners make big money off these stars!) It's an arm's-length deal. CEOs, however, are paid by directors not out of their own pockets but with other people's money, a clear example of the agency problem in our investment system, and our focus on business conduct rather than professional conduct.

A Lack of Accountability

The root problem is that corporate shareholders have played little, if any, role in setting executive pay. A long time ago, Benjamin Graham got this issue exactly right. He observed that in terms of legal rights, "the stockholders as a class are king. Acting as a majority they can hire and fire managements and bend them completely to their will." But in terms of the assertion of these rights in practice, "stockholders are a complete washout . . . they show neither intelligence nor alertness . . . and vote in sheep-like fashion for whatever the management recommends, no matter how poor the management's record of accomplishment may be." That was true when he wrote those words in 1949; it is no less true today.

Driven by the growing lack of accountability of corporate boards to shareholders, this agency problem permeates corporate governance in three major ways. First is the indifference of the (themselves highly paid) institutional money managers, who in the aggregate now hold effective voting control of corporate America. Next are the conflicts of interest faced by these managers, in which their fiduciary interest in representing the mutual fund shareholders and pension beneficiaries they are duty-bound to serve seems to have been overwhelmed by their financial interest in gathering and managing the assets of these mutual funds and pension funds. And, finally, is the fact that most institutional shareholders no longer practice long-term investing (which logically demands attention to corporate governance issues). They have turned instead to short-term speculation, in which they hold corporate shares for an average of a year or less (which logically leads to indifference about governance issues).

One step that might mitigate all three problems would be to allow nonbinding shareholder votes on executive compensation. Implementation costs would be relatively modest, and it would force the institutional shareholders who own corporate America to act as responsible corporate citizens, to the benefit of our society at large.

Intrinsic Value, Not Stock Price

It's hardly surprising that CEOs managing companies whose stocks have provided higher returns have received systematically higher compensation. After all, given the heavy role played by stock options in compensation packages, it would be little short of astonishing were that not the case. But I take issue with the heavy reliance on stock prices as the principal basis of CEO compensation. The short-term and momentary price of a stock, as we now know, is as illusory as it is precise. CEO performance should be based on the long-term building of enduring intrinsic value, which is as real as it is imprecise. (Now there's a paradox!)

Basing compensation on increasing the intrinsic value of business would be a far better way than flighty stock prices to reward executives for durable long-term performance. For example, CEO compensation might be based on corporate earnings growth, corporate cash flow (even better, for it is far more difficult to manipulate), dividend growth (ditto), and return on corporate capital relative to peers and relative to corporations as a group (say, the S&P 500). Such measurements should be taken only over an extended period of time. What's more, CEO incentive pay should be subject to exceeding a sort of hurdle rate, earned only when the firm's returns exceed the corporation's cost of capital. To be sure, those standards are challenging, but meeting challenges is what real business success should be all about.

Performance, Not Peer Groups

Much of the responsibility for our flawed system for CEO compensation can be attributed to the rise of the compensation consultant. It must be clear, first, that compensation consultants who consistently recommend lower pay or tougher standards for CEO compensation would likely not hold on to many clients. To make matters worse, the well-known methodology of consultants—grouping CEOs into peer groups measured in quartiles—leads inevitably to a ratchet effect.

It has been observed, correctly I believe, that boards of directors typically fall in love with their CEOs (at least until something big goes wrong). When a board finds that its own CEO's pay reposes in the fourth quartile, it raises his (or her) compensation to bring it into, say, the second quartile, which, of course, drops another CEO into the fourth quartile. And so the cycle repeats, onward and upward over the years, almost always with the encouragement of the ostensibly impartial consultant (who of course makes his or her living not by recommending less, but by recommending more).

Such a methodology is fundamentally flawed, and has the obvious effect: The figures in these compensation grids almost always go up for the peer group, and almost never go down. Warren Buffett pungently describes the typical consulting firm by naming it, tongue in cheek, "Ratchet, Ratchet, and Bingo." Until we pay CEOs on the basis of corporate *performance* rather than on the basis of corporate *peers*, CEO pay will, almost inevitably, continue on its upward path.

Finally, CEO compensation should have a contingent component. Incentive pay should be spread out over an extended period of years, and stock options should be phased in as well—for example, 50 percent exercisable on the first exercise date, with 10 percent exercisable annually over the subsequent five years. There should also be clawback provisions under which incentive compensation is returned to the company when earnings are restated downward. If CEOs are going to expose their corporations to aggressive strategies and high risks in order to win maximum compensation, whether based on intrinsic shareholder value or on stock price, then when the strategies backfire, shareholder value collapses, and the risks come home to roost (as tragically exemplified in the current financial crisis), executives should be required to pony up from their own earlier rich rewards.

Principals and Principles

Returning professional conduct to a more important role in business affairs will be no easy task. One avenue to pursue, curiously enough, was suggested by a mailing that arrived on my desk with a typographical error that I just couldn't ignore. Sent out by the Center for Corporate Excellence to announce that General Electric would receive its Long-Term Excellence in Corporate Governance award, the flyer quoted GE president Jeffrey Immelt on the importance of "sound principals of corporate governance."

Clearly, the quotation should have read *principles*, not *principals*. But as I thought about the error, it seemed almost prophetic. After all, no matter how strong the ethical *principles* of the world of business may be, of what use are they without ethical *principals* to honor them? Corporate America is in dire need of more leaders who will assume the responsibility of assuring that these ethical principles permeate and dominate the culture of our corporate world.

We can all agree, I'm sure, on a basic set of ethical principles that should guide businesses and their leaders toward traditional professional standards. Indeed, virtually all of our large publicly held corporations already have ethical codes, published for all to see, paying lip service to high ideals. Yet we have also witnessed far too many examples in which these standards have been ignored by the very managements that brag about them, in order to meet ambitious—often overly ambitious—goals for growth in corporate revenues and earnings.

Our corporate directors also pay lip service to their duty to responsibly represent the shareholders of the companies whose proxies they vote. How could they say otherwise? But preserving, protecting, and defending the corporation's resources with the interests of its owners as the highest priority seems the exception rather than the rule. While the fact is that the CEO is an employee—albeit the senior employee—of the corporation, responsible, through the board of directors, to the owners, rare are the CEOs who see themselves in those terms. Rather, the paradigm is those imperial CEOs who view themselves as solely responsible for the creation of shareholder value—forgetting the immense contribution made by all those millions of employees who commit themselves to the task of building corporate value every day, and worse, are paid as if their contribution were small.

We see corporations preach the so-called balanced scorecard that calls for fair dealing with the corporation's other constituencies—customers, employees, suppliers, the local community, government, and the public. But the news-papers are full, every day it seems, of stories of companies that have gone in exactly the opposite direction. And how about the integrity of the firm's financial statements, let alone the true independence of the independent auditor who attests to their conformity with generally accepted accounting principles? Small wonder that the engineering wonder of our age is *financial* engineering.

Am I arguing that our business *principals* of today are less ethical than their predecessors? No, not necessarily. But I am arguing that our business *principles* have been compromised. It wasn't so many decades ago that the standards in the conduct of business were close to absolute:

There are some things that one simply doesn't do.

But today we place our reliance on relative standards:

Everyone else is doing it, so I can do it, too.

Our society cannot and should not tolerate the substitu-tion of moral relativism for a certain form of moral absolut-ism, and its debasement in the ethical standards of commerce.

"Only Capitalists Can Kill Capitalism"

We who are or have been principals in the world of busi-ness have a high obligation not only to establish unspar-ing principles modeled along professional lines for our firms and colleagues, but to preserve and protect and defend those principles. When we fail to do so, as we too often have of late, cynicism spreads widely across the populace and social ills are magnified. I can't make the case any better than did Felix Rohatyn, the widely respected former managing director of Lazard Freres, in the *Wall Street Journal* a few years ago:

> *I am an American and a capitalist and believe that market capitalism is the best economic system ever invented. But it must be fair, it must be regulated, and it must be ethical. The last few years have shown that excesses can come about when finance capitalism and modern technology are abused in the service of naked greed. Only capitalists can kill capitalism, but our system cannot stand much more abuse of the type we have witnessed recently, nor can it stand much more of the financial and social polarization we are seeing today.*

We are now seeing in our corporations and our financial markets the result of the triumph of business standards over professional standards—far too much of the former, not nearly enough of the latter. No, we can't deny—nor should we—that the primary requirement for any business is to earn a profit. But we can demand that a business conduct its affairs with ethical professionalism. Our society has a huge stake in striving to return to the professional values that, a mere 40 years ago, ruled triumphant in this nation.

Chapter 6

Too Much Salesmanship, Not Enough Stewardship

It is especially painful for me to acknowledge that the mutual fund industry is in many respects the exemplar of the deterioration in business values and investment values that I have just described. So allow me to turn here to the very industry that I entered in 1951 and in which I have served ever since, and discuss the vast changes that have swept through it during my more than half-century in the field. First, let's chronicle these changes, which together have tipped the balance away from the stewardship of yore to the salesmanship that clearly characterizes the industry today.

The most obvious change is that the fund industry has enjoyed enormous growth. Once a midget, it is now a giant. In 1951, mutual fund assets totaled $2 billion. Today, assets total more than $12 *trillion*, an astonishing 17 percent average rate of annual growth over more than a half-century—a rate that has been exceeded by few, if any, other industries. In 1951, equity funds held about 1 percent of all U.S. stocks; by 2008, they held a stunning 35 percent, making the mutual fund industry the nation's most dominant financial institution.

Far less obviously, the fund industry has significantly changed its investment focus. Then, almost 80 percent of stock funds (60 of a mere 75 funds) were broadly diversified among investment-grade stocks. These funds pretty much tracked the movements of the stock market itself and lagged its returns by only the amount of their then-modest operating costs. Today, such large-cap blend funds—about 500 in all—are vastly outnumbered by 3,100 U.S. equity funds diversified in other styles, another 400 funds narrowly diversified in various market sectors, and 800 funds investing in international equities—some broadly diversified, some investing in specific countries. Some of these new fund categories (e.g., the global stock market) have served investors well; others have had disastrous consequences. In any event, the challenge to investors in picking funds has become almost equivalent to the challenge in picking individual stocks.

Investors Change Their Spots; So Do Managers

In part responding to this change, the behavior of investors who own mutual funds has also changed. Fund investors no longer just *pick* funds and *hold* them. They *trade* them. In 1951, the average fund investor held his or her shares for about 16 years. Today, that holding period averages about four years. To make matters worse, fund investors don't trade very successfully. Because they usually chase good performance and then abandon ship after bad performance, the asset-weighted returns—those actually earned by *fund investors*—have trailed the time-weighted returns reported by the *funds themselves* by the astonishing gap mentioned previously, in which the 10 percent annual return of the average fund over 25 years was 37 percent higher than the 7.3 percent return earned by fund shareholders.

The investment process utilized by fund managers, too, is radically different from the process prevailing when I entered this field. In 1951, management by investment committee was the rule; today it is the exception. This is the age of the portfolio manager, with the vast majority of funds (some 60 percent) managed by a single individual or a team of about three managers.* While committee management was hardly a guarantor of superior returns, the system served investors well, with the vast majority of funds producing returns that were relatively marketlike. And while a system of individual portfolio managers may not be bad in and of itself, this evolution—really a revolution—has led to costly discontinuities. A star system among mutual fund managers has evolved, with all the attendant hoopla, encouraging hyperactivity by fund investors. The average portfolio manager serves a fund for but five years, aggressively managing a portfolio the returns of which often depart sharply from the returns of the broad stock market—sometimes positively for a while, and then sharply negative. But most of those stars have turned out to be comets.

Given this change from the collective to the individual, it is hardly surprising that fund investment strategies have also been drastically altered. In 1951, the typical mutual fund focused on the wisdom of long-term investing, holding the average stock in its portfolio for about six years. Today, the holding period for a stock for *actively*

---

*In a refinement of this system, some giant fund managers employ groups of "portfolio counselor" teams, each handling a relatively small portion of the fund's assets. Whether these teams can be multiplied ad infinitum in order to produce superior returns remains to be seen.

managed equity funds is just one year. (More charitably, on a dollar-weighted basis, the average holding period is just over 1.5 years.) Either way, the typical mutual fund of today is focused on the folly of short-term speculation.

With these changes, fund costs have soared. On an *unweighted* basis, the expense ratio of the average actively managed equity fund has almost doubled, from 0.77 percent in 1951 to 1.50 percent in 2007. To be fair, when *weighted* by fund assets, the expense ratio has risen from 0.60 percent to 0.93 percent, a lower, but still staggering, increase of more than 50 percent. Put another way, if we apply those ratios to equity fund assets of $2 billion in 1951 and to $7 trillion in 2007 respectively, an industry that once provided its services—rather more effectively—for $12 million a year now does so—less effectively—for $65 *billion* a year.

Good for Managers, Bad for Shareholders

However calculated, this astonishing rise in costs constitutes a major drag on the returns earned by fund investors. Despite the quantum growth in industry assets since 1951, managers have arrogated to themselves the lion's share of the extraordinary economies of scale available in the field of money management, rather than directing that lion's share of economies to the fund owners, who, to state the obvious, made them possible. As noted earlier, money managers—led by the giant global financial conglomerates that dominate the industry (those conglomerates now own 32 of the 50 largest fund organizations, and another nine firms are publicly owned)— hold as their highest priority the return earned on *their own capital*, rather than the return earned on the *capital they are investing for their fund shareholders*. This change in the industry's character—from privately owned managers to managers largely owned and controlled by conglomerates—brings into sharp relief the fact that what is good for the fund industry is generally bad for fund shareholders.

Each one of these profound changes has fostered a new and far less lofty mission for the industry. Over the past half-century-plus, the fund business has turned from stewardship to salesmanship, from *managing* assets to *gathering* assets. We have become largely a marketing industry, engaging in a furious orgy of product proliferation. Our apparent motto: "If you will buy it, we will make it."

During the 1950s and 1960s, some 240 new equity funds were formed, and during the 1970s and 1980s, about 650 were formed. But in the 1990s alone, 1,600 new equity funds were created. Most of them, alas, were technology, Internet, and telecommunications funds, and aggressive growth funds focused on these areas. It was such funds, of course, that then took the brunt of the 2000–2002 bear market. Such product proliferation has engendered the expected reaction: Funds are born to die. Whereas

13 percent of all funds failed during the 1950s, the failure rate for the present decade is running at near 60 percent.

Toward a Better World

This combination of asset growth, truncated investment focus, counterproductive investor behavior, real-time portfolio management process, hair-trigger investment strategies, soaring costs, conglomerate ownership, and product proliferation (inevitably followed by deproliferation) has constituted a serious disservice to fund investors.

Simply put, we, the trustees of the investment dollars of American families—pension funds, mutual funds, and other financial institutions—have failed to live up to the faith investors have placed in us. We have become blind to our excessive intermediation costs; deaf to the fact that, given the level of those costs, investment managers as a group are destined to fail at the task of providing adequate returns; and insensitive and unforthcoming to the multitudinous ways in which we as an industry fail our clients.

We pander to the public taste by bringing out new funds to capitalize on each new market fad, and we magnify the problem by heavily advertising the returns earned by our hottest funds. In a phrase, salesmanship has trumped stewardship, and our investors are the ones who have suffered. Our trade association, the Investment Company Institute (ICI), has *never* noted the gap between the returns reported by mutual funds and the returns actually received by fund shareholders, even as it claims to be the advocate for those very shareholders. Nor, for that matter, has the ICI noted the huge returns earned by fund management companies regardless of whether fund shareholders are making any money.

These are but two of the many examples that add to the evidence that belies the consistent claim of the industry, articulated over and over again at the annual membership meetings of the ICI, that "the interests of mutual fund managers are directly aligned with the interests of mutual fund shareholders." It is simply not true.

It must seem obvious that there is an urgent need to face up to these and other failures in the changing world of capitalism, and especially the rapidly changing world of the mutual fund industry. Yet it is remarkable to me that a situation so dire has occasioned such a dearth of public discourse. While we drown in innovation, we starve for introspection, the one quality that might allow us to truly see where we have been, where we are going, and what we must do to earn the trust of the investors.

In the investment community, I have seen no defense of the inadequate returns delivered by mutual funds to investors, nor of the industry's truly bizarre, counterproductive ownership structure; no attempt by fund managers to explain why the rights of ownership that one would think are implicit in holding shares of stock in our portfolios remain largely unexercised; no serious criticism of the virtually unrecognized turn away from the once-conventional and pervasive investment strategies that relied on the wisdom of long-term investing, toward strategies that increasingly rely on the folly of short-term speculation; and, until 2007, almost no discussion of the huge deficits that we are facing in our public and private systems of retirement plan funding in which our funds play such an important role.

While these are not problems that lack solutions, it would be absurd to claim that solutions will be easily achieved. But I now want to set out my views as to the new direction this industry ought to take—indeed, ultimately *must* take, in its own enlightened self-interest—to establish a new beginning for reform.

Let's Dream Together

"I have a dream." Or rather, five dreams—five dreams for redesigning the mutual fund industry in the years ahead so that it can return to the focus on management of its early history and minimize the marketing focus that has come to dominate the business today—a dream, that is, of an industry that once again values stewardship more highly than salesmanship.

Dream 1: A Fair Shake for Shareholders

The first dream is to design a new industry in which we give our investors a fair shake in terms of costs. As I have noted, although equity fund expense ratios recently have leveled off, despite the staggering increase in assets under management they remain at least 50 percent higher than in the infinitely smaller industry of 50 years ago. Clearly, the vast economies of scale that come hand in hand with the management of other people's money have done far more to benefit managers than to benefit investors. I dream that that trend will be reversed.

Dream 2: Serving the Investor for a Lifetime

My second dream is that we design an industry that will serve the investor not for a season but for a lifetime. Technologically, we are well prepared to do just that. The industry's ability to handle the complex record keeping for the nearly 50 million participants in our multifaceted defined-contribution plans, for example, has been something of a triumph. And the services we provide to our fund investors through communications and transactions over the Internet have been truly remarkable. But the vast menus of funds we offer and the wide array of strategies we create almost of necessity encourage investors to restlessly move their money around, a strategy that favors the house far more than it favors the player.

We have too many investors who are too aggressive—401(k) plan participants working for Fortune 100 companies allocate an average of 36 percent to company stock, not only concentrating their investment risk but aligning it with their career risk. We also have too many investors who are too conservative. Investors who have so-called stable value funds and money market funds as an investment option allocate nearly 24 percent to these funds. What is more, 401(k) investors are notorious for performance chasing, and we seem not to care. Traditionally, the most popular funds in our retirement plans have been those with extraordinary past performance—but, alas, their returns are destined to revert to the market mean at best, and more likely well below it. We also offer too many choices, sowing confusion among participants. We allow too much borrowing, and we now know that, in today's world of high employee turnover, fully 45 percent of those who leave their jobs simply take their money and run. And we are only now developing annuity-linked programs that allow our clients a seamless move from their years of accumulating assets to their years when they begin to draw those assets down, secure from the risk of exhausting them.

Most important of all, we need to recognize that pooled investment funds such as mutual funds now constitute the dominant element of the nation's overall retirement system, including not only individual retirement plans but also corporate benefit plans and federal, state, and local government plans. With each passing year, they will become even more dominant. Instead of merely looking after our own parochial interests, farsighted industry leaders ought to be leading the way to rationalizing the entire retirement services system. So my dream of providing lifetime services to investors includes a vision that our industry leaders begin to act as statesmen and at last step forward with proposals and designs that will create for our citizens a sound, integrated, disciplined, and secure retirement system. We owe no less to our investors and to our nation.

Dream 3: Long-Term Investment Horizons

My third dream is that our money managers turn back the clock, reverting to our traditional focus on long-term investment strategies. As I wrote earlier, the average fund portfolio turns over at an annual rate of nearly 100 percent—a holding period of barely *one year* for the average stock! Who benefits from such frantic turnover? Not our fund shareholders as a group. Indeed, to state the obvious (again), such trading *must*—and *does*—dilute the returns of our owners in the aggregate. So the fund industry's conversion from its historic focus on the long term to today's focus on the short term has been detrimental to the interests of our shareholders.

There's another great benefit in again becoming an own-a-stock industry. We would be forced to recognize that the interests of our shareholders demand that we act as responsible corporate citizens, carefully examining company financial statements; making our views known on matters such as stock options, executive compensation, and corporate governance; and ensuring that the corporations whose shares we hold are operated in the interests of their shareholders rather than their managers. In today's rent-a-stock industry, focused on speculation, stocks are treated as mere pieces of paper to trade back and forth rather than as the talisman of ownership. As a result, those governance issues are too often ignored. So my dream is that we return to our roots as *investors*, not only because it will be to the economic benefit of our clients, but because we can play the determining role in returning corporate America to its own roots of democratic capitalism.

Dream 4: Serving Long-Term Investors

My fourth dream is that we again focus on serving long-term shareholders. That is not how it works today. For even as the investment horizons of our fund managers have diminished, so, too, have the horizons of our mutual fund owners. Small wonder, since we have shaped our business to meet the demands of short-term investors. Just look at our mad, ongoing rush to offer investors funds that are designed to be traded rather than funds designed to be held for a lifetime. The contrast of yesteryear's fund industry—consisting largely of marketlike portfolios holding blue-chip stocks—to today's could hardly be more stark. We think in terms of *sizes* and *styles*, terms more suggestive, when you think about it, of the field of high fashion than of the field of investing.

So in my fourth dream, we abandon the fashion-model-runway approach to investing. How can we even pretend to foster responsibility for our clients' long-term well-being when nearly 2,800 of the 6,126 mutual funds that existed in 2001—only seven years ago—are already dead and gone? Instead of narrowly defined *products*, the industry needs to be providing more broadly diversified mutual funds—*trust accounts* that can be bought and held forever. That's where our roots lie. If that change leads us to greater emphasis on broad-market index funds—which clearly meet that definition—well, so be it. But even if it leads to other investment strategies with a similar orientation, the index fund remains the purest paradigm to which we must return.

Dream 5: Putting Fund Investors in the Driver's Seat

My fifth dream is putting the investors in the driver's seat of fund governance. Only in this way can we honor the express demand of the Investment Company Act of 1940—the federal statute that governs our industry—that mutual funds be "organized, operated, and managed in the best interests of their shareholders rather than in the interest of their advisers and underwriters." Yet for all of the Act's noble intentions, that's simply *not* the principle under which our industry operates today. The blunt fact is that funds are organized, operated, and managed to benefit their advisers.

So what's to be done? Shareholder education is painfully slow, yet time is money. The conglomerates that dominate the industry today will not soon accept eroded returns on their own capital, nor will they willingly return their profits to their clients. So I see no recourse but to demand that the governance of mutual funds comports with precisely what the 1940 Act demands: a largely independent board of directors that is beholden, first and foremost, to the shareholders who elect it.

That structure exists, but it doesn't operate that way. Contrary to the Act's language, the adviser controls the fund. So we must eliminate the blatant conflict of interest that exists when the chairman of the fund board is the same person as the chairman of the management company board. (As Warren Buffett says, "Negotiating with one's self seldom produces a barroom brawl.") For the same reason, we need a board *wholly* independent of the manager. (The requirement that 75 percent of the directors must be independent is a good beginning. But at Vanguard, our external advisers have *zero* board representation, obviously without adverse consequences for our shareholders.) SEC regulations already require an independent legal counsel and a chief compliance officer for the funds themselves, and I strongly favor, at least for the larger fund complexes, a *fund* staff, responsible to the board, that provides the board with objective and unbiased information on fund costs, performance, marketing, and the like. Note those key words: *objective* and *unbiased*. What a breath of fresh air that would be!

Of, By, and For the Shareholder

What I'm ultimately looking for is an industry that is focused on stewardship—the prudent handling of other people's money solely in the interests of our investors—an industry that is *of the shareholder, by the shareholder, and for the shareholder.* We need a mutual fund industry with both *vision* and *values*: a vision of fiduciary duty and shareholder service, and values rooted in the proven principles of long-term investing and of trusteeship that demands integrity in serving our clients.

How do we get there, in addition to the five-step (well, five-dream) program I have just outlined? First, we do so by having faith in the majesty of simplicity, helping investors to make the uncertain but necessary judgments to determine their allocation between stocks, with their opportunity for growth of capital and the attendant risks, and bonds, with their income productivity and relative stability, and then doing everything in our power to diversify these investments and minimize the costs—management fees, operating costs, marketing expenses, turnover impact—promising only to give investors their fair share of financial market returns: no more, no less. Again, if index funds are the best way to assure the realization of these goals, so be it.

We also need to build, not just fund companies that are amalgamations of financial products, but *companies that stand for something*. As one who has been at that task for better than five decades, I can tell you that it is a tough, demanding, never-ending task. My own goal has been to build a company that stands for *stewardship*. Let me be clear, however, that this goal is not without a self-serving aspect. For only to the extent we adequately serve the human beings who have entrusted us with the management of their wealth will Vanguard itself survive and prosper.

Others will have to define their own firms, but I hope that stewardship will become at least part of their character, because stewardship pays off. In this industry, we tend to define success in terms of dollars under management, cash flow, market share, and new accounts opened. But real success can't be measured by such numbers. Rather, success must be defined in terms of service quality, and of providing investors with their fair share of whatever returns our financial markets are generous enough to bestow on us. Success must also be measured by the character and values of our firms, not only in our words but in our deeds.

Above all, our success depends on keeping the faith—the faith of those human beings who have entrusted us with their precious hard-earned dollars—and then going out and earning that faith, every single day. In the fund field, to say nothing of the financial field at large, we have had quite enough—indeed, far too much—salesmanship. It's stewardship—of which we have had not nearly enough—that holds the key to our future.

Chapter 7

Too Much Management, Not Enough Leadership

It has been observed that most of our larger corporations are overmanaged but underled. I believe that's accurate, not only with respect to our nation's businesses, but to our financial institutions as well. Of course every group, every organization, and every nation requires a healthy cadre of both managers and leaders. Each role is essential. But each role is different, and recognizing the difference is equally essential. Hear management guru Warren Bennis on this point:

> There is a profound difference between management and leadership, and both are important. To manage means to bring about, to accomplish, to have charge

of or responsibility for, to conduct. Leading is influenc-
ing, guiding in a direction, course, action, opinion. The
distinction is crucial.

Bennis lays out a number of critical distinctions
between the two:

- *The manager administers; the leader innovates.*
- *The manager is a copy; the leader is an original.*
- *The manager focuses on systems and structure; the*
  leader focuses on people.
- *The manager relies on control; the leader inspires*
  trust.
- *The manager has a short-range view; the leader has*
  a long-range perspective.
- *The manager has his or her eye always on the*
  bottom line; the leader has his or her eye on the
  horizon.
- *The manager imitates; the leader originates.*
- *The manager accepts the status quo; the leader*
  challenges it.

Professor Bennis ends his litany with this clear summation: "The manager does things right; the leader does
the right thing."

While the thrust of Dr. Bennis's litany is generally on
the mark, I believe that the dichotomy is overdrawn. Woe to
the leader who ignores the bottom line, for example.

Woe to the manager who fails to inspire trust, or who focuses only on the short range. So let me present a more subtle thesis, one that encompasses, in many instances, both sets of talents.

For the enterprise to achieve its fullest expression, good stewardship, high professional standards, and trust must suffuse an entire organization, from the mail room to the boardroom. The qualities must be built into the character of the enterprise, not grafted onto its exterior. Of necessity, those qualities must begin with leadership—with leaders who do more than count, leaders whose highest priorities include the deeper values of their organizations.

Of course, in order to function with efficiency and excellence, all enterprises also need skilled and dedicated managers at every level of the organization. And they too must be committed to those values. And both leaders and managers must learn to view those who work with them—from the highest to the humblest—not just as pawns on a corporate chessboard but as human beings with the same needs and concerns that all of us have. Without strong and determined leaders to set the firm's character, direction, and strategy, even the best managers will be trying to push water up a hill.

What, then, are the characteristics of good leadership and of good management? On that subject, I have (surprise!) strong opinions, most of them formed in the crucible of my own six decades of business experience, including four decades as a leader—nine years as chief executive of

Wellington Management, 22 years as chief of Vanguard, and (if you will) now nine years running Vanguard's admittedly tiny Bogle Financial Markets Research Center, with its crew of three plus me. So here I speak from my own broad, firsthand, and often hard-won experience.

Of course I'm especially proud of the extraordinary accomplishments of our Vanguard crew members, not only when I ran the firm, but up to this very moment. Their intense involvement in, and contribution to, those accomplishments testify to the merit of the wonderful wisdom I culled from a 1972 speech given by Howard W. Johnson, then the chairman of the Massachusetts Institute of Technology. It put into words what I believed, long before I read them.

> *The institution must be the object of intense human care and cultivation. Even when it errs and stumbles, it must be cared for, and the burden must be borne by all who work for it, all who own it, all who are served by it, all who govern it. Every responsible person must care, and care deeply, about the institutions that touch his life.*

Building a Great Organization

So, at heart, my central message begins with a sense of caring—a message reflected in these 10 rules for building a great organization, many of which, as you will see, apply to both leaders and managers.

Rule 1: Make Caring the Soul of the Organization

When I first spoke to our Vanguard crew about caring in 1989, I used these words: "Caring is a mutual affair, involving: (1) Mutual respect from the highest to the humblest among us: Each one of you deserves to be—and *will* be—treated with courtesy, candor, friendliness, and respect for the honorable work you perform. (2) Opportunities for career growth, participation, and innovation: While Vanguard is an enterprise in which so many are asked to do jobs that are routine and mundane but always essential, the simple fact is that we need your enthusiastic participation in your job—whatever it may be—if we are to make Vanguard work effectively. After all, you on the firing line know a lot more about problems and solutions than the rest of us will ever know." The list continues: maintaining an attractive, efficient work environment; providing a meaningful communication program; and paying fair compensation. Then, I was expressing nothing more than these commonsense principles. Today, nearly 20 years later, I'm not sure I would alter a single one of them. In an increasingly impersonal world, I have come to believe, with Howard Johnson, that success depends on a deep sense of caring for the institution by all who are affected by it.

Rule 2: Forget about Employees

At our outset in 1974, I tried to capture the spirit of our new organization by eliminating the word *employee*—a word that hardly suggested teamwork and cooperation—from our lexicon, substituting "crew member," another nautical nod to our patron saint, Lord Nelson, and to his flagship after which our company is named. To me, an *employee* suggested someone who came in each day at nine, left promptly at five, did what he was told, kept her mouth shut, and got paid, just like clockwork, when the workweek ended. A *crew member*, while it may sound sort of, well, corny, suggested to me an excited, motivated, committed—yes, caring—person who was part of a crew in which we all worked together on a worthwhile voyage, part of a chain that could be no stronger than its weakest link. That's the kind of crew I wanted to lead, one linked together, each dependent on the other.

Rule 3: Set High Standards and Values—and Stick to Them

Way back in 1980, at a celebration of Vanguard's $3 billion milestone, I called on our crew to offer "skill in what we do; imagination in what we create; integrity in what we produce; judgment in the goals we set for ourselves; courage in times of peril and good humor in adversity; and humility in accomplishment." If I were starting over today, I would not hesitate to set those same standards.

As for values, I was determined from the outset to make human beings the focus of our firm. How often I have said over these long years that those whom we serve—and, let's never forget, those *with* whom we serve as well—must be treated as "honest-to-God, down-to-earth human beings, all with their own hopes and fears and financial goals." In practice, that means together serving the human beings who are our clients to the best of our ability; being prudent stewards of the assets they have entrusted to us; treating them as we would like the stewards of our own assets to treat us; and serving them with candor, with empathy, with fair dealing, and with integrity.*

In my time as head of Vanguard, none of these standards and values was ever written down in a manual. Rather, I proposed a single overarching but simple rule: "Do what's right. If you're not sure, ask your boss." Why so? Because as I've said a thousand times: "Good ethics *is*

---

*I've often observed that while 100 percent of our business leaders describe integrity as the essential characteristic of leadership, less than 100 percent actually deliver on that claim.

good business." A new thought? Hardly. In the *Odyssey*, Homer reminds us,

> *Take it to the heart, and pass the word along:*
> *Fair dealing brings more profit in the end.*

I've read untold numbers of books and articles about business management and corporate strategy, but I've never seen the phrase *human beings* as representing the key to business leadership. But when I think of both our clients and crew, that phrase has been the key to everything we've accomplished.

Rule 4: Talk the Talk. Repeat the Values Endlessly.

If building a great workforce demands leadership, and if leadership requires virtue—and I have no doubt that the best leadership does require virtue—then a leader can be defined as *a person who initiates and directs an endeavor in the principled pursuit of a project of consequence.* To lead at all levels—from chief executives to senior managers to project directors, even to those souls responsible for the most mundane of tasks—requires inspiring and persuading other human beings to work together on a journey toward a worthwhile destination.

Building a great organization demands finding the right words to communicate the best ideas and the highest ideals, words that convey purpose and passion and vision. In the effort to do so, we have all been given a priceless gift: the English language. Let's use the inspirational words and cadences it has given us to build an organization that lasts, an organization in which leaders, managers, and those who do the hard work of routine can take great pride.

Rule 5: Walk the Walk. Actions Speak Louder than Words.

Whether manager or leader, there are few more self-defeating courses of action than "talking the talk" without "walking the walk." So whatever you *preach*, you'd darn well better *practice*. The principle is simple: If you want to be trusted, be trustworthy. If you demand hard work, work hard. If you want your colleagues to level with you, level with them. It's not very complicated!

But there's another aspect to walking the walk—its literal meaning. Walk around your company, or department, or unit, or group. Personal visibility is one of the key elements of leadership, and it doesn't happen when you're sitting behind your desk. And if you're an executive—a "suit," in common parlance—don't limit your ambit to conference rooms filled with other suits. Get out and meet the people who are doing the real

work: those in the mail room, the security guards, the programmers, the accountants, the money managers, everyone upon whom your daily work depends.

Rule 6: Don't Overmanage

As I have earlier noted, the most important things in life
and in business can't be measured. The trite bromide "If
you can measure it, you can manage it" has been a hindrance in building a great real-world organization, just as
it has been a hindrance in evaluating the real-world economy. It is character, not numbers, that make the world
go 'round. How can we possibly measure the qualities of
human existence that give our lives and careers meaning?
How about grace, kindness, and integrity? What value do
we put on passion, devotion, and trust? How much
do cheerfulness, the lilt of a human voice, and a touch
of pride add to our lives? Tell me, please, if you can, how
to value friendship, cooperation, dedication, and spirit.
Categorically, the firm that ignores the intangible qualities
that the human beings who are our colleagues bring to
their careers will *never* build a great workforce or a great
organization.

Lord Keynes got it just right on this score, too: "It is
the merest pretense to suggest that an enterprise is based
on an exact calculation of benefits to come.... [We need]

animal spirits, a spontaneous urge to action. If animal spirits are dimmed and spontaneous optimism falters, leaving us to depend on nothing but a mathematical expectation, the enterprise will fade and die." And so it will. We must allow those animal spirits to triumph within our organizations and within ourselves.

Rule 7: Recognize Individual Achievement

In Vanguard's early days, we were among the first firms to create a formal employee recognition program. It began, as I recall, in about 1980, and remains intact and virtually unchanged today. Each quarter, I would appear before a group of crew members and present the Vanguard Award for Excellence to one of the inevitably astonished colleagues. The award, based on nominations from one's peers and reviewed by a committee of officers, is given for special team spirit, cooperation, exemplary service to clients and crew members, initiative, and resourcefulness. Some six to ten awards were presented each quarter and included a $1,000 check, $500 to the crew member's favorite charity, and a plaque with the motto "*Even one person can make a difference*." The Award for Excellence remains in place to this day.

The point isn't to make recipients rich, but to recognize achievement, reinforcing an unshakable belief in the value of the individual to the organization as a whole. Even though I am no longer the company's chief executive, I continue to sit down in my office with each award winner for an hour or so of conversation, at once listening and talking, learning and teaching, getting acquainted, and giving each winner a special signed copy of one of my books with a bookplate commemorating the award. Small as they may seem, these human touches in a now giant enterprise will, I'm certain, help to preserve the legacy I've tried to create.

Rule 8: A Reminder—Loyalty Is a Two-Way Street

Rare is the high-ranking corporate officer who doesn't call on his or her workforce to display loyalty, but too many managers stop there. The best leaders, however, make certain they give loyalty back in equal measure. As I told our crew back in 1988, "It is really incredible that it has taken most American companies so long to realize that it is simply *not right* to ask those who do the daily work to be loyal to the corporation without making the same commitment, with the same fervor, that the corporation will be loyal to them in return. And that concept of two-way loyalty must itself become a Vanguard tradition."

Talk without action is hollow and meaningless. So once Vanguard reached a solid financial footing in the early 1980s, we acted to demonstrate the firm's loyalty to its crew. Through the Vanguard Partnership Plan, each and every member of our crew, from the moment of signing on, shares in the rewards we generate for our shareholders. I know of no other company in which every member of the workforce—without putting up one cent of capital—shares in its earnings.

These earnings are derived from: (1) our low-cost advantage (that is, our fund expense ratios relative to those of our major competitors); (2) the extent to which our fund performance exceeds or falls short of the returns of our competitors; and (3) the size of our asset base. So as our cost advantage has increased, as the returns of our funds have exceeded those of their peers, and as our assets have grown, our earnings have grown—substantially! Each crew member holds a specific number of partnership units, which we increase with years of service and job grade level, and each June receives a check that, with some significant exceptions, typically comes to 30 percent of a crew member's annual compensation. (The plan's provisions are proprietary.)

Rule 9: Lead and Manage for the Long Term

Leading a business is a serious, rugged, flaw-ridden, demanding task. Dog-eat-dog competition keeps managers and the members of the workforce on their toes, and the inevitable fluctuations and vicissitudes in an industry's affairs, as well as in the general level of economic activity, often seem to compel painful decisions and trade-offs to meet the exigencies of the day. But leading a business is also thrilling, challenging, and rewarding. The key to the difference, I believe, lies in doing everything possible to focus on long-term opportunities, doing your best to ignore the inevitable short-term difficulties. Scores of times I've reminded our crew: "Once you decide whether you expect to be in business for a short time or a long time, most of the right decisions are easy."

Think about it: The *ephemeral perception* of a business is based largely on images, superficial headlines in the press, the momentary challenges—all of those hiccups and diversions that take our eye off the proverbial ball. The *eternal reality* of a business, in contrast, is its ability to provide good products or services that meet client needs at a fair price. Yes, client perceptions may change as tough times and hard circumstances take their toll. But, over time, with businesses (even as with stock prices), any gap between perception and reality will be reconciled *in favor of reality*.

So a great workforce must be managed as a long-term asset, and anyone who aspires to be a great leader or a great manager must ever keep in mind that long-term perspective. Some guidelines: Avoid layoffs in temporary downturns; beware of excessive stringency in compensation; don't slash benefits to meet short-term budgetary constraints; and never demand that some arbitrary percentage of the workforce must unilaterally be rated unsatisfactory. *Never!* (In the trade, this is called "rank and yank.") If you focus on the long term, you can create the right environment for building a great organization. *Character* is the bedrock of the firm that lasts.

Rule 10: Press On, Regardless

If there were a single phrase that best articulates the attitude of business leaders and managers who both deserve and reward a great workforce, it would be "press on, regardless." It is a rule of life that has been a motto of my family for as long as I can remember, and has sustained me through times thick and times thin alike.* The motto's provenance was an old lobster boat named *Press On* owned by my uncle, investment banker Clifton Armstrong Hipkins. On the little bridge was a framed copy of these words from President Calvin Coolidge:

> *Nothing in the world can take the place of persistence. Talent will not; nothing is more common than unsuccessful*

---

*When I was in danger of losing my scholarship and having to leave Princeton during my sophomore year—struggling, at first unsuccessfully, with, yes, Paul Samuelson's *Economics: An Introductory Analysis* in my first course in what would become my major—I sure as heck pressed on. I graduated with high honors.

*men with talent. Genius will not; unrewarded genius is
almost a proverb. Education will not; the world is full of
educated derelicts. Persistence and determination alone
are omnipotent. The slogan "Press on" has solved, and
always will solve, the problems of the human race.*

A caution: Many leaders intuitively understand the
need to press on when the weather is stormy and the going
is hard. Far fewer, it seems to me, understand the need also
to press on when the weather is sunny and the going is
easy. Yet leaders and managers alike need to be reminded
that the good times as well as the bad will pass away. The
best course that I know is to keep pressing forward, no
matter the circumstances.

Like all great sentiments, the idea of pressing on is
hardly new. St. Paul urged his flock to do as he did, and
"press to the mark." Two and a half millennia earlier, the
last words written by Buddha expressed the identical sentiment: "Strive on, diligently."

The Superior Company

If its leadership and management alike can learn from
these rules and act on them—and do so consistently and
with conviction—any firm has the opportunity to build
what Robert Greenleaf, the creator of the concept of

servant-leadership, liked to call "the superior company." Here's how he described such an enterprise:

What distinguishes a superior company from its competitors are not the dimensions that usually separate companies, such as superior technology, more astute market analysis, better financial base, etc.; it is unconventional thinking about its dream—what this business wants to be, how its priorities are set, and how it organizes to serve. It has a radical philosophy and self-image.

The company's unconventional thinking about its dream is [often] born of a liberating vision. Why are liberating visions so rare? Because a powerful liberating vision is difficult to deliver. That difficulty of delivery, however, is only half of the answer. The other half is that so few who have the gift for summarizing a vision, and the power to articulate it persuasively, have the urge and the courage to try. But there must be a place for servant-leaders with prophetic voices of great clarity who will produce those liberating visions on which a caring, serving society depends.

I leave to far wiser—and more objective—heads than mine the judgment about the extent to which Vanguard may meet the definition of a superior company. Of course, I hope it does. But I have no hesitancy in saying it is the product of unconventional thinking about what we wanted to be, about how we set our priorities, and about how we organized to serve our clients.

Values and Profits

By now, it probably goes without saying that I'm deeply convinced other firms—be they mutual fund firms, other financial firms, or even firms engaged in manufacturing goods and providing services—can learn from Vanguard's example. I'm pleased to say that I'm not alone in that conviction. In *The Value Profit Chain*, three Harvard Business School professors describe Vanguard as one of only two organizations (the other was Wal-Mart) whose "remarkable accomplishments . . . were based on value profit chain concepts *from the onset of their development* . . . [and] have risen to leadership positions in their respective industries."

The authors' value profit chain is a concept that includes a series of "interrelated phenomena: customer loyalty and commitment, [driven by] high levels of value compared to competition; value created by satisfied, committed, loyal, and productive employees; employee satisfaction [based on] the 'fairness' of management, the opportunity for personal growth on the job, and the capability of employees to deliver service to customers. . . .

When organizations get the elements of the value profit chain right, the results"—citing Vanguard's superior returns, low costs, and high shareholder satisfaction—"are dramatic."

The Gale of Creative Destruction

I'm sure that our competitors—even the most successful of them—look with a sort of detached bemusement and skepticism at our emergence as one of the fund industry's largest and most respected leaders; at our unique corporate structure and our focus on holding costs to a minimum (in an industry that hardly strives for that goal); and at our missionary zeal, our contrariness, and our feistiness. But we have dared to be different. We have strived to build an enterprise in which trust, stewardship, and professionalism are woven into the very fabric of the place—indeed, even into the name itself—and it seems to be working just fine. Most of all, I did my best to build a company that would endure, an enterprise that would last for at least a century. (We're not that far off. Wellington Fund celebrates its 80th birthday this very year. I'm sure that, from his perch in Heaven, Walter Morgan, Wellington's founder and my great mentor, will be accepting congratulations. Such a milestone is no mean testimonial!)

Few corporations indeed have ever met the century test. Witness, for example, the changes in the Fortune 500 (an annual list of America's 500 largest corporations) even over a period as short as a half-century. Of the 2,000 companies that made the list at one time or another since it was first published in 1955, the vast majority are gone. Only 71 companies of the original 500 remain on the list today. Clearly, this turnover is what Joseph Schumpeter, the first economist to recognize entrepreneurship as the vital force that drives economic growth, called "the gale of creative destruction," in which established companies that are ill prepared for change are replaced by new companies inspired by new ideas and new technologies and driven by visionary entrepreneurs.

Yet there is no inherent reason why any firm with the commitment and boldness to build the kind of positive culture I have tried to describe here can't defy the ever-present danger of creative destruction. Jim Collins, the author of *Good to Great*, agrees: "When you've built an institution with values and a purpose beyond just making money—when you've built a culture that makes a distinctive contribution while delivering exceptional results—why would you surrender to the forces of mediocrity and succumb to irrelevance? And why would you give up on the idea that you can create something that not only lasts but also deserves to last? . . . No law of nature dictates that a great institution must inevitably fail, at least not within a human lifetime."

My hope, then, is not merely that Vanguard will endure, but that it will deserve to endure. Further, I hope that other firms that deserve to last will also fight the unremitting gale of creative destruction and endure. To do so, of course, the institutions that survive and prosper must have values and a purpose beyond just making money. They will also require both managers and leaders who suffuse vision and character into every element of the firm, men and women who bring not only their heads but their hearts to the challenge.

By avoiding the consequences of overmanaging, well-qualified managers, of whom we have a good supply (although even in this age of the MBA, never quite enough), must do things right, for only outstanding management can effectively implement the policies and practices that are required to build the superior firm. But only genuine leadership, of which we will never have nearly enough, can focus on doing the right things: establishing caring human principles, setting the course of action, and providing the vision that will inspire the members of the organization to follow.

LIFE

Chapter 8

Too Much Focus on Things, Not Enough Focus on Commitment

For as long as I can remember, I've been inspired by the great truths of human existence. Sometimes I find them in the expected places: the ancient Greek philosophers, the Bible (especially the King James version), Shakespeare. But often, too, I find that great truths pop up in unexpected places. One such instance came a decade ago, when I was watching a hit film in a suburban Philadelphia movie theater.

The film was *A Civil Action*, based on Jonathan Harr's book chronicling a lawsuit that was the aftermath of deadly water pollution in a Massachusetts town. An

183

ambitious personal injury lawyer (played by John Travolta) at first seeks to earn fame and riches for himself by winning millions for the families of the victims. But as the case develops, he becomes involved with the families and spends huge amounts of his resources on scientific investigation of the pollution's impact, putting himself and his small firm deeply in debt. As the movie progresses, the search for right and justice begins to consume him until, finally, by standing up for principle, he risks financial failure. Alas, he goes down in flames, and the film's final sequence finds him in personal bankruptcy court.

There, the judge finds it hard to believe that the only assets owned by this successful and once-wealthy litigator are $14 and a portable radio. Incredulous, she asks, "Where are the things by which one measures one's life?" I almost jumped out of my seat at the profundity of the question. *Where are the things by which one measures one's life?* But he no longer has any things. He has stood up for the worthy cause of children who have died and families who have been devastated. He has put his career on the line, and he has lost everything. Should we measure him by what he *has*, or by who he *is*?

It seems rather out of character for Hollywood to deal with how we measure our lives. But the question remains: What *are* the things by which we should measure our lives? I'm still searching for the ultimate answer to that question. But I know that we can never let things as such—the material possessions we may come to accumulate—become the measure of our lives. In a nation as rich with material abundance as ours, a cornucopia of things almost beyond measure, it is an easy trap to fall into. Two and a half thousand years ago, the Greek philosopher Protagoras told us that "man is the measure of all things." Today, I fear, we are becoming a society in which "things are the measure of the man."

Indeed, there's a perhaps tongue-in-cheek aphorism that whoever dies with the most toys wins. Such a measure is absurd; it is superficial; and, finally, it is self-defeating. The world has far too many calls on its limited resources to expend them on things trivial and things transitory. There are literally billions of human beings out there, all over the globe, who cry out for support and for salvation, for security and for compassion, for education and for opportunity—those intangibles that carry a value far in excess of so many tangible things whose nature is, finally, inconsequential. One of my favorite hymns, "God of Grace and God of Glory," says it better than I can: "Cure Thy children's warring madness, bend our pride to Thy control; Shame our wanton, selfish gladness, rich in things and poor in soul."

If it is surprising that a Hollywood film would be concerned with the things by which one measures one's life, it might be even more surprising that a businessman—particularly one in the investment arena, where greed seems the order of the day—would echo that concern. But I have had cause enough to know that the road of life is rarely smooth and that we need to be prepared for the inevitable reversals in our fortunes, whether constituted by wealth, or health, or family.

Now at 79 years of age, I've also lived long enough to recognize the wisdom of that pointed warning from Ecclesiastes: "The race is not to the swift, nor the battle to the strong,* neither yet bread to the wise, nor yet riches to men of understanding, nor yet favor to men of skill, but time and chance happeneth to them all." Put another way, time and chance can bestow things on you, and take them away from you as well. But even as *what you have* may come and go, *who you are*—your character—will endure.

Boldness, Commitment, and Providence

If things are by nature ephemeral (after all, "you can't take them with you"), what is it that does matter? What are the characteristics by which we should measure our lives? Surely the nineteenth-century German philosopher Goethe identified one of them: boldness.

---

*Referring to the same passage from Ecclesiastes, Damon Runyon added this caution: "The race may not always be to the swift nor the battle to the strong, but that's the way to bet."

Are you in earnest? Seize this very minute;
What you can do, or dream you can do, begin it;
Boldness has genius, power and magic in it.

Goethe's inspirational words inspired a strong ampli-
fication from Scottish author W. H. Murray, which I paraphrase here:

Until one is committed, there is hesitancy, the chance
to draw back, always ineffectiveness. Concerning all
acts of initiative and creation, there is one elementary
truth, the ignorance of which kills countless ideas and
splendid plans: that the moment one definitely com-
mits oneself, then providence moves too.

A whole stream of events issues from the deci-
sion, raising in one's favor all manner of unfore-
seen incidents and meetings and material assistance,
which no man could have dreamt would have come
his way. Whatever you do, or dream you can, begin it.
Boldness has genius, power and magic in it. Begin
it now.

And so the combination of boldness and commitment
magically seems to summon what we might call *providence*.

It is all true, and my own life has been the proof of
it, better than any dream. Whenever I have committed
myself with boldness, providence has followed, whether it

was the providence of stumbling on that *Fortune* magazine article on the mutual fund industry way back when
I was searching for a topic for my senior thesis, and then
committing myself wholeheartedly to the project; the
providence (yes, the providence!) of being fired by my
Wellington partners that demanded of me the commitment to recapture my career in the industry and gave
me the opportunity to start Vanguard; the providence of
receiving a new heart, just as mine was about to expire;
and the commitment to making the most of my second
chance at life; and the many other examples I've cited
throughout this book—the "acres of diamonds" that were
always providentially there, waiting to be discovered but
requiring commitment to capitalize on their value.

Equally, for every act of boldness at Vanguard, I have
indeed been rewarded with gifts of genius, power, and
magic—not my own, but the genius, power, and magic
of my fellow crew members and of the ideas that drove
us on: building a better mousetrap and finding that clients
would beat a path to our door, slashing costs, and investing for the long term, firmly committed to doing it all
the right way, even when shortcuts were popping up all
around us.

My inherent resistance to shortcuts was greatly amplified by a hard experience as a police-beat reporter for
the old *Philadelphia Bulletin*. In 1950, while working at a

summer job, I got a call from the news desk to cover a house fire that was two trolley rides away from my location in a firehouse. (I had no car.) It was about midnight; I was tired and uninspired by the story; so I waited until the firemen returned, got the story from them, and called it in. But my rewrite man, observing my lack of detail and sensing my strategy, caught me short with a single question: "What color was the house, Bogle?" Mortified by my conduct and scared that I might lose my job, I replied simply: "I'll get over there right away." And I did. It was a great lesson—I owe that rewrite man a hearty salute!—to beware of the apparently easy shortcuts of life. *If a job is to be done, best to do it right.*

Commitment and boldness—these are among the things that truly matter, the things by which we can measure our lives, the things that help turn providence in our favor. Their reach goes far beyond how we earn our living, for never forget that none of us lives by bread alone.

Commitment to Family and Community

The well-rounded life requires other commitments, too. These commitments begin with our families. Until we are committed, there is the chance to draw back, but once we commit ourselves to family, all sorts of things occur that might never have otherwise occurred. For me, commitment to family has brought the blessings of marriage (Eve and I have now enjoyed nearly 52 magical years together), the blessings of children, the blessings of grandchildren, and perhaps one day even the blessings of great-grandchildren.

Commitment to our neighbors and our community is also vital. In this increasingly individualistic age, community spirit—once exemplified by the barn raising, the quilting bee, the fence-mending—seems almost a quaint anachronism. But a spirit of cooperation and togetherness is today more important than ever, especially in our urban areas where enormous wealth and grinding poverty exist side by side, and where, paradoxically, both extremes seem to lead away from the kind of community spirit that is at the core of the civility that has made living in American communities so worthwhile.

I am not at all embarrassed to mention the constructive role of religion in fostering these higher values. While I won't dwell now on the Judeo-Christian values that I deeply cherish, I would note that virtually all religions preach the existence of a supreme being, the virtues of a Golden Rule, and standards of conduct that parallel the Ten Commandments. We thrive as human beings and as families not by *what faith* we happen to hold, but by *having faith*, faith in something far greater than ourselves.

The Commitment to Citizenship

In my day, I've met many successful men and women, too many of whom express their pride in having done it all themselves. But I don't believe that any one of us can take sole credit for our success. Most of us have been blessed by the nurture and love of our families, the support of our friends and colleagues, the dedication of our teachers, and the inspiration and guidance of our mentors, to say nothing of the providence that brought us the opportunity to realize our goals. "We did it *ourselves*." Really? When I hear that, I'm bold enough to ask, "Now just how did you arrange to be born in the United States of America?"

And so I come to my final affirmation of commitment: commitment to our nation—"America the Beautiful," in the words of the hymn. Please neither derogate our heritage as Americans nor take it for granted. And, for that matter, never think that we have arrived at perfection, as this splendid verse of the hymn—my favorite—warns: "America! America! God mend thine every flaw. Confirm thy soul in self-control, thy liberty in law." The moment we boldly commit ourselves to doing all we can, every day, to measure up to the elementary principles of good citizenship, magic follows for our nation, too.

So, it's up to each of us to summon our unique genius, our own power, and our personal magic. Just as it has done so unfailingly for me, providence will respond for you. It really will! So in everything you do, be bold. Each of us must decide for ourselves how much to focus on things, and indeed what things to focus on. But I know that each one of us can profit by some moments of quiet introspection about whether our lives are driven far too much by the accumulation of things, and not nearly enough by the exercise of bold commitment to our family, to our work, to a worthy cause, to our society, and to our world.

Chapter 9

Too Many Twenty-First-Century Values, Not Enough Eighteenth-Century Values

A few summers back, a book that the late Neil Postman—prolific author, social critic, and professor at New York University—had autographed and given me. The central message of *Building a Bridge to the Eighteenth Century* is encapsulated in its opening epigraph:

Soon we shall know everything the 18th century didn't know, and nothing it did, and it will be hard to live with us.[*]

Postman's book presents an impassioned defense of the old-fashioned liberal humanitarianism that was the hallmark of the Age of Reason. His aim was to restore the balance between mind and machine, and his principal concern was our move away from the era in which the values and character of Western civilization were at the forefront of the minds of our great philosophers and leaders, and when the prevailing view was that anything that's important must have a moral authority.

To Postman's way of thinking, truth is invulnerable to fashion and the passing of time. I'm not so sure. While that is the way things work in the long run—of course reality ultimately prevails—perception often wins in the short run. Indeed, I would argue that we have moved away from *truth*—however one might define it—to (with due respect to television commentator Stephen

---

[*]While we met only once, Postman knew enough about my own values to inscribe his book: "To Jack, whom I am delighted to have met in the 21st century, but who hasn't forgotten the glorious 18th century. A toast to common sense!"

Colbert) *truthiness*, the presentation of ideas and numbers that convey neither more nor less than what we wish to believe in our own self-interest, and persuade others to believe, too. This self-interest on the part of the wealthiest segments of our society, in turn, has been used to justify what I described in *The Battle for the Soul of Capitalism* as a "pathological mutation" from *owners'* capitalism to *managers'* capitalism in our business and financial systems—in corporate America, investment America, and mutual-fund America alike, the book's three principal targets.

But I fear, too, that this pathological mutation has spread more broadly across society, into the texture of so many of our lives. With Wikipedia at our fingertips and Google waiting online to serve us, we are surrounded by information, but increasingly cut off from knowledge. Facts (or, more often, factoids) are everywhere. But wisdom—the kind of wisdom that was rife in the age of this nation's Founding Fathers—is in short supply.

When I first expressed this skepticism about our Information Age more than a decade ago, I naively believed that it was an original thought. But there is nothing new under the sun, and I was delighted to learn recently that T. S. Eliot had expressed the same ideas—much more poetically, of course—in *The Rock* (1934):

> *Where is the Life we have lost in living?*
> *Where is the wisdom we have lost in knowledge?*
> *Where is the knowledge we have lost in information?*
> *The cycles of Heaven in twenty centuries*
> *Bring us farther from God and nearer to the Dust.*

To paraphrase Neil Postman's essential message, soon we shall know everything that doesn't count, and nothing that does.

The Age of Reason

The Age of Reason that Postman applauded—what we now often describe as the Enlightenment—centered in the eighteenth century, and became central to western philosophy and society. The great intellectuals and philosophers who then populated western civilization didn't always agree with one another, but together they managed to implant in society a reliance on reason, a passion for social reform, and the belief that moral authority is integral to the successful functioning of education and religion as well as to commerce and finance.

These thought leaders also believed in the primacy of the nation-state and the liberty of human beings, exemplified by two of Thomas Paine's powerful and influential tracts, *The Age of Reason* and *The Rights of Man*. Paine's impassioned essay *Common Sense* played an important role in the founding of our nation, helping to awaken the American colonists to the understanding of the absurdity "in supposing a continent can be perpetually governed by an island," to the need for "a government that contained the greatest sum of individual happiness with the least national expense," and to the understanding that "the more simple anything is, the less liable it is to be disordered."[*]

Like Paine, Thomas Jefferson and Alexander Hamilton spoke eloquently of reason, rights, and reform. The correspondence of John Adams, George Washington, James Madison, and others among our Founding Fathers is punctuated with the values of the Enlightenment. These men were strongly influenced by its proponents in Great Britain and throughout Europe, a "who's who" of the era, including Edmund Burke, David Hume, Immanuel Kant, John Locke, Sir Isaac Newton, Jean-Jacques Rousseau, and Adam Smith.

The ideas of those philosophers sprang, in turn, from their predecessors of yore, another Hall of Fame that stretches from Homer, Sophocles, Socrates, Plato, Aristotle,

---

[*] You'll recognize, I think, the frequent appearances in this book of these final two themes.

and Virgil, to Dante, William Shakespeare, Sir Francis Bacon, and John Milton—all great thinkers and writers who expressed their ideas with a force and clarity that continues to impress us to this day. The eighteenth-century heroes of the Age of Reason stood on the shoulders of these earlier heroes, and it is hard to imagine our modern world without their contributions.[*]

The Prototypical Eighteenth-Century Man

Perhaps the paradigm of the eighteenth-century man was Benjamin Franklin. I cite him here not only as a remarkable illustration of the values of the Enlightenment, but also as the most famous citizen of my adopted City of Brotherly Love.

Franklin's extraordinary accomplishments as Founding Father, framer, statesman, diplomat, scientist, philosopher,

---

[*]I believe that without *The Federalist Papers,* numbering some 85 essays, our Constitution would have failed to gain approval by 9 of the 13 states that was required for its adoption. (It was ultimately ratified by all 13, although often by paper-thin margins.) Alexander Hamilton, author of 52 of the essays, chose the pen name *Publius,* after one of the founders and great generals of the Roman republic, whose name came to mean "friend of the people."

author, master of the epigram, and fount of earthy wisdom are widely known and justly celebrated. But his astounding entrepreneurship—remarkable for *any* era—offers the greatest contrast in some ways with our own age.

In today's grandiose era of capitalism, the word *entrepreneur* has come to be commonly associated with those who are motivated to create new enterprises largely by the desire for personal wealth or even greed. But in fact *entrepreneur* simply means "one who undertakes an enterprise," a person who founds and directs an organization. At its best, entrepreneurship entails something far more important than mere money.

Please do not take my word for it. Again heed the words of the great Joseph Schumpeter. In his *Theory of Economic Development*, written nearly a century ago, Schumpeter dismissed material and monetary gain as the prime mover of the entrepreneur, finding motivations like these to be far more powerful:

> *(1) The joy of creating, of getting things done, of simply exercising one's energy and ingenuity, and (2) The will to conquer: the impulse to fight, . . . to succeed for the sake, not of the fruits of success, but of success itself.*

Entrepreneurs and Capitalists

There is a difference, then, between entrepreneurs and capitalists. As Franklin biographer H. W. Brands put it, "Had Franklin possessed the soul of a true capitalist, he would have devoted the time he saved from printing to making money somewhere else." But he did not. For Franklin, the getting of money was always a means to an end, not an end in itself. The other enterprises he created, as well as his inventions, were designed for the public weal, not for his personal profit. Even today, Dr. Franklin's idealistic eighteenth-century version of entrepreneurship is inspirational. When he reminded us that "energy and persistence conquer all things," Franklin was likely describing his own motivations to create and to succeed, using Schumpeter's formulation, for the joy of creating, of exercising one's energy and ingenuity, the will to conquer, and the joy of a good battle.

Franklin's creation of a mutual insurance company was the classic example of his community-minded approach to entrepreneurship. In the eighteenth century, fire was a major and ever-present threat to cities. In 1736, when barely 30 years of age, Franklin responded to that threat by founding the Union Fire Company, literally a bucket brigade that protected the homes of its subscribers. In a short time, other Philadelphia fire companies had formed and begun to compete with one another, so in April 1752, Franklin joined with his colleagues in founding the Philadelphia Contributionship, which continues today as the oldest property insurance company in the United States. And he didn't stop there. He also founded a library, an academy and college, a hospital, and a learned society—none for his personal enrichment, all for the benefit of his community. Not bad!

Like many entrepreneurs, Franklin was also an inventor. Once again, his goal was to improve the community's quality of life. Among other devices, he created the lightning rod and the Franklin stove (to say nothing of bifocals and swim fins). He made no attempt to patent the lightning rod for his own profit, and he declined the offer by the governor of the Commonwealth for a patent on his Franklin stove, the "Pennsylvania fireplace," his 1744 invention that revolutionized the efficiency of home heating with great benefit to the public at large. Benjamin Franklin believed that "Knowledge is not the personal property of its discoverer, but the common property of all. As we enjoy great advantages from the inventions of others, we should be glad of an opportunity to serve others by any invention of ours, and this we should do freely and generously."

As the first decade of the twenty-first century comes to a close, Franklin's noble eighteenth-century values stand in bold contrast to the bitter patent wars of today, to the obscene salary demands of the executives of our giant corporations and the enormous compensation paid to hedge fund managers (often whether they win or lose, or even survive), and to the nonmutuality, if you will, of so much of our civic life. In fact, the differences verge on the appalling.

The Impartial Spectator

As much as Benjamin Franklin is the personal embodiment of the Age of Reason, his eighteenth-century contemporary, Adam Smith (17 years Franklin's junior), is surely the intellectual embodiment of how economies work. Smith's analogy of the invisible hand and how it moves the economy, described in *The Wealth of Nations*, remains an important element of economic philosophy to this day.

As Smith wrote:

Every individual intends only his own security; by directing his industry in such a manner as to produce its greatest value, he intends only his own gain but is led by an invisible hand to promote an end which was no part of his intention . . . promoting the interests of the society more effectively than when he really intends to promote it.

The invisible hand remains almost universally known to this day. But in our time, Smith's "impartial spectator," which first appears in his earlier *Theory of Moral Sentiments*, is today almost universally unknown. Yet the impartial spectator uncannily echoes the values by which Franklin lived.

That impartial spectator, Smith tells us, is the force that arouses in us values that are so often generous and noble. It is the inner man, shaped by the society in which he exists—even the soul—who gives us our highest calling. In Smith's words, "It is reason, principle, conscience, the inhabitant of the breast, the man within, the great judge and arbiter of our conduct."

[The impartial spectator] calls to us, with a voice capable of astonishing the most presumptuous of our passions, that we are but one of the multitude, in no respect better than any other in it; and that when we prefer ourselves so shamefully and so blindly to others, we become the proper objects of resentment, abhorrence, and execration. It is from him only that we learn the real littleness of ourselves. It is this impartial spectator . . . who shows us the propriety of generosity and the deformity of injustice; the propriety of reining the greatest interests of our own, for the yet greater interests of others . . . in order to obtain the greatest benefit to ourselves. It is not the love of our neighbour, it is not the love of mankind, which upon many occasions prompts us to the practice of those divine virtues. It is a stronger love, a more powerful affection, the love of what is honourable and noble, the grandeur, and dignity, and superiority of our own characters.

Smith's magnificent cadences can hardly help but inspire us citizens of this twenty-first century with the very values that we are ignoring and in danger of completely losing. The impartial spectator is one of the central metaphors that define those values, the high values of the eighteenth century.

"The Moral History of U.S. Business"

The evidence suggests that the values held high by Franklin and Smith were not uncommon among the businessmen of that era. Indeed, it seems almost providential that the very same 1949 issue of *Fortune* that inspired my Princeton University thesis included a feature essay entitled "The Moral History of U.S. Business." Although I had no clear recollection of the contents of the essay when I reread it a few years ago, I'm certain that I read it at the time. Still, I quickly found myself reflecting on Vanguard's founding principles, which seem to me to be related to the kind of moral responsibility of business that was expressed in that ancient *Fortune* essay.

The essay began by noting that the profit motive is hardly the only motive that lies behind the labors of American business leaders. Other motives include "the love of power or prestige, altruism, pugnacity, patriotism, the hope of being remembered through a product or institution." Even as I freely confess to all of these motives—life is too short to be a hypocrite—I also agree with *Fortune* on the appropriateness of the traditional tendency of American society to ask: "What are the moral credentials for the social power that the businessman wields?"

The *Fortune* article quotes the words of Quaker businessman John Woolman of New Jersey, who in 1770 wrote that it is "good to advise people to take such things as were most useful, and not costly," and then cites (almost inevitably) Benjamin Franklin's favorite words, industry and frugality, as "the means of producing wealth and receiving virtue."

Moving to 1844, the essay cites William Parsons, "a merchant of probity," who described the good merchant as "an enterprising man willing to run some risks, yet not willing to risk in hazardous enterprises the property of others entrusted to his keeping, careful to indulge no extravagance and to be simple in his manner and unostentatious in his habits, not merely a merchant, but a man, with a *mind* to improve, a *heart* to cultivate, and a *character* to form."

A Merchant and a Man

I found Parsons' definition of *merchant* and *man*, set out more than 160 years ago, to be more than inspiring; it seemed aimed directly at me. The words about the prudence, trustworthiness, and simplicity of the enterprising man struck me as apt descriptions of the goals of my own career and my life. And the three qualities that defined the merchant as a man were, I think, equally appropriate. As for the mind, I still strive every day—I really do!—to improve my own mind, reading, reflecting, and challenging even my own deep-seated beliefs, and writing about the issues of the day with passion and conviction.

As for the heart, no one—no one!—could possibly revel in the opportunity to cultivate it more than I, having discovered that diamond of a new heart more than a dozen years ago. And as for character, whatever moral standards I may have developed over my long life, I have tried to invest my own soul and spirit in the character of the little firm that I founded all those years ago.

On a far grander scale than just one human life, these standards of mind, of heart, and of character resonate—as ever, idealistically—in how I hope the leaders of our productive businesses and our financial managers will again seek to manage the trillions of dollars of capital entrusted to their stewardship, putting the will and the work of our business and financial enterprises in the service of others.

Returning Stewardship to Capitalism

My fear—and part of what compels me to continue to press on in my chosen mission of returning capitalism, finance, and fund management to their roots in stewardship—is that in this computer-driven, information-overloaded age, we have forgotten the old truths that so successfully guided us in the past. But while our society's commitment to eighteenth-century values continues to fade, that commitment is hardly nonexistent. I'm heartened by the few—but strong—voices rising to the defense of those values.

For example, listen again to the widely respected businessman Bill George:

> *Authentic leaders genuinely desire to serve others through their leadership . . . are more interested in empowering the people they lead to make a difference than they are in power, money, or prestige for themselves . . . are as guided by qualities of the heart, by passion and compassion, as they are by qualities of the mind . . . lead with purpose, meaning, and values . . . build enduring relationships with people . . . are consistent and self-disciplined. When their principles are tested, they refuse to compromise.*

As George shows in his best-selling book, *Authentic Leadership*, these are more than stirring words. Authentic companies led by authentic leaders create solid business performance, building the intrinsic value of the enterprises they lead. These leaders build moral integrity into the fabric of the organization, and they create not just stock-price spikes but sustained growth in revenues and earnings per share. "The best path to long-term growth in shareholder value," George writes, "comes from having a well-articulated mission that inspires employee commitment and the confidence and trust of clients."

Listen, too, to legendary Boston College law professor Tamar Frankel in her impassioned book *Trust and Honesty: America's Business Culture at a Crossroad*:

> *The real test for an honest and productive society is not what a society has achieved, but what it aims to achieve. It can put honest people on a pedestal even if they do not maximize their personal benefits and preferences . . . and discard and shun as models of failure dishonest people who achieve their highest ambitions by fraud and abuse of trust.*

That echo of the impartial spectator helps provide the perspective we need. Bill George and Tamar Frankel exemplify the voices that will allow us to blend the best ideals of the eighteenth century with the compelling realities of the twenty-first century. These are the kinds of thinkers who will lead us to perhaps the most forgotten of all the qualities of that long-ago century—the central characteristic that those eighteenth-century versions of entrepreneurship, mutuality, and invention for the public weal have in common: *virtue.*

On Virtue

Today, *virtue* is a word that tends to make us uneasy. But it surely didn't embarrass Benjamin Franklin. In 1728, when he was but 22 years of age, he tells us that he "conceived the bold and arduous project of arriving at moral perfection. . . . I knew, or thought I knew, what was right and wrong, and I did not see why I might not *always* do the one or avoid the other." The task, he tells us, was more difficult than he imagined, but he ultimately listed 13 virtues—including temperance, silence, order, frugality, industry, sincerity, and justice—even ranking them in order of importance. He began each day with "The Morning Question: What Good shall I do this day?" and ended with "The Evening Question: What Good have I done today?" It is hard to imagine a philosophy of self-improvement cast in a more ethical fashion.

Even viewed through the lens of twenty-first-century cynicism rather than eighteenth-century idealism, I confess a sense of wonder at the young Franklin's moral strength and disciplined self-improvement. While few of us in today's society would have the will to pursue a written agenda of virtue, Franklin had established, in his own words, the "character of Integrity" that would give him so much influence with his fellow citizens in the struggle for American independence.

That character was also central to his dedication to the public interest, so easily observable in his entrepreneurship, in the joy he took from his creations and from exercising his ingenuity, his energy, and his persistence. And that character also found its expression in Franklin's ongoing struggle to balance pride with humility—a battle that in this age of bright lights, celebrity, and money we seem to have largely abandoned. As Franklin wrote in his autobiography:

> *In reality, there is, perhaps, no one of our natural passions so hard to subdue as pride. Disguise it, struggle with it, beat it down, stifle it, mortify it as much as one pleases, it is still alive, and will every now and then peep out and show itself; you will see it perhaps often in this history; for even if I could conceive that I had completely overcome it, I should probably be proud of my humility.*

In candor, these words serve to remind me that my own pride too often peeps out and shows itself, and that my own humility could use a little more development.

Franklin's mind is indeed the eighteenth-century mind at work—a model for our times. It is a contrast that reminds us that we have steeped ourselves quite enough in twenty-first-century values, driven largely by self-interest, and not nearly enough in the values of the eighteenth century, when the impartial spectator was our guide and a sense of common purpose pervaded our society.

Chapter 10

Too Much "Success," Not Enough Character

The Reverend Fred Craddock, a remarkable preacher from Georgia, may have been imagining things—the way preachers are wont to do—but he says this story really happened. Dr. Craddock was visiting in the home of his niece. There was this old greyhound, just like the ones who race around a track chasing those mechanical rabbits. His niece had taken the dog in to prevent it from being destroyed because its racing days were over, and Dr. Craddock struck up a conversation with the greyhound:

I said to the dog, "Are you still racing?"
"No," he replied.

"Well, what was the matter? Did you get too old to race?"

"No, I still had some race in me."

"Well, what then? Did you not win?"

"I won over a million dollars for my owner."

"Well, what was it? Bad treatment?"

"Oh, no," the dog said. "They treated us royally when we were racing."

"Did you get crippled?"

"No."

"Then why?" I pressed. "Why?"

The dog answered, "I quit."

"You quit?"

"Yes," he said. "I quit."

"Why did you quit?"

"I just quit because after all that running and running and running, I found out that the rabbit I was chasing wasn't even real."

A true story? Well, perhaps not. But I expect that most of us know just how that old greyhound felt. How many times have we gone around and around the track, chasing the false rabbit of success, only to discover that the real rabbit was under our nose, waiting to be discovered all along?

Flawed Measures of Wealth . . .

To be clear, I'm not against success. But because there are so many possible definitions of success, I try to avoid using the word whenever possible.* In bull sessions with my classmates when I was attending Princeton University, the conventional definition of success was said to be achieving wealth, fame, and power. All those years ago, that definition seemed reasonable enough to me, and even though more than a half century has passed since my college days, that definition still seems pretty reasonable. Indeed, the dictionary confirms that definition: "Success: the prosperous achievement of something attempted, the attainment of an object, usually wealth or position, according to one's desire."

So I accept the fact that wealth, fame, and power remain the three main attributes of success, *but not in the conventional way in which we still define those elements.* I have come to recognize that wealth is ill measured by mere dollars, that fame is ill measured by public accolades, and that power is ill measured solely by control over others.

---

*Curiously, I don't ever recall thinking much about becoming a success in life, any more than I ever worried much about failure. I just never focused on those abstract ideas. Rather, I believed that if I did my best, every day, more than I was asked to do, better than I was expected to do it, my future would take care of itself.

Financial wealth, in fact, is a shallow measure of success. If we accept dollars as our standard, then "money is the measure of the man," and what could be more foolish than that? So how *should* wealth be measured? What about a life well lived? What about a family closely bound by love? Who could be wealthier than a man or woman whose calling provides benefits to mankind, or to his fellow citizens, or to her community or neighborhood?

It is not that money doesn't matter. Who among us would not seek the resources sufficient to fully enjoy our life and liberty? We desire the security of freedom from want, the ability to pursue our chosen careers, the wherewithal to educate our children, and the comfort of a secure retirement. But how much wealth do these goals require? Indeed, we ought to wonder whether the super-wealth we observe at the most extreme reaches of our society—the ability to acquire an infinite number of the things of life—is not more bane than blessing.

. . . and of Fame and Power

Fame, too, is a flawed measure of success. Yet fame, sadly, seems to be the great ego builder of our age. If only those who strive for fame would ask themselves two essential questions: From what *source*? To what *avail*? Yes, of course the momentary fame of our sports heroes and the glittering fame of our entertainers give us the joy of seeing human beings operating at the very peak of their potential. But in today's fast-paced world, much of that glow rarely lasts more than the metaphorical 15 minutes of fame that Andy Warhol promised each one of us. Fame for real accomplishment is one thing. Fame based on self-aggrandizement, fame that is ill deserved, fame that is gained through wealth extracted from our corporate and financial institutions (and investors!), and fame that is used for base purposes are entirely different matters.

I'm only human, so I must confess to having enjoyed my own occasional heady brushes with fame. Of course I was amazed and delighted when in April 2004 I opened *Time* magazine and learned that I had been included on its first annual list of "The World's 100 Most Influential People," sandwiched in the "Heroes and Icons" group with Bono, Nelson Mandela, Tiger Woods, and the Dalai Lama. I knew I hadn't been chosen for my golf swing (only fair) or my serenity (nonexistent!), and learned that creating Vanguard and the first index mutual fund landed me on the list. I much appreciated the honor.

But I also knew that, as much wealth as Vanguard and our index funds may have created for investors, there were far more than 99 other individuals—many thousands more—who have had greater influence on contemporary society than I have had, and still millions of others who have received little or no recognition, yet have had an enormous and positive impact on their own communities. The fact is that most of those who make the greatest contributions to the daily working of our society never experience even a moment of the kind of fame that involves favorable recognition and public adulation.

And that brings us to *power*. Sure, few souls are more aware than I am of the thrill in having the power to run an enterprise. Exercised wisely, power over the *person* who serves the firm and power over the corporate *purse* are great fun, breeding self-confidence and the thrill of getting things done. But when power is used capriciously and arbitrarily, when power is reflected in grossly excessive perquisites, and when power is employed to create ego-building (and compensation-enhancing!) mergers and unwise capital expenditures that are more likely to detract from corporate value than to increase it, not only the shareholders of the corporation but its loyal employees—indeed society as a whole—are the losers.

What we ought to respect is power for a worthy purpose—the power of the intellect; the power of moral conduct; the power to enable the people with whom we work to grow in skill and spirit alike; the power that assures respect for the humblest to the highest souls who dedicate themselves to an enterprise; the power to help one's fellowman; power that is, using Adam Smith's ancient words, "[s]omething grand and beautiful and noble, well worth the toil and anxiety, to keep in motion the industry of mankind, to invent and improve the sciences and arts, which ennoble and embellish human life." Now *that's* power worth seeking.

So what are we to make of all of these mixed measures of success? Just this: Success cannot be measured solely—or even primarily—in monetary terms, nor in terms of the amount of power one may exercise over others, nor in the illusory fame of inevitably transitory public notice. But it *can* be measured in our contributions to building a better world, in helping our fellow man, and in raising children who themselves become loving human beings and good citizens. Success, in short, can be measured not in what we attain for ourselves, but in what we contribute to our society.

The Means, Not the End

I admit to a bias in favor of a business career—in part, for selfish reasons (business has been my own life's work) and in part out of genuine conviction. Businesses produce the goods and services that make our society work—indeed, that make so many of our lives so comfortable. Finance lubricates the machinery of capitalism. And entrepreneurship is the major force for innovation. What's more, businessmen and businesswomen at all levels of an organization have been the driving force of American capitalism that has made our incredibly wealthy economy the envy of the world. All that's to the good, but only so long as those of who have chosen business careers continue to ask ourselves whether we're chasing the fake rabbit of *success* or the real rabbit of *meaning*, defined by the contributions to our society that stem from principle, virtue, and character.

No career is the right career if it is undertaken solely to get rich, or to gain public fame, or to throw one's weight around. Nor is it the right career if it is undertaken to meet the expectations of others. And no success is the right success if it is achieved at society's expense. The proper measure? Your own expectations, and making the most of your talents.

A Special Burden

It's my conviction that those of us who do engage in business and financial careers carry a special burden, for it is in business and finance where most of the people in our society make the most money. Yet money itself can easily deceive us about what we do and why we do it. As René Descartes reminded us four full centuries ago, "A man is incapable of comprehending any argument that interferes with his revenue." So of course we must challenge ourselves as to whether the rabbits we are chasing are real.

Contrast businessmen and businesswomen with others who *are* chasing what I believe are the real rabbits of life—physicians and surgeons and nurses, teachers and scientists, sculptors and painters, historians and musicians, authors and poets, jurists and true public servants, ministers and priests and rabbis, and on and on. Perhaps these responsible, dedicated souls earn our respect because they serve our society knowing that accumulating great wealth is almost out of the question, that great fame is rare, and that great power—at least temporal power—is conspicuous by its absence.

But don't stop there. Think too about the humble folk of this life who do the world's work—electricians and carpenters, soldiers and firefighters, plumbers and mechanics, computer programmers and train conductors, pilots and navigators, landscapers and stonemasons, technicians and farmers, and on and on. Our society wouldn't function without these good souls who get up with the sun and do an honest day's hard work, usually with neither complaint nor accolade, and are rarely rewarded with any of those elusive fruits of so-called success. Yet surely few of them need wonder about whether the rabbits they chase are real. *Of course they are real!*

"I long to accomplish a great and noble task," the ever-inspiring Helen Keller once wrote, "but it is my chief duty to accomplish humble tasks as though they were great and noble. The world is moved along, not only by the mighty shoves of its heroes, but also by the aggregate of the tiny pushes of each honest worker."

Woodrow Wilson said it perhaps even more eloquently:

The treasury of America does not lie in the brains of the small body of men now in control of the great enterprises. . . . It depends upon the inventions, upon the originations, upon the ambitions of unknown men and women. Every country is renewed out of the ranks of the unknown, not out of the ranks of the already famous and powerful in control.

Competition for What?

Life has a way of creating new challenges, and the wealth of American life today has created its own challenges—a feeling of entitlement, of economic power, and of military might that has earned for our nation the admiration, the envy, and, yes, the hatred of much of mankind. I freely concede that the world in which our young people today are growing up is far more demanding than the more innocent world of six decades ago when I could still count myself as a youth. High schoolers double and triple up on studies, sports, and extracurricular activities so they can gain admission to the so-called best colleges. Once in college, students continue to strive for grades so they will get into the best graduate schools, and on and on the cycle of competition goes.

Up to a point, that's fine. Competition is part of life. But again I ask, competition for what? For test scores rather than learning? For form rather than substance? For prestige rather than virtue? For certainty rather than ambiguity? For following someone else's stars rather than one's own? What does all that mean if you lack honor and character? And there is the problem. For while our best and brightest are exquisitely trained to pursue the false rabbits of success, on the whole they are being poorly trained in the intangible qualities that become the virtues that bring real success.

"Without Character and Courage, Nothing Else Lasts"

In a *New York Times* essay in November 2004, David Brooks put it well:

> *Highly educated young people are tutored, taught, and monitored in all aspects of their lives, except the most*

important, which is character-building. But without
character and courage, nothing else lasts.

If character is not taught, how can it possibly be
learned? The affluent world in which so many young
citizens exist today doesn't easily create the ability to
build character. Often character requires failure; it requires
adversity; it requires contemplation; it requires determination and steadfastness; it requires finding one's own space
as an individual. And it surely requires honor. Yet we
rarely seem to emphasize character, even though in our
society today there are priceless sources of inspiration
right at hand. In fact, the challenge isn't finding useful
sources of inspiration, but sorting out the very good from
the best. While the Old Testament, for example, may not
use the word *character*, it describes character beautifully in
these words:

What is man that you are mindful of him, the son of
man that you care for him? Psalms 8:4

The fear of the Lord teaches a man wisdom, and
humility comes before honor. Proverbs 15:33

Humility and the fear of the Lord bring wealth and
honor and life. Proverbs 22:4

He who pursues righteousness and love finds life,
prosperity and honor. Proverbs 21:21

The New Testament is rich with sources as well. Recall, for example, St. Paul's warning, "They that will be rich fall into temptation and a snare and into many foolish and hurtful lusts, which drown men in destruction and perdition. For the love of money is the root of all evil." Or St. Luke's demand of those who have been blessed with plenty (which, defined broadly, includes the substantial majority of us Americans today): "For unto whomsoever much is given, of him much shall be required.... And to whom men have committed much, of them they will ask the more."

William Shakespeare did his part, too, summing it all up so beautifully in these familiar words from *Hamlet*, profound words of advice that Polonius gives to his son, Laertes, as the young man is about to depart for France:

> *This above all, to thine own self be true,*
> *And it must follow as the night the day,*
> *Thou canst not then be false to any man.*

So be true to yourself. *Be yourself!* And if you're not the kind of person you know you should be—the kind of person you want to be and can be—make yourself a *better* person. You can do it, whether you're 16 or 60 or, like me, headed into your ninth decade, maybe even beyond!

Like Dr. Craddock's old greyhound, age might slow us down on the track, but if anything, it should give us a keener awareness of which rabbits count. The point is this: Each one of us has within our own selves and our own souls the ability to be the exemplar of the dictionary definition of *honor:* "High in character, nobility of mind, scorn of meanness, magnanimity, a fine sense of what is right, and a respect for the dignity of virtue."

Wondering about the Rabbit We Chase

Most of us should not have to spend much time wondering whether the rabbits we are chasing are real or false. The guideposts are all around us. Yet in the quiet of the evening and the sometime loneliness of the soul, many of those who shouldn't *need* to wonder about the value of hard work and a life well lived doubtless do exactly that. But whether *they* wonder or not, surely any one of us who—by the blessings of birth, genes, talents, luck, determination, and the help of others—achieves the financial rewards of what passes for commercial success deserves no such exemption. (Perhaps it will surprise you to learn that I do a lot of lonely wondering about the worth of my own life and career.) We'll be better human beings and achieve greater things if we challenge ourselves to pursue careers that create value for our society—with personal wealth not as the goal, but as the by-product. Best of all, by setting that challenge for ourselves, we'll build the character that will sustain us in our labors.

We're *all* in the human race together—those who undertake the nobler missions of life, those unsung heroes who make our world work, and those of us who are lucky enough to earn a good living through our careers in business and trade, in finance, and in the other highly paid sectors of American life. So rather than running after a rabbit and finally finding that it's fake, and, like that greyhound we met earlier, quitting in dismay, let's just make sure that we are chasing the *real* rabbit of life, doing our best—in a complicated, risky, and uncertain world—to serve our fellowman.

Once we do that, let's keep running—and running, and running, and running!—the long race of a life well lived. We have quite enough lionizing of the notion of success as popularly defined by a certain kind of material wealth, fame, and power. But we do not have nearly enough of a more elevated notion of success, defined by a more spiritual kind of wealth, fame, and power, simply summed up in one word: character. And there can never be enough character. Our society needs every one of us to be part of the mission that will place character at the top of our national agenda. We can do it. We can make that noble task our own.

KNOWING ENOUGH (IF YOU CAN)

What's Enough
For Me? For You?
For America?

I n a book entitled *Enough.*, you may be wondering: What's enough for Jack Bogle? What's enough for you? And the giant question that looms over the United States today, what's enough for our society?

The idea of enough *wealth* was clearly on Joseph Heller's mind when he commented on Kurt Vonnegut's observation about the financial riches of their billionaire host. But, as you now know, I've taken the idea of *enough* far beyond money, to our business system and to the lives we live. So before I talk about the wealth issue for me, for you, and for the United States, let's think a bit further about the relationship between happiness and success, especially the right kind of success.

Albert Schweitzer got it exactly right. *"Success is not the key to happiness. Happiness is the key to success."* Honestly, I think that nearly all of us have a pretty good notion of what happiness is, and the extent to which we have found happiness in our lives. And all of us have experienced, to one degree or another, both the joys and sorrows of life, its pleasures and its pains, its bright surprises and its profound disappointments. Yet we come to realize, again, in almost all cases, that "this too shall pass away." So we survive and we move on. By and large, we human beings are a resilient bunch.

Psychologists have pretty accurately described the three major factors that define human happiness. Money, it turns out, does provide happiness, but as we quickly get used to our higher level of material wealth, it turns out to be a transitory sort of happiness. According to an authoritative article in *American Psychologist* magazine, it's not money that determines our happiness, but the presence of some combination of these three attributes: (1) *autonomy*, the extent to which we have the ability to control our own lives, "to do our own thing"; (2) *maintaining connectiveness* with other human beings, in the form of love of our families, our pleasure in friends and colleagues, and an openness with those we meet in all walks of life; and (3) *exercising competence*, using our God-given and self-motivated talents, inspired and striving to learn.

Some unfortunate human beings, tragically, are never able to develop these traits or may never even have the opportunity to develop them. But nearly all of us fortunate citizens, to one degree or another, share these traits and revel in their blessings.

Now that we've considered the important thing—the meaning of happiness in our lives—let's look at *enough* in a money context.

Enough for Me?

Let me open up my confession about what is enough for me by saying that, in my now 57-year career, I've been lucky to earn enough—actually, more than enough—to assure my wife's future well-being; to leave some resources behind for my six children (as it is sometimes said, "enough so that they can do anything they want, but not enough that they can do nothing"); to leave a mite to each of my 12 grandchildren; and ultimately to add a nice extra amount to the modest-sized foundation that I created years ago. The choice to share my financial blessings with those less fortunate reflects my profound conviction that each of us who prospers in this great republic has a solemn obligation to recognize his or her good fortune by giving something back.

I've been able to accumulate this wealth despite giving, for about the past 20 years, one-half of my annual income to various philanthropic causes. I don't look at these contributions as charity. I look at them as an attempt to repay the enormous debts I've accumulated over a lifetime, including (in no special order), the spiritual strength enhanced by the church in which most members of our family express their faith; the hospitals whose guardian angels nursed me through my five-decade struggle with heart disease, and the Greater Philadelphia community, through the United Way.

I've also supported the major causes that have given me the opportunity to serve our society, most notably the magnificent National Constitution Center on Independence Mall in Philadelphia, whose goal is to bring the values of our U.S. Constitution back into the mainstream of American Life. I've served the Center for 20 years, including almost eight years as its chairman, and was proud to preside at its opening in 2003.

I've also done my best to support the educational institutions that paved the way for my adult life and my career: Blair Academy, which fostered my academic discipline, opened my mind to a better understanding of mathematics, history, science, and the English language, and opened the door to opportunity; and Princeton University, which helped hone my mind and my character, and instilled in me the enormous respect and appreciation I've developed for the enlightenment of Western civilization—thinkers, writers, musicians, and artists—to say nothing of our Founding Fathers and the, yes, eighteenth-century values that I hold to this day.

"What goes around comes around." And so my greatest philanthropic delight has come with endowing Bogle Brothers scholarships for the remarkable students at Blair and Princeton who have been the beneficiaries. I've been at this task for a long time, ever since the moment came, years ago, when my income began to nicely exceed my family expenses.

At both institutions, I was given scholarships, and I figured that I darn well had an obligation to return the favor by funding scholarships for others who needed them every bit as much as my brothers and I did. (Our need was exemplified by some correspondence between Dr. Breed, then Blair's headmaster, and my father. Dr. Breed wrote to remind my father that he must pay $100 toward our tuitions; my father had to write back, "I'm sorry, but I don't have $100." The matter was dropped.) So far, some 128 Blair students and 110 Princeton students have been beneficiaries of those Bogle Brothers scholarships.

It's been the thrill of a lifetime to meet so many of these exceptional young men and women, and I've vicariously enjoyed their academic accomplishments. These fine citizens have already begun, or will soon begin, to realize their potential to serve not only our U.S. society but our global society as well. As I observe our younger generation in action, my confidence in our nation and my hopes for our future soar to the skies.

Now a bit of context regarding my financial assets: Some 87 members of the elite now named on the *Forbes* 400 listing the nation's wealthiest individuals have made their fortunes in the financial field—through either entrepreneurship, or speculation, or hard work, or sheer good luck. As it happens, most founders of investment management firms (and often their successors, too) have accumulated truly enormous wealth. The lowest-ranking financial person on the list has wealth estimated at $1.3 billion, and the highest-ranking (Fidelity's Johnson family) is worth some $25 billion.

I have never played in that billion-dollar-plus major league; nor, for that matter, even in its hundred-million-dollar-plus minor league. Why not? Simply because as the founder of Vanguard, I created a firm in which the lion's share of the rewards would be bestowed on the shareholders of the truly *mutual* mutual funds that compose the Vanguard Group. In fact, cumulative savings to our shareholders vis-à-vis the shareholders of our peers will soon exceed $100 billion.

These savings arise largely because we operate, as you have read earlier, on an "at-cost" basis. As a result, our management company, Vanguard—which is owned not by me but by our mutual funds—essentially earns a net income of zero. Nonetheless, through the Partnership Plan I described earlier, I've been paid generously,* sharing in the enormous growth of our fund assets, the superior returns earned by our funds, and our successful quest to slash the unit costs borne by our shareholders.

So, in comparison to nearly all, if not all, of my peers in this business, I'm something of a financial failure. (Perhaps they are amused by the fact that they are so much wealthier than I!) I suppose you could say that failure was intentional (not that I had any premonition that we would grow to such a huge size, nor, in truth, any idea of how much I might be giving up by creating Vanguard's mutual structure).

But I'm doing just fine, thank you, for three reasons. First, I was born and raised to save rather than spend.

---

*Full disclosure: I feel compelled to acknowledge that I've deferred some of my own compensation, a widespread practice among senior executives of most of our corporations. The deferred amounts compound tax-free but the final value of the account will be fully taxed when withdrawn. (Some deferred compensation plans accrue interest not at the going rate—as my own does—but at annual rates as high as 13 percent!) Both situations call for reform, with limitations on accumulated deferrals to a reasonable amount, and with the rate of interest to be accrued limited to the market interest rate.

I don't go for extravagance, and it still hurts me a bit to spend on things that are not necessities. I confess, however, that I have periodically, if reluctantly, broken those two rules. I have, for example, a weakness for flag paintings, indulged largely through my acquisition of reproductions of the classic works of Jasper Johns and Childe Hassam. But I can't remember a single year during my long career in which I've spent more than I earned.

Second, I've been blessed, ever since I began working in 1951, with a fabulous defined-contribution retirement plan, provided at the outset by Wellington Management, and then carried over to Vanguard, where I've continued to invest to this day. Wellington's first contribution to the plan was made in July 1951, 15 percent of my first month's salary of $250, or just $37.50. I've continued investing 15 percent of my compensation—which grew substantially during the late 1980s through the mid-1990s—in my retirement plan (to which a thrift plan was later added).

After stepping down as Vanguard's chief executive, I've continued to put away that 15 percent of the modest annual retainer I receive from the firm. I'm not yet retired, so I'm not required to draw down any distributions. My experience is a living testimony of how the humble wonders of the tax-deferred retirement plan, soundly invested over the long-term, can build the accumulation of wealth. My own retirement plan is by far the largest single item on our family balance sheet, and while I prefer not to tell the world the exact amount, its current value is little short of awesome.

Third, I've invested wisely, eschewing speculation and focusing exclusively on (you guessed it!) conservatively invested, low-cost mutual funds, first at Wellington and then at Vanguard. During my early career, I invested in Wellington Fund (shares that I hold to this day) and then, for most of my later career, largely in Vanguard's equity funds. But late in 1999, concerned about the (obviously) speculative level of stock prices, I reduced my equities to about 35 percent of assets, thereby increasing my bond position to about 65 percent. While stock and bond market fluctuations have swung that ratio around a bit, I haven't made a single change in my asset allocation ever since. And, even in today's turbulent markets, I do my best to avoid the temptation to peek at the value of my fund holdings. (A good rule for all of us!)

So I've been truly blessed by the magical combination of my Scottish thrift genes; my generous compensation; my propensity to save whatever remains each year; the mathematical miracle of tax-free compounding; the knowledge that in investing, costs matter enormously; and enough common sense to focus on a balanced asset allocation. I've talked this talk endlessly. Now that I've walked its walk personally, I can assure you that it's true. It works!

Enough for You?

Whoever cultivates the Golden Mean avoids both the
poverty of a hovel and the envy of a palace.

That's the standard that the Roman poet Horace urged
upon us some two millennia ago, and it is an equally valid
standard today. My own resources surely place me within
that Golden Mean, if clearly on the high side; indeed, relative to those in our society at large, in the higher reaches
among U.S. citizens.

I'm confident that virtually all of you who are reading
this book also fall within the Golden Mean that Horace
described. Over years of meeting thousands of Vanguard
shareholders—and receiving letters and e-mails from
thousands more—I've learned that many of them (indeed,
most of them) are confident that they have accumulated
enough to satisfy their own needs and desires. I can hardly
find the words to express how delighted I am that my
humble vision of how to invest successfully has played a
key role in that outcome.

When John D. Rockefeller was asked how much
was enough, he answered, "Just a little bit more." But for
most of us, as it is said, *enough* is $1 more than you need.
And that's a pretty good way to look at it. But the question is more complicated than that. A *Wall Street Journal*
book review of *Whatever Happened to Thrift?* recently tried

to answer the question "Do Americans have enough?" with this wise answer: "That depends on what the meaning of the word 'enough' is. Enough for our own good? Enough for that of our neighbors? Our grandchildren? Our neighbor's grandchildren and our grandchildren's neighbors? . . . By any standards," the review concludes, "we save too little." And, of course, for nearly all of us, saving—early, often, and regularly—is the key to wealth accumulation. It *is* as simple as that.

Another proven way to improve your savings accumulations is to postpone for as long as possible your first payments from Social Security. (The maximum yearly benefit for a married couple at age 62 is roughly $28,800 in 2008; at age 70—when payments *must* begin—it would be $47,700.) Still another way (you've heard this before!) is to invest rather than speculate. Always manage investment costs. Even that *Wall Street Journal* book review cited two tenets. "Moral: stick with low-fee funds. Bigger moral: there are some very simple things we can all do to become wiser investors."

When you plan your financial future, don't fool yourself by focusing on the nominal *gross* returns on stocks and bonds; subtract the costs you expect to be assessed, and work with net returns. Then assume that even those returns will be reduced by inflation. (You pick the number: 2.5 percent? 3.5? 4.5? More?) Set realistic goals that you can reasonably expect to achieve. I could give you dozens of additional tips on how to have enough, but I'd just be repeating what I've written in *Bogle on Mutual Funds* (1993), *Common Sense on Mutual Funds* (1999), and *The Little Book of Common Sense Investing* (2007).

Enough for America?

It seems probable—perhaps even likely—that most of you have enough to live at a reasonable, enjoyable standard of living, or are sufficiently financially savvy to reach the *enough* standard by the time your retirement comes, when the accumulation of wealth slows and the distribution of wealth begins. But, in conscience, I dare not fail to acknowledge the plight of literally millions of our fellow citizens who *don't* have enough, and who will *never* have enough to live at such a relatively lofty standard.

While all across society the rich are growing richer, there are vast segments of the American citizenry where the poor remain abjectly poor. For example, according to a recent study in the *New York Times*, the wealthiest 5 percent of residents of Manhattan earned more than $500,000 in 2006, and the top 20 percent earned more than $300,000. But the poorest 20 percent of wage earners took home an average pay of just $8,855. Think of that!

I share the concern of *New York Times* columnist David Brooks about what he describes as "this stark financial polarization."

> *On the one hand, there is the investor class. It has tax-deferred savings plans, as well as an army of financial advisers. [On the other hand,] there is the lottery class, people with little access to 401(k)s or financial planning but plenty of access to payday lenders, credit cards and lottery agents. . . . The loosening of financial inhibition has meant more options for the well-educated but more temptation and chaos for the most vulnerable. Social norms, the invisible threads that guide behavior, have deteriorated. Over the past years, Americans have been more socially conscious about protecting the environment and inhaling tobacco. They have become less socially conscious about money and debt.*

We who are members of what David Brooks describes as the investor class can feel proud of our good fortune and our thrift. But even as we thrive on the great benefits of our American civilization, we must remind ourselves that these benefits are not shared by far too large a portion of our citizenry. The Declaration of Independence assures us "that all men are created equal, that they are endowed by their Creator with certain unalienable Rights, that among these are Life, Liberty and the pursuit of Happiness."

While we all may be created equal, however, we are born into a society where inequality—of family, of education, and, yes, even of opportunity—begins as soon as birth takes place. But our Constitution demands more. "We the People" are enjoined "to form a more perfect Union, establish Justice, insure domestic Tranquility . . . promote the general Welfare, and secure the Blessings of Liberty to ourselves and our Posterity." These commitments—especially to a *more perfect* Union, to *justice* for all, to domestic *tranquility*, and to the *general* welfare—are not mere words; they represent the challenge of our age.

In all, of course, Americans seem to have quite enough of the things that we can measure! With 4 percent of the world's population, we produce 21 percent of the world's output, consume 25 percent of it, and earn 26 percent of the world's income. Our wealth is unsurpassed, as is our military might, although wars in far-off countries are consuming staggering amounts of our treasure. We continue to import far more from foreign lands than we export to them, the result of our *de minimis* national savings rate (as calculated by our government, about zero). The weakness of our U.S. dollar in world currency markets bodes ill for the future.

What's more, the real growth rate of our economy—about 3 percent per year currently—lags far behind the growth rates of the emerging giants of China (9 percent) and India (6 percent). While these high rates of growth from a small base are unsustainable, we should be clear that our domination of the global economy—and the global financial markets on which that economy is ultimately based—will not endure forever.

But, in the spirit of the analysis that has permeated this book, while we seem to have quite enough things in the United States, our traditional values seem to be eroding, and soon we'll not have nearly enough of them. So let's never forget that over the long term it is not things, nor power, nor money that forms the heart of any nation. Rather, it is values, the very values, applied to our society, that I have described here for us as individuals: the persistence, resilience, moral standards, and virtue that have made this nation great. The question, in short, is not whether the United States has enough money—enough productive wealth—to maintain and enhance its global presence and power, but whether it has enough character, values, and virtue to do so.*

As H. L. Mencken once observed, "the chief value of money lies in the fact that one lives in a world where it is overestimated." (That was 60 years ago; imagine what he'd say today.) And that's why I want to leave you with this message: What can be counted and weighed and spent is only a small part of *enough*. To understand what *enough*

---

*Former President Bill Clinton has expressed the idea well. "People the world over have always been more impressed by the power of our example than by the example of our power."

means in the larger picture of existence, we must all keep in mind the many other things that count in this life, even though (after that sign in Einstein's office) they can't be counted.

The idea that money isn't everything returns us to the Kurt Vonnegut story with which I opened this book. When I finally tracked down the source of the story, it turned out to be a poem, published in the *New Yorker* magazine in 2005. It's delightful; even better, it's only 92 words long:

True story, Word of Honor:
Joseph Heller, an important and funny writer
now dead,
and I were at a party given by a billionaire
on Shelter Island.
I said, "Joe, how does it make you feel
to know that our host only yesterday
may have made more money
than your novel 'Catch-22'
has earned in its entire history?"
And Joe said, "I've got something he can never have."
And I said, "What on earth could that be, Joe?"
And Joe said, "The knowledge that I've got enough."
Not bad! Rest in Peace!

Rest in Peace indeed, for both Heller and Vonnegut, who went to his reward early in 2007. These two men brought much laughter into the world, captured many of the ironies of human existence, and punctured many over-inflated egos. But not R.I.P. for the rest of us. There's too much of the world's work still to be done, and there are never enough citizens with determined hearts, courageous character, intelligent minds, and idealistic souls to do it.

Yes, our world already has quite enough hate, guns, political platitudes, arrogance, disingenuousness, self-interest, snobbishness, superficiality, war, and certainty that God is on our side. But it never has enough love, conscience, tolerance, idealism, justice, and compassion, nor enough wisdom, humility, self-sacrifice for the greater good, integrity, courtesy, poetry, laughter, and generosity of substance and spirit. If you carry nothing else away from your reading of this book, remember this: The great game of life is not about money; it is about doing your best to join the battle to build anew ourselves, our communities, our nation, and our world.

My Own Exciting Odyssey

Before I close this book, I'd like you to consider these excerpts from a poem that, when I first read it late in my career, seemed (rather like that 1949 *Fortune* article on the moral credentials of U.S. business) to be aimed directly at me. The words are a part of Alfred, Lord Tennyson's *Ulysses*, as the poet describes the adventurer's remarkable ancient odyssey. My hope is that they may explain to you, far better than could any words of my own, the exciting adventures I've enjoyed, the conflicting emotions I've endured, and the single-minded determination with which I await, with eager anticipation, the still-unwritten final chapters of my long career.

Ulysses begins by reflecting on his odyssey:

I cannot rest from travel: I will drink
Life to the lees: All times I have enjoy'd
Greatly, have suffer'd greatly, both with those
That loved me, and alone.
I am become a name;
For always roaming with a hungry heart
Much have I seen and known; cities of men
And manners, climates, councils, governments,
Myself not least, but honour'd of them all;
And drunk delight of battle with my peers.
I am part of all that I have met.

Then he considers what may lie ahead:

How dull it is to pause, to make an end,
To rust unburnish'd, not to shine in use!
As tho' to breathe were life! Life piled on life
Were all too little, and of one to me
Little remains: But every hour is saved
From that eternal silence, something more,

A bringer of new things;
And this gray spirit yearning in desire
To follow knowledge like a sinking star,
Beyond the utmost bound of human thought.
Old age hath yet his honour and his toil;
Death closes all: but something ere the end,
Some work of noble note, may yet be done.

Then, determined to take on one final mission, Ulysses summons his followers:

So come, my friends
'Tis not too late to seek a newer world.
Push off, and sitting well in order smite
The sounding furrows; for my purpose holds
To sail beyond the sunset, 'til I die.
Tho' much is taken, much abides; and tho'
We are not now the strength which in old days
Moved earth and heaven, that which we are, we are;
One equal temper of heroic hearts,
Renewed by time and fate, still strong in will
*To strive, to seek, to find, and not to yield.**

---

*In the penultimate line of the poem, I've taken the liberty of revising Tennyson's words. He actually wrote, "*made weak* by time and fate, *but* strong in will." He never could have imagined that a beating heart could be transplanted from one human being to another.

To be "strong in will, to strive, to seek, to find, and not to yield" is what this whole life of mine has been about. Yes, I've surely been blessed with enough—in wealth, in wonderful family and friends, in a career that's been aimed at giving investors a fair shake, and in a mission designed to open the eyes of our citizens to the serious flaws and inequities in our business and financial system.

Enough, I hope it's fair to say, to inspire others to some thoughtful introspection about the human condition and human aspirations. But never—never!—enough to be self-satisfied and self-indulgent. Perhaps this book will help each of you find more than enough in the way of enlightenment and idealism, virtues that will further enrich your own life and the lives of your loved ones.

Bonus Content from
If You Can

How Millennials Can Get Rich Slowly

Would you believe me if I told you that there's an investment strategy that a seven-year-old could understand, will take you 15 minutes of work per year, outperform 90% of finance professionals in the long run, and make you a millionaire over time?

Well, it is true, and here it is: Start by saving 15% of your salary at age 25 into a 401(k) plan, an IRA, or a

---

taxable account (or all three). Put equal amounts of that 15% into just three different mutual funds:

- A U.S. total stock market index fund
- An international total stock market index fund
- A U.S. total bond market index fund

Over time, the three funds will grow at different rates, so once per year you'll adjust their amounts so that they're again equal. (That's the fifteen minutes per year, assuming you've enrolled in an automatic savings plan.)

That's it; *if* you can follow this simple recipe throughout your working career, you will almost certainly beat out most professional investors. More importantly, you'll likely accumulate enough savings to retire comfortably.

But You're Still Screwed

Most young people believe that Social Security won't be there for them when they retire, and that this is a major reason why their retirements will not be as comfortable as their parents'. Rest assured that you *will* get Social Security; its imbalances are relatively minor and fixable, and even if nothing is done, which is highly unlikely in view of the program's popularity, you'll still get around three-quarters of your promised benefit.

The *real* reason why you're going to have a crummy retirement is that the conventional "defined benefit" pension plan of your parents' generation, which provided a steady and reliable stream of income for as long as they lived, has gone the way of disco. There's only one person who can repair the gap left by the disappearance of these plans, and you know who that is. Unless you act with purpose and vigor, your retirement options may well range between moving in with your kids and sleeping under a bridge in the rain.

Further, the most important word in this entire guide is the

if

in the above "if you can follow this simple recipe," because, you see, it's a very, very big *if*.

At first blush, consistently saving 15% of your income into three index funds seems easy, but saying that you can become comfortably well-to-do and retire successfully by doing so is the same as saying that you'll get trim and fit by eating less and exercising more. People get fat because they like pizza more than fresh fruit and vegetables and would rather watch Monday night football than go to the gym or jog a few miles. Dieting and investing are both *simple*, but neither is *easy*. (And I should know, since I've been much more successful at the latter than at the former.)

In your parents' day, the traditional pension plan took care of all the hard work and discipline of saving and investing, but in its absence, this responsibility falls on your shoulders. In effect, the traditional pension plan was an investing fat farm that involuntarily limited calorie intake and made participants run five miles per day. Too bad that, except for the luckiest workers, such as corporate executives and military personnel, these plans are disappearing.

Bad things almost inevitably happen to people who try to save and invest for retirement on their own, and if you're going to succeed, you're going to need to avoid them. To be precise, five bad things—hurdles, if you will—must be overcome if you are to succeed and retire successfully:

Hurdle number one: People spend too much money. They decide that they need the newest iPhone, the most fashionable clothes, the fanciest car, or a Cancun vacation. Say you're earning $50,000 per year, 15% of which is $7,500, or $625 per month. In this day and age, that's a painfully thin margin of saving, and it can be wiped out simply by stringing together several seemingly innocent expenditures, each of which might nick your savings by $100 or so per month: a latte per day, a too-rich cable package, an apartment that's a little too tony, a dress or pair of brand-name sneakers you really don't need, a few unnecessary restaurant meals, and, yes, an excessive smartphone plan you could, if you had to, not only live without, but also function better without. Life without these may seem spartan, but it doesn't compare to being old and poor, which is where you're headed if you can't save. You might even save the whole $625 in one fell swoop just by living with a roommate for a while longer, instead of renting your very own place. Again, as bad as having a roomie may be, it's not nearly as awful as living on cat food at age 70.

Let's assume you *can* save enough. You're not home free, not by a long shot. You've got four more barriers to get by.

Hurdle number two: You'll need an adequate understanding of what finance is all about. Trying to save and invest without a working knowledge of the theory and practice of finance is like learning to fly without grasping the basics of aerodynamics, engine systems, meteorology, and aeronautical risk management. It's possible, but I don't recommend it. I'm not suggesting that you need to get an MBA or even read a big, dull finance textbook. The essence of scientific finance, in fact, is remarkably simple and can be acquired, if you know where to look, pretty easily. (And rest assured, I'll tell you exactly where to find it.)

Hurdle number three: Learning the basics of financial and market *history*. This is not quite the same as the above hurdle; if learning about the theory and practice of finance is akin to studying aeronautics, then studying investing history is akin to reading aircraft accident reports—something every conscientious pilot does. The new investor is usually disoriented and confused by market turbulence and the economic crises that often cause it; this is because he or she does not realize that there's nothing really new under the investment sun. A quote often misattributed to Mark Twain has it that "History doesn't repeat itself, but it does rhyme." This fits finance to a tee. If you don't recognize the landscape, you *will* get lost. Contrariwise, there's nothing more reassuring than being able to say to yourself, "I've seen this movie before (or at least I've read the script), and I know how it ends."

Hurdle number four: Overcoming your biggest enemy—the face in the mirror—is a daunting task. Know thyself. Human beings are simply not designed to manage long-term risks. Over hundreds of thousands of years of human evolution, and over hundreds of millions of years of animal development, we've evolved to think about risk as a short-term phenomenon: the hiss of the snake, the flash of black and yellow stripes in the peripheral vision. We were certainly *not* designed to think about financial risk over its proper time horizon, which is several decades. Know that from time to time you *will* lose large amounts of money in the stock market, but these are usually short-term events—the financial equivalent of the snake and the tiger. The *real* risk you face is that you'll be flattened by modern life's financial elephant: the failure to maintain strict long-term discipline in saving and investing.

Hurdle number five: As an investor, you must recognize the monsters that populate the financial industry. They're very talented chameleons; they don't *look* like monsters; rather, they appear in the guise of a cousin or an old college friend. They are also self-deluded monsters; most "finance professionals" don't even realize that they're moral cripples, since in order to function they've had to tell themselves a story about how they're really helping their customers. But even if they're able to fool others and often themselves as well, make sure they don't fool you.

Only if you can clear all five of these hurdles can you successfully execute the deceptively simple "three-fund strategy" I've outlined above.

How can you defeat these five demons? No financial expert, no matter how smart, or how well he or she writes, can tell you exactly how to do this within a few dozen pages of a guide like this. To torture a metaphor, I can show you the road to Jerusalem, but since the journey takes longer than I have within these relatively few pages, I can't take you all the way there.

In other words, this inexpensive, small guide is not a taxi cab or an airliner; it's a map.

Acquiring the tools to make you a competent investor will take you at least several months. You can't learn to pilot an airplane in an hour, which is all it'll take for you to finish this guide, and neither can you become a competent investor in an hour either. The good news is that you're young and in no particular hurry, and that the effort of following the road map will be time well spent.

Now, for full disclosure. First, I've written a few investment books that continue to earn me royalties. I don't want you to buy them, since it's tacky for an author to recommend the purchase of his or her works. I'll shortly tell you what other books you should read, and in what order. Second, I'm also a co-principal in a money management firm. My partner and I specialize in individuals who already have millions; you very well might get there, but I'm old enough that by the time you do, I'll be pushing up the daisies. I am writing this book for my children, my grandchildren, and for the millions of young people who don't have a prayer of retiring successfully unless they take control of their saving and investing.

How to Read This Guide

This is, as you can see, a very short guide and although it will take you very little time to read, you're going to have to read it twice, and the second time will take a while if you do it properly.

After you've completed this guide, about an hour from now, take another ten minutes and reread the next section, beginning with "Hurdle Number One." At the end of that section, you'll encounter your first reading assignment, which will take you at least a week or two. If you have a busy schedule, it may even take you a month or two.

Then reread the following section, and then complete *its* reading assignment, which again will take you a few weeks or months. And so on, through to the end of the guide.

This may take you up to a year, but you're in no hurry, since you are just beginning to think about your retirement and you likely have little in the way of assets; you may even be in hock up to your ears with debts from school and car loans. So there's plenty of time, and the months you take to complete the course laid out in the guide will be the most profitable reading you will ever do; it may not be too much of an exaggeration to suggest, in fact, that your financial life depends on it.

With that out of the way, let's get started.

Hurdle Number One: Even If You Can Invest Like Warren Buffett, If You Can't Save, You'll Die Poor

How much do you need to save? We'll get into deeper math in the next section, but, as already mentioned, if you're starting to save at age 25 and want to retire at 65, you'll need to put away at least 15% of your salary.

Before you can save, you'll of course have to get yourself out of debt. In thinking about just how to do this, it helps to compare your expected investment return with the interest you're paying on your debt.

Every situation is different, but a few basic principles apply to everyone. First, no matter how much debt you have, always, always max out the employer match on your 401(k), 403, or other defined contribution retirement plan, since the "return" on this money is usually between 50% and 100%, which is higher than even the worst credit card interest rates. (From now on, I'll use the term "401(k)" to refer to any employer-sponsored deferred compensation plan.)

Next, eliminate your credit card debt, followed by your car loan. What about your educational loans? Since your long-term investment return on your retirement savings will be around 5%, which is likely lower than your loan interest rate, you should make paying off those your next priority. When, and only when, you've gotten rid of all your debt are you truly saving for retirement.

The above paragraph raises a subtle but important point about retirement savings. Note that I quoted an "expected return" of 5% for your retirement saving. We'll skip over for now how I arrived at that figure, but for the moment, I'll point out that this 5% number is *not* adjusted for inflation; that is, it is a "nominal" rate of return. I did this so as to more accurately compare it to the loan and credit card interest rates you may be facing.

For the purposes of retirement savings, though, it's better to think about returns that have been adjusted for inflation, that is, "real" rates. Currently, for example, long-term inflation appears to be running at around 2%, so the above 5% expected *nominal* return of your investments calculates out to a 3% *real* return, and what matters is the spending power of your portfolio, that is, its *real* value, not the *nominal* value you'll see on your brokerage or mutual fund statements. From now on, we're only going to talk about real returns and dollar amounts, not nominal returns and dollar amounts; every time you see a dollar figure, you'll have to remember that this is in terms of spending power in the year 2025. One final point: this means that in the above example, planning on saving $625 per month beginning in 2025 means you'll have to increase that savings amount with inflation; this should not be difficult, since you can expect that your salary should increase by at least that rate.

I'll end this section, as I mentioned above, with a reading assignment: Thomas Stanley and William Danko's *The Millionaire Next Door*. This is the most important book you'll ever read, because it emphasizes the point that there's an inverse correlation between spending and saving. (Statisticians and economists like to pooh-pooh this book for its methodological flaws, which admittedly are many. These blemishes, though, in no way detract from the lucid way in which *Millionaire* dissects the corrosive effects of our consumer-oriented society on both personal and societal well-being.)

My father was a modestly successful attorney who, because he began his career a few years before the onset of the Depression, became a compulsive saver. Consequently, our house, vacations, and automobiles were not as fancy as those of our neighbors. When I'd ask him why this was, he'd reply that our neighbors *owned* a lot, but didn't *have* a lot. In fact, he'd slyly add, he knew for a fact that more than a few *owed* a lot. (When I was younger, I'd ask him if we were rich: "Your mother and I are comfortably well to do. You don't have a dime.")

Stanley and Danko systematically studied the characteristics of millionaires. Some not-so-surprising facts: the most common millionaire car was an F-150 truck, which offered the most pounds of vehicle per dollar. A plumber making $100,000 per year was far more likely to be a millionaire than an attorney with the same income, because the latter's peer group was far harder to keep up with. And so forth. If this book doesn't scare your spending habits straight, nothing will.

Hurdle Number Two: Finance Isn't Rocket Science, But You'd Better Understand it Clearly

Do you know the difference between a stock and a bond? Maybe you do, and maybe you don't, but a little review never hurts.

Say you're starting a business. It'll be a bit before it starts making money, but from day one it'll have expenses, and you'll need money for that up front.

You can get that money in one of two ways: you can borrow it from relatives, friends, or from a bank, or you can sell an ownership interest to a friend or family member. For example, if your brother is half owner, he's entitled to half of all of your business's future earnings.

Nothing prevents you from doing both, and in fact that is what most large corporations do. If you do both borrow money *and* sell shares, then both legally and morally, you have to pay the lenders' interest and principal first. Only after they have been paid, and only after your other ongoing business expenses have been met, can you then pay out the remaining profits to yourself and your brother.

You and your brother are thus the "residual owners" of the business; if, and only if, you can pay off your lenders and your expenses do you make any money. *From the investors' perspective, an ownership stake (a stock) is much riskier than a loan to your business (a bond), and so the stock deserves a higher expected return than a bond.*

The term "expected return" causes a lot of grief among neophyte investors. It's only what's *expected*, i.e., the average result; the *risk* is the chance that it will fall short. A coin toss that offers a dollar for heads and nothing for tails, for example, has an expected return of fifty cents, but there's also the 50/50 *risk* you'll get nothing.

Here's a good way to think about the relationship between expected return and risk. You'd probably prefer a certain fifty cents for each and every coin flip rather than a 50/50 chance of a dollar or nothing. In fact, most people would prefer even a certain forty cents; only at twenty or thirty cents of certain payoff would the average person prefer the coin flip; this is the point where the higher expected return of the coin flip adequately compensates for the 50% chance of getting nothing. (Economists use examples like this to gauge "risk aversion." The person who will not take a penny less than a certain fifty cents to avoid the coin toss has zero risk aversion; the person who will take a certain ten cents to avoid the coin toss is highly risk averse. This paradigm is a good way to think about your own risk aversion—that is, how much risk you can tolerate.)

Put another way, bond ownership has no other upside beyond the full repayment of interest and principal, so it needs to be safe; stocks, on the other hand, need to have their potentially unlimited upside to entice investors who must endure their high risk. Put yet another way, if stocks and bonds were equally risky, no one would own the bond, with its limited upside; conversely, if stocks and bonds had the same return, no one would want to own the stocks, with their higher risk.

This raises a more subtle point, and one that is often not well understood by even sophisticated investors, which is that the interests of the owners of stocks, who are willing to take considerable risks to get higher returns, and the owners of bonds (or, in the case of a small business, the folks loaning it money), who care only about safety, are very different, and it's a company's stock owners who get to vote, not the bond owners. For this reason, loans to businesses—corporate bonds—are in general a bad deal, and it is a good idea to confine your bond holdings to government offerings.

How risky are stocks? You've *no* idea. During the Great Depression, stocks lost, on average, around 90% of their value; during the recent financial crisis, they lost almost 60%. Although you might think that you can tolerate this kind of loss, guess again. It's one thing to think about temporarily losing 60% or even 90% of your savings, but the actual experience, in the moment, is unimaginably upsetting. In the words of Fred Schwed, one of the most astute observers of the investment scene (and certainly the funniest):

> *There are certain things that cannot be adequately explained to a virgin either by words or pictures. Nor can any description I might offer here even approximate what it feels like to lose a real chunk of money that you used to own.*

Is it possible to predict when such declines might occur, and so avoid them? Don't even think about it: in the past 80 years, no one, and I mean no one, has ever done so reliably. Like a broken clock that is right twice a day, many have predicted a single bear market fall, but their future forecasting ability always evaporates, exactly what you'd expect from a lucky guess, and not from skill.

Is it possible to find a mutual fund manager or advisor who can beat the market? Again, no: several decades of careful research have shown that managers with superb prior performance usually fall flat on their faces going forward. (Over the past decade, even Warren Buffett has failed to beat the market by any significant margin.)

The simplest way to think about investing "skill" is to imagine a stadium containing 10,000 people. Everyone stands up and flips a coin: heads you stay up, tails you sit down. The laws of probability tell us that after 10 coin flips, on average about 10 flippers will still be standing. Were they skillful? Of course not. The poster child for this phenomenon is a money manager named William Miller, whose Legg Mason Value Trust mutual fund beat the S&P 500 index of stocks for 15 straight years before giving back nearly all of his cumulative advantage over that index in just three short years.

Think about it another way. Say you could time the market or successfully pick stocks. Would you be publishing a newsletter, telling people about your predictions on TV, running a mutual fund, or, ha ha, working as a stock broker? Of course not. You'd borrow as much money as you could, bet on your predictions with that borrowed money, and go to the beach. (You might also run a hedge fund, and so direct much of the upside to yourself and all of the downside to your clients.) When all is said and done, there are only two kinds of investors:

those who don't know where the market is headed, and those who don't know that they don't know. Then again, there is a third kind: those who know they don't know, but whose livelihoods depend on *appearing* to know.

If you don't find that convincing, think about investing in yet another way: When you buy and sell stocks, the person on the other side of the trade—the person or organization you're buying from or selling to—almost certainly has a name like Goldman Sachs or Fidelity. And that's the *best* case scenario. What's the worst case? Trading with a company insider who knows more about his or her employer than 99.9999% of the people on the planet. Trading stocks and bonds is like volleying with an invisible tennis opponent. More often than not, that person turns out to be one of the Williams sisters.

If I had to summarize finance in one sentence, it would go something like this: if you want high returns, you're going to occasionally have to endure ferocious losses with equanimity, and if you want safety, you're going to have to endure low returns. At the end of the investing day, only two kinds of assets exist: risky ones (high returns and high risks, namely stocks), and what are known in finance as "riskless" ones (low risks and low returns, like T-bills, CDs, and money market funds). Job one for the investor is to figure out the appropriate mix of the two. For example, the three-fund portfolio presented at the beginning of this book consists of two-thirds risky assets and one-third riskless assets.

While it's impossible to estimate the returns of the stock or bond markets tomorrow, or even next year, it's actually not too difficult to estimate them in the very long term. First, government bonds. The 30-year U.S. Treasury bond, as of this writing, yields around 3.6%. This is a pretty good estimate of its return over the next 30 years. But this is a nominal return, and recall I just told you that you want to think in real, inflation-adjusted terms. Well, the Treasury also offers a 30-year inflation-protected security (TIPS), that currently has a real 1.4% yield and return of real principal, both of which rise over time with inflation. So the expected real return of the 30-year bond is . . . 1.4%.

Stocks are only slightly more complicated. Domestic stocks currently yield a dividend of around 2%, foreign stocks around 3%. This is a *real* yield, since historically the *real* dividend payout increases at around 1.5% per year. Since the stock price should increase roughly in line with this growth in dividends, the real return of stocks should be the sum of the current yield and the growth rate—that is, for domestic stocks, the 2% yield plus the 1.5% growth rate, or 3.5%, and for foreign stocks, about 4.5% (their current 3% dividend plus the 1.5% dividend growth).

Thus, a portfolio that is two-thirds stocks and one-third bonds *should* have a long-term expected real return of around 3%, and this is also where the suggested 15% savings rate for someone who starts saving at age *25* comes from. Most young people are familiar with Microsoft Excel, so I've uploaded a spreadsheet that shows the effects of varying returns rates and saving rates in terms of real, accumulated assets after 20, 30, and 40 years to www.efficientfrontier.com/files/savings-path.xls. The name of the game is to accumulate around 12 years of living expenses (cells H12–H16), which, combined with Social Security, should provide for a reasonable retirement. How did I arrive at 12 years of living expenses? The average person needs to accumulate about 25 years of living expenses, and I'm assuming you'll be getting about half of that from Social Security.

So much for an introduction to basic finance. Your next reading assignment is Jack Bogle's *Common Sense on Mutual Funds*, perhaps the best introduction to basic finance that's ever been written.

I'll end this section with one more bit of full disclosure. I was proud to call Jack Bogle an acquaintance, but he also the founder of the Vanguard Group, which is now the world's largest mutual fund company. Four decades ago, he made a fateful decision, which was to give ownership in the company to the *shareholders of the mutual funds*. That is to say, when you own a Vanguard mutual fund, *you* are the owner of the company that offers it. Because Vanguard's shareholders own it, the company has no incentive to gouge them with excessive fees and hidden expenses.

This is the only mutual fund company for which this is true; when you own the shares of any other fund company, you are *not* the owner, and it is in the interest of the company's real owners—the stock shareholders or private owners of the fund company—to keep fees high.

Consequently, Vanguard's fund expenses are generally the lowest in the industry, and the company is my go-to for most investors, whether they have a few thousand dollars or hundreds of millions. I have occasionally been accused of being a "shill" for Vanguard; if wanting to be the owner of my fund company and so pay rock-bottom fees makes me a shill, then I plead guilty.

Jack Bogle, while not a poor man, would almost certainly have been a billionaire many times over had he retained ownership in the company, instead of giving it away to the fund shareholders. He is the only person in the history of the financial services industry to have done so and, as you might expect, he remained to the end a strong and clear voice for the rights of small investors everywhere.

Hurdle Number Three (With Apologies to George Santayana): Those Who Ignore Financial History Are Condemned to Repeat It

There is no greater cause of mischief to the small investor than the confusion between the health of the economy and stock returns. It's natural for people to assume that when the economy is in good shape, future stock returns will be high, and vice versa.

The exact opposite is in fact true: market history shows that when there's economic blue sky, future returns are low, and when the economy is on the skids, future returns are high; it is a truism in the market that the best fishing is done in the most stormy waters. In the late 1990s, for example, people thought that the Internet would change everything. It did, but it didn't help the economy that much, and over the next decade stocks suffered not one, but two bone-crushing bear markets that resulted in more than a decade of negative real returns. By contrast, investors who bought stocks in the depths of the Great Depression (and in the depths of the more recent financial crisis) made out like bandits.

By now you know enough investment theory to understand this paradox: since risk and return are inextricably intertwined, high risk and high returns go hand in hand, and so do low risk and low returns. When the economy looks awful, risks seem high, and so stocks must offer high returns to entice people to buy them; contrariwise, when the economy looks great and stocks seem safe, they become more attractive to people, and this yields low future returns. Another way to put it is that the biggest profits are made by buying at the lowest prices, and stocks only get cheap when bad economic news abounds; therefore, the highest returns are earned by buying when the economy is in the toilet, and vice versa.

Learning market history isn't just about knowing the past pattern of returns (though that's helpful). In addition, it's about learning to recognize the market's emotional environment, which also correlates with future returns.

The 1929 market peak offered a classic example of the value of being attuned to sentiment; when asked how he knew to sell stocks the year before, Joseph Kennedy Sr. was said to have answered that when the shoeshine boys started offering him stock tips, he knew it was time to get out. In the 1990s, I had two "shoeshine boy moments." The first came when I saw a TV advertisement for an online brokerage featuring a day trader who had just acquired his own island; the second came when a relative who did not know the first thing about investing joined her first stock club. (One version of the island commercial is available here: http://www.youtube.com/watch?v=1lnwkXb3B-k.)

Similarly, you may have observed how during the early 2000s it seemed as though half your friends were flipping houses and brokering real estate and mortgages.

Why the correlation between popular interest and subsequent low returns? Simple: Driving the price of any asset higher requires the entry of new buyers, and when *everyone* is invested in stocks, real estate, or gold, there's no one left to join the party; the entry of naïve, inexperienced investors usually signals the end.

Market bottoms behave the same way; when everyone is afraid of stocks, then there's no one left to sell, so prices are much more likely to move up than down.

Put another way, we often depend on the recommendations of others for, say, restaurants, movies, doctors, or accountants; when all your friends report favorably on one, there's a pretty good chance that the recommendation is valid. Finance, though, for the reasons explained above, is the exact opposite; when all your friends are enthusiastic about stocks (or real estate, or any other investment), perhaps you shouldn't be, and when they respond negatively to your investment strategy, that's likely a good sign.

A working knowledge of market history reinforces this sort of profitable but highly counterintuitive behavior— i.e., to have seen the movie before.

Does the ability to recognize excessive market optimism or pessimism mean that you can "time" the market?

No, it does not. Rather, you should use your knowledge of financial history simply as an emotional stabilizer that will keep your portfolio on an even keel and prevent you from going all-in to the market when everyone is euphoric and selling your shares when the world seems to be going to hell in a handbasket.

Then again, the discipline of maintaining a fixed allocation, such as the 33/33/33 portfolio mentioned at the beginning of the book, is an easy and effective form of market timing, since it of necessity means that you will be buying more stocks after significant market falls, when pessimism reigns, and selling some stocks after prolonged and dramatic price rises, when the market seems to be making everyone rich. The real purpose of learning financial history is to give you the courage to do the selling at high prices and the buying at low ones mandated by the discipline of sticking to a fixed stock/bond allocation.

Section Three's homework is a pair of treats, *Devil Take the Hindmost* by Edward Chancellor, a compendium of stock market manias; and its bookend, *The Great Depression: A Diary*, by Benjamin Roth, a portrait of how things look at the bottom. The lives of most investors encompass the two different kinds of markets described in these books, and they will provide a beacon that will guide you through both the best of times and the worst of times.

Hurdle Number Four (With Apologies to Walt Kelly, Creator of the *Pogo* Cartoon): We Have Met the Enemy and He Is Us

As you may already have guessed, the person most liable to screw up your retirement portfolio is you. A superb example of just how this happens is found in the March 29, 2013, edition of *The Wall Street Journal*, in which reporter Jonathan Cheng described an agreeable, attractive married physician couple, Lucie White and Mark Villa. Wrote Mr. Cheng,

> Feeling "sucker punched," [by the global financial crisis] they swore off stocks and put their remaining money in a bank. This week, as the Dow Jones Industrial Average and Standard & Poor's 500-stock index pushed to record highs, Ms. White and her husband hired a financial adviser and took the plunge back into the market. "What really tipped our hand was to see our cash not doing anything while the S&P was going up," says Ms. White, a 39-year-old dermatologist in Houston. "We just didn't want to be left on the sidelines."

This story speaks volumes about just how human nature can derail even the best designed portfolio.

In order to understand just how this happens, we need to consider the basics of human evolution. In a state of nature, the biggest risks to human existence tend to be attacks by predators and by other humans, and an ability to react instinctively and quickly carries real survival value. As human beings advanced from agricultural to industrial to postindustrial societies and as health and longevity improved, survival and the quality of life began to depend on a shift to long-run decision making—up to a time horizon of several decades.

Long-term planning, of course, is what investing is all about, and it's a predisposition that our maker most definitely did *not* endow us with. The nearly instantaneous emotional responses that served us so well on the prehistoric African plains turn out to be fatal in finance, as manifested in the buy-high sell-low behavior epitomized by the Villa-Whites.

And that's just for starters. Human nature turns out to be a virtual Petrie dish of financially pathologic behavior. People tend to be comically overconfident: for example, about 80% of us believe that we are above average drivers, a logical impossibility. (Men tend to be much worse on this count, and thus worse investors than women.) We tend to extrapolate the recent past indefinitely into the future; in the 1970s, investors thought that inflation would never end, and by 2021, most people thought it would never occur again. Surprise! The first viewpoint was proven wrong within a few years, and the latter viewpoint was rudely disconfirmed in 2022. In the same way, both long bear and bull markets seem to take on a life of their own.

Most importantly of all, humans are "pattern-seeking primates" who perceive relationships where in fact none exist. Ninety-five percent of what happens in finance is random noise, yet investors constantly convince themselves that they see patterns in market activity.

Statistics professors use this classic demonstration in introductory courses: the instructor leaves the room and asks all but one of the students to record the results of 30 coin tosses. The one remaining student, chosen by the class without the knowledge of the professor, is asked to *simulate* the tosses with pen and paper.

The professor returns and is able to quickly identify the single student who simulated the coin tosses. How? His or her simulations almost never contain 4 or more straight heads or tails, which almost always occur within 30 *random* coin tosses. The point here is that runs of 4 or more heads or tails are *perceived* as a nonrandom pattern, when in fact they are the rule in random sequences, not the exception. Stock market participants frequently make this mistake, and an entirely bogus field of finance known as "technical analysis" is devoted to finding patterns in random financial data.

Once again, your homework in this section is a real piece of chocolate cake, *Your Money and Your Brain*, by *The Wall Street Journal*'s Jason Zweig; I can guarantee you that you'll enjoy it immensely, and if Jason can't save you from yourself, then no one can.

Hurdle Number Five: The Financial Services Industry Wants to Make You Poor and Stupid

It's sad but true: by the time you've completed the reading for the previous four hurdles, you'll know more about finance than the average stock broker or financial advisor.

You should avoid them, since their main goal is to transfer your wealth to them. This advice also applies to most mutual fund companies, for the reason mentioned previously: they exist to make profits for their owners, not you.

In fact, the prudent investor treats almost the entirety of the financial industry landscape as an urban-combat zone. To be avoided at all costs are: *any* stock broker or "full-service" brokerage firm; *any* newsletter; *any* advisor who purchases individual securities; *any* hedge fund. *Most* mutual fund companies spew more toxic waste into the investment environment than a third-world refinery. *Most* financial advisors can't invest their way out of a paper bag.

Brokers and advisors may appear to be skilled professionals, but don't be fooled. Doctors, lawyers, and accountants all have the equivalent of post-graduate degrees and had to study for years to pass grueling exams, yet your broker was not required to graduate high school. Further, people do not go into the financial services industry for the same reasons that attract individuals to social work, government service, or elementary education.

Why isn't the public as well protected from malfeasance in the brokerage industry as it is in medicine, dentistry, accounting, and the law? The reason is that all four of these professions are highly regulated, and their practitioners deviate from standard procedure only at great peril to their livelihood. If a physician fails to recognize and treat with powerful antibiotics more than one or two cases of obvious bacterial pneumonia, his license will get yanked with gusto. Ditto for the accountant or attorney who regularly falls below the standard of practice.

The message of the preceding pages couldn't be clearer; don't come anywhere near a stock broker or a brokerage firm; sooner rather than later you will get fleeced. It's a little known fact that stock brokers do not owe their clients what is known as "fiduciary duty"—the obligation that most other professionals have to put their clients' interests above their own. Without this, you'll have little legal protection from a broker's incompetence and mendacity absent outright fraud or the sale of an outrageously unsuitable investment. (Technically, investment advisors are required to meet a fiduciary standard, but many stock brokers now call themselves "advisors" and are not required to act as fiduciaries.)

Avoiding brokers and advisors is harder than it seems, since they're liable to be your old college roommate, brother-in-law, or church or service organization member. The best way of solving this problem is to deftly change the subject when these folks bring the conversation around to finance or, if you don't mind a little fibbing, to tell them that you have no interest in money management. However you choose to handle this, a ready routine for deflecting approaches from friends and relations in the finance industry is an essential survival skill.

The terrain presented by the mutual fund industry is only slightly less hostile, but because it features greater transparency and the legal protections offered by the 1940 Investment Company Act, it offers you at least a fighting chance of emerging with your wealth intact.

Still, all is not well in the mutual fund world; since fund company revenues flow proportionately from assets under management (AUM), mutual fund companies focus primarily on growing the size of their funds, not on your returns. The good news is that the linkage between these two is far tighter than it is with a brokerage account.

Since funds regularly report performance and fees, and since you can so easily move your assets from a fund family's stock fund to your money market fund, from which a check can be written, there is less opportunity for monkey business.

Still, you'll need to exert extreme care with mutual funds. Except for the Vanguard Group, a mutual fund or brokerage company has two sets of masters: the clients who purchase the mutual funds or stocks and bonds in the funds and brokerage accounts, and the shareholders who own the stock of the brokerage or fund company itself. Every company's goal is to maximize the bottom line of the latter—its real owners—and mutual fund and brokerage firms can only do this at the expense of their clients—that is, you. And if you think that your interests are the same as the fund company's—high investment returns—then guess again. By the time you figure out how it's fleecing you, it will have made far more in excessive management fees than it might have made with the higher returns that come from lower expenses. (In other words, if a fund company raises its fund fees from 1.0% to 1.5%, it has just raised its revenues by 50%, but you are unlikely to notice its effect on your performance for many years, if ever.) This same logic applies in spades to brokers, as well, who are very highly trained—in selling, not in finance.

To summarize, you are engaged in a life-and-death struggle with the financial services industry. Every dollar in fees and expenses you pay them comes directly out of your pocket. (Be aware that you're often getting charged far more in mutual fund fees than that "expense ratio" listed on the prospectus or annual report, which is often exceeded by the "transactional costs," that is, adverse price changes that result from moving around millions of shares, much of which accrues indirectly to the fund company.) Act as if every broker, insurance salesman, mutual fund salesperson, and financial advisor you encounter is a hardened criminal, and stick to low-cost index funds, and you'll do just fine.

Now for the good news: you've already done the homework for this section, which is the same as for Section Two, *Common Sense on Mutual Funds*. So you've almost finished the reading list.

What About the Nuts and Bolts?

So, how do you actually implement the investment plan outlined above? As mentioned in the first section, your biggest priority is to get yourself out of debt; until that point, the only investing you should be doing is with the minimum 401(k) or other defined contribution savings required to "max out" your employer match; beyond that, you should earmark every spare penny to eliminating your student and consumer debt.

Next, you'll need an emergency fund placed in T-bills, CDs, or money market accounts; this should be enough for six months of living expenses, and should be in a taxable account. (Putting your emergency money in a 401(k) or IRA is a terrible idea, since if you need it, you'll almost certainly have to pay a substantial tax penalty to get it out.)

Then, and only then, can you start to save seriously for retirement. For most young people, this will mean some mix of an employer-based plan, such as a 401(k), individual IRA accounts, and taxable accounts.

There are two kinds of IRA accounts: traditional and Roth. The main difference between the two comes when you pay taxes on them; with a traditional account, you get a tax deduction on the contributions, and pay taxes when the money is withdrawn, generally after age 59½. (You can withdraw money before 59½, but, with a few important exceptions, you'll pay a substantial tax penalty for doing so.) With a Roth, it's the opposite: you contribute with money you've already paid taxes on, but pay no taxes on withdrawals in retirement.

There's thus not a lot of difference between a 401(k) and a traditional IRA; in fact, you can seamlessly roll the former into the latter after you leave your employer. In general, the Roth is a better deal than a traditional IRA, since not only can you contribute "more" to the Roth (since $7,000—the current annual contribution limit — of after-tax dollars is worth a lot more than $7,000 in pre-tax dollars), but also you're hopefully in a higher tax bracket when you retire.

Your goal, as mentioned, is to save at least 15% of your salary in some combination of 401(k)/IRA/taxable savings. But in reality, the best strategy is to save as much as you can, and don't stop doing so until the day you die.

The optimal strategy for most young people is thus to first max out their 401(k) match, then contribute the maximum to a Roth IRA (assuming they're not making too much money to qualify for the Roth, approximately $200,000 for a married couple and $120,000 for a single person), then save in a taxable account on top of that.

A frequent problem with 401(k) plans is the quality of the fund offerings. You should look carefully at the fund expenses offered in your employer's plan. If its expense ratios are in general more than 1.0%, then you have a lousy one, and you should contribute only up to the match. If its expenses are in general lower than 0.5%, and particularly if it includes Vanguard's index funds or Fidelity's Spartan-class funds (which have fees as low as Vanguard's), then you might consider making significant voluntary contributions in excess of the match limits. For most young savers, fully maxing out voluntary 401(k) contributions (assuming you have a "good" 401(k) with low expenses) and the annual Roth limit will get them well over the 15% savings target.

Your contributions to your 401(k), IRA, and taxable accounts should be made equally to the indexed U.S. stock, foreign stock, and bond funds available to you. Once per year, you should "rebalance" them back to equal status. In the good years, this will mean selling some stocks, which you should avoid doing in a taxable account, since this will incur capital gains taxes. In practice, this means keeping a fair amount of your stock holdings in a tax sheltered 401(k) or IRA. This will not be a problem for the typical young investor, since he or she will have a relatively small amount of his or her assets in a taxable account.

The following are some examples of the kinds of index funds you'll want to use. If your 401(k) is lucky enough to have Vanguard funds, look for, respectively, the (U.S.) Total Stock Market Index Fund, Total International Stock Index Fund, and either the Short-Term Bond Index or Total Bond Market Index Fund. As already mentioned, the Fidelity Spartan series is also excellent: the Total Market Index, International Index, and U.S. Bond Index (or Short-Term Treasury Bond Index) funds.

Increasingly, 401(k) plans are making "target funds" the default contribution choice. For example, Vanguard offers Target Retirement funds, which carry fees of 0.16–0.18%, aimed at those retiring between 2010 (geezers) and 2060 (20-year olds) in 5-year increments (2060, 2055, 2050, and so forth, down to 2010). The 2060 fund, for example, has a 90% allocation to stocks, which will then fall by a percent or so each year as the saver gets older.

This is about as far as I can take you in this book with the nuts and bolts. There's nothing magic about a portfolio consisting of equal parts U.S. stocks, foreign stocks, and bonds; you might want a higher or lower allocation to each of these, and you might even want to "slice and dice" the U.S. and foreign stock components into smaller component pieces such as real estate investment trusts (REITs), emerging and developed markets for foreign stocks, and so forth. And, as I've said, there's nothing wrong with an all-in-one target retirement fund, as long as it has low expenses.

Since Section Five had no homework assignment, I'm going to double up the reading assignment with two books: Allan Roth's *How a Second Grader Beats Wall Street* and Rick Ferri's *All About Asset Allocation*.

That's it. As I told you in the beginning, if you've completed your first pass through the guide, take a deep breath and start with the Section One reading assignment, *The Millionaire Next Door*, then continue with the rest.

There are a number of things I haven't told you, the most important of which is how to spend down your money in retirement. At present, the best way of doing this is the purchase of an inflation-adjusted fixed annuity, which mimics the payout of a traditional pension plan, or a "ladder" of inflation-protected bonds (TIPS) that matures every few years, to provide you with an inflation-adjusted income stream. Estate planning is another issue I haven't discussed, since it's even further out in the future.

The reason I haven't talked about either retirement spending or estate planning is that both will not become important to you for many decades, by which point the relevant investment options and tax law will almost certainly be very different from today's. So it's just not worth thinking about these two issues now. In other words, you're way too young for these things to matter, for the simple reason that they'll be very different by the time they do.

Back to the present; if this is the end of your second pass through the guide, and you have thus completed all of the sectional reading lists, then you're ready to start on your journey to a reasonably well-to-do retirement.

Good fortune!

William J. Bernstein
Portland, OR
March 2025

Bonus Content from
Stay the Course

What Really Matters

A Memoir (Written at Dusk)

Advice. This ancient Persian proverb offers the best advice that I know for dealing with the inevitable ups and downs of life, the best times and the worse times alike: *This too shall pass away*.

American Indian College Fund. The more that I've studied our nation's history, the more that I've come to recognize that America's early Anglo-European colonists claimed that a land that belonged to others belonged to them. Ever since Columbus, American Indians have been shabbily treated by our invaders, by our own federal government, and by our society. I felt obligated to try to help right this wrong, and have made modest (if large for me) annual contributions to the American Indian College Fund, helping to support, I'm told, some 500 scholarships for young Native American men and women.

I served as a Trustee of the American Indian College Fund from 1996 to 2002, and each year I continue to receive photos of the smiling/serious faces of those young students, doing their best to find their place in our society.

"The Eagle and the Bear"

In 1996, while awaiting my heart transplant, I decided that, "just in case," I'd like to leave a remembrance at our family retreat on Placid Lake in the Adirondacks. Through the Lummi tribe of northwestern Washington State, I ordered a totem pole for my purpose. Carved by Native American artist Dale James, its height came to some 25 feet. For 22 years it has rested on a knoll overlooking the lake.

The totem pole, carved from a great cedar tree, came with its own legend, "The Eagle and the Bear."

Eagle called to the carvers of the people and said, "My time could be short. I am feeling the pull of two worlds, and when I see my wife and children I feel

*a great love and tenderness. I would have you carve
me a great pole of remembering for them. A pole that
tells of the family. A pole which speaks of the love of
a man with the spirit of Eagle and a woman with the
spirit of Bear, and their six children who will tell his
story to their children's children."*

Blair Academy.   This fine New Jersey boarding school
was – and remains – among the principal cornerstones of
my long life. Twin brother David and I began our studies
at Blair in September 1945, and graduated in June 1947.
(Brother William graduated in June 1945.)

Being away from our stressed home was the best thing
for us. There was no way we could pay our tuition, but
my beloved mother somehow persuaded Blair to take us
in *gratis.* We held scholarships and worked jobs – waiters in
the dining hall; in my senior year, waiter captain.

My experienced masters at Blair (four of whom had
joined the faculty in 1912) seemed to see something
worthwhile in me. They would not accept flawed work.
Jesse Gage crushed me with a 40 on my first exposure
to algebra, but I ended the year earning 100 on my final
exam. Henry Adams and Marvin G. Mason corrected
my English papers with a fury, and with red pens. The
markups of my papers were not pretty sights, but my
ability to write began under their tutelage.

Determined to overcome that slow start, I worked hard, graduated cum laude, and was named "best student." That may have been the first hint that I had the grit to stay the course.

Giving Back

Having been given so much, I wanted to give back. The Bogle Brothers Scholarship Fund has now helped enable more than 160 young men and women to attend Blair, and each year we add a dozen or so more. Bogle Hall (1989) and the Armstrong-Hipkins Center for the Arts (1999) were named to honor my parents, and then my grandparents.

I've also sought to serve my alma mater, mostly as an active member of the board of trustees from 1973 through 2002, and then as chairman emeritus to this day – 45 years of board membership, including 16 years as chairman. Leading a school board has its challenges. But I was lucky. My mentor was my remarkable predecessor, the late J. Brooks Hoffman MD, Blair Class of 1936. Brooks showed me the way.

Blair's Renaissance

The most important task for a chairman is when the time comes to select a new Head of School. For me, that time came in 1989. I sought a personable, energetic, young person who could lead Blair to the realization of its great potential. T. Chandler Hardwick (age 36) accepted our offer. With his wife Monie, Chan led Blair's renaissance, returning the Academy to its rank as one of the nation's top college preparatory schools.

A solid relationship between board chairman and Head of School is the key to good governance. It was essential to Blair's ascendance, and it was strengthened, I trust, by a self-imposed rule that I followed (most of the time!): "The Head of School is the boss. The chairman is there to help him whenever he asks." After giving Blair Academy 24 years of their lives, the Hardwicks moved on in 2013. The close friendship that Eve and I developed with them endures to this day.

What is the mission of Blair Academy? I can do no better than offer these words from a speech I gave to our alumni in 2007:

> *The task before our school is large, . . . to preserve, to protect and to defend this fount of liberal education, this island of opportunity, this community of teaching and learning. At Blair Academy, we give some of the most promising young men and women in our land the opportunity to learn more than they might otherwise have learned, to accomplish more than they*

might otherwise have accomplished, and to develop
their character and their values more than they might
otherwise have developed them. If these seem like
unremarkable goals, I assure you that they are any-
thing but. Such young citizens are the core of our civ-
ilization, our hope for years to come. . . .

Books. I love writing books, and I have a "lover's
quarrel" with the mutual fund industry. That combination has resulted in 12 books, 10 of which have helped
to drive Vanguard's success as an industry rebel creating a
new industry, one among those companies that consider
"themselves insurgents, waging war . . . on behalf of an
underserved customer," as described in Chapter 10.

Why do I write? Because I love to do it. Because
writing takes those inchoate, rambling thoughts we all
have rattling around in our brains and demands that they
be focused and articulate, even impassioned. Because
books outlive one's short existence on this planet.

My first book, *Bogle on Mutual Funds* (1993), and
my sixth book, *The Little Book of Common Sense Investing*
(2007), have been particularly popular with readers, and
the nine others have also done well.[1] Sales of my books

---

[1]You're reading my 12th and last (yes!) book, *Stay the Course: The Story of Vanguard and the Index Revolution* (Hoboken, NJ: Wiley, 2019).

– so far! – total about 941,000 through mid-2018. Almost 1,000 readers have offered comments on Amazon, overwhelmingly positive (74% 5-star, 16% 4-star). I remember the pans better than I do the pats, but I won't soon forget two particular accolades for my *Little Book of Common Sense Investing* (Tenth Anniversary Edition, 2018). How could an author fail to revel in the headline and the review that follow:

> 1. *The oasis where every successful investor must eventually drink.*

> 2. *Wow, I just finished the book and never expected to be so entertained, I'm almost sad it's not longer just because I loved reading it so much. . . . Great advice for investing and written in a very easy to read style (it was like a close friend was giving me their honest advice). I also love that the book has been recently updated. But even if it's 10 years in the future and you're reading this review I think the book will still be very accurate and topical. John has done the investing world another great service with this book and I highly suggest everyone read it (I already bought a second copy to give to a family member).*

Buffett, Warren. The oracle of Omaha has been described as a better salesman than I am for the Vanguard

500 Index Fund. He's boosted it in seven Berkshire Hathaway Annual Reports. He's also put his money where his mouth is, including a winning bet that the S&P 500 would outpace a select group of hedge funds, and directing the trustee of his wife's estate to invest 90% of its assets in the Vanguard 500 Index Fund. Warren, that down-to-earth gentleman whom I first met 25 years ago, has also endorsed many of my books.

My personal highlight: at the Berkshire Hathaway 2017 annual meeting, held in a giant arena in Omaha before some 40,000 investors, Mr. Buffett gave me a generous "shout out."

> Jack Bogle has probably done more for the American investor than any man in the country. . . . Jack could you stand up?

The applause was thunderous. I was embarrassed, overwhelmed, and delighted.

Communication. I've always recognized the need for us human beings to communicate with one another, directly, empathetically, honestly, personally, and, at best, elegantly. For an appraisal of my approach to communications, I rely here on my long-time aide and friend Jeremy Duffield. He is surely among the finest, best-schooled, and most integrity-laden individuals who have ever crossed my path.

Jeremy, an Australian who came to the United States in 1969, joined Vanguard in 1979, founded our Australian subsidiary in 1996, and ran it with entrepreneurial excellence until he left the firm in 2010. Here's how he described my communications style:

> *It helps to be compulsive about it – to be absolutely maniacal and disciplined about being a great communicator. . . . So the first lesson is you've got to work very, very hard at it . . . his books . . . his 575 speeches, [now 29] papers published in the* Journal of Portfolio Management *and the* Financial Analysts Journal*, 100 television appearances, 250 annual reports that he wrote to shareholders. . . . Perhaps the secret to Jack's impact is his ability to bring drama into the equation. A lot of that derives from his state of constant agitated moral indignation about the plight of the investor. There's no gray in Jack's thinking. It's moral absolutism.*

"On Vanguard's Seas"

On a sobering note, Jeremy also wrote a poem to be read when I leave this mortal coil – a fine example of his own communications ability. I was deeply touched when I read, "On Vanguard's Seas":

> *On Vanguard's seas, the waves still flow*
> *With foaming crests, row by row*
> *That cover his resting place; and in the sky*
> *The gulls, still bravely singing, fly*
> *Scarce heard amid the guns below. . . .*
> *Take up my quarrel with our foe*
> *To you from failing hands I throw*
> *The torch; be yours to hold it high*
> *If ye break faith with those who die*
> *I shall not sleep, though winds still blow*
> *O'er Vanguard's seas.*

Determination. Years ago I asked some friends and most members of my family what they thought was my single most important trait. Each came up with the same word: *determination*. I think they are likely on the right track, even as I recognize that while determination is necessary to achieve one's goals, it can sometimes result in a single-mindedness that is not particularly attractive. I'm also known for my contrarianism. ("There must be a better way.") I've also been cited for decisiveness, resilience, grit, and self-confidence (which, I pray, does not cross the line and become arrogance).

Dylan Thomas.   *Do not go gentle into that good night. Rage, rage against the dying of the light.*

Engine.   *The Little Engine That Could* offers the best brief advice for a successful career that I can imagine:

> *I think I can. I think I can. I think I can. . . . I knew I could. I knew I could. I knew I could.*

Family.   My family has been an utter blessing, giving me a life that is as complete as it could possibly be. The center of ours is Eve, my wife of 62 years. She is loving, kind, strong, smart, and resilient. A few years back, I was introduced to an audience that had been told that we were then celebrating our 50th wedding anniversary. In the Q&A period, the fifth question was "What's the secret?" Without a moment's hesitation, I gave an answer that I could hardly improve on, even a dozen years later, "Two secrets," I said. "First, marry a saint. Second, never forget the two most important words in the English language: 'Yes, dear.'"

We've been infinitely blessed. Six children, 12 grandchildren, good citizens all, healthy, happy, and dealing well with the challenges that are part of the lives of every human being on our planet. And now six great-grandchildren, all boys, two born in 2018.

Today, we see a lot written about the "work/life balance." As if work were not part of life! But if the test is "the work/family balance," I have little doubt that I have been overbalanced on the work side of the scale. Nonetheless, I did my best with family, and I believed that they would all agree that I've earned more than a passing grade.

Forgiveness. I confess that I always kind of liked the simple message "an eye for an eye and a tooth for a tooth." But I soon retreated to the less severe "there can be no forgiveness without repentance." In 1974, my former Boston partners abruptly cut short my career at Wellington Management Company. It was hardball politics, for it was their investment failures that almost sank the company. So I returned to my earlier philosophy: "The heck with asking for repentance, get revenge!" I soon realized that heeding this maxim was eating away at me.

Then I learned of the mutual enmity between former U.S. presidents John Adams and Thomas Jefferson. They were political enemies until 1801, when Jefferson's presidency ended. Then their rift healed. They became friends. Their long years of correspondence ended only when both died on the same day, July 4, 1826, exactly 50 years after the signing of the Declaration of Independence.

I was inspired by that story. So in 1991, 25 years after our merger agreement was signed on June 6, 1966, I decided to take the initiative to mend the rift and forgive my successors, even without their repentance. I met with Bob Doran and Nick Thorndike, leaders of the (dare I say) cabal that had axed me. My words were simple: "Twenty-five years is enough. Let's be friends." And so it would be. Indeed, when I spoke to a large audience at The Country Club (near Boston, for those not in the know), my forgiveness must have played a role in their graciously hosting a lovely small dinner there in Eve's and my honor. (I'm no hero. I confess that I can't quite get "an eye for an eye" out of my mind.)

God.   Is there a God? Yes.

Guardian angels.   As you read at the conclusion of Chapter 10, *No man is an island, entire of itself.* All my life I've depended on the support of others, never more than in my long struggle with heart disease. My first heart attack came on the tennis court in 1961, when I was but 32 years of age. The genetic disease, undiscovered for another decade, was arrhythmogenic right ventricular dysplasia (ARVD). Potentially fatal if not treated promptly, the heart fibrillations struck out of nowhere. Eve had to rush me to the hospital maybe 10 times (not easy for a mother of three, and later six, young children), where my heart would be electrically shocked into a normal rhythm.

This routine got rather tiresome. So I sought the top cardiologist in the nation. By consensus, it was Dr. Bernard Lown of Boston's Peter Bent Brigham (now Brigham and Women's) Hospital. Beginning in 1967, I became a patient of this superb physician (and remarkable human being who shared the Nobel Peace Prize – yes! – in 1985). He watched over me with intensity and deep caring, my prototypical guardian angel for two decades until 1987, when he could see that my frequent hospitalizations and visits to his Boston office were taking their toll on me.

Heart Transplant Wanted!

By then, my ARVD attacks, now treated in Philadelphia by experimental medicines, had become less frequent. But by 1996, half of my heart had stopped functioning. (Providentially, it was the right half; the left side does the pumping.) It was time to get a new heart.

At 65, I was but a marginal candidate, but Dr. Susan Brozena accepted me into the transplant program at Philadelphia's Hahnemann Hospital. (One door in the transplant unit said, "NO EXIT." That worried me.)

Potential recipients of new hearts are pretty much date-stamped, when they enter the hospital in a process (as I observed) "as democratic as a traffic jam." With continuous intravenous medicine, my flawed heart kept pumping for

128 days before a new heart (from a 26-year-old male, bless him) arrived on February 21, 1996. Two weeks later, after a bit of a struggle adapting to the transplant, I was home again. I knelt down and kissed the earth.

"Dr. B"

Since then, my cardiologist has been Dr. Susan Brozena ("Dr. B."), another prototypical guardian angel. Smart, experienced, professional, vivacious, charming, and up-to-the-moment with the pharmacology and complexity of transplant treatment (including anti-rejection drugs for the remainder of my life), she is primarily responsible for the extra 22 years of life that I've enjoyed to the fullest – likely a record for a 65-year-old transplant recipient.

Yes, Drs. Brozena and Lown have been incredible guardian angels. In my long life with two hearts, the first one flawed, the second less than perfect, I've also been watched over by a dozen or more other guardian angels. They know who they are, and to all of them I offer bountiful gratitude, from the bottom of my . . . well, heart.

There's apparently a psychological basis for survival over nearly six decades in dealing with heart disease and its aftermath. I'll let Dr. Lown describe it.

> *How were your major achievements possible with a heart struggling for the next uncertain pulse, for the next*

hesitating contraction? I marveled at your iron will and still do. The advances in medical science certainly added years to your life. Yet science alone does not account for the miracle of John Bogle.

You taught me a deeper truth: that surviving against great odds demands intangibles not readily measured by the metrics of science — above all the might of the human spirit that defines our self-awareness. It includes a commitment to serving others, a fearless sense of transience, and a joy in making a difference. Such a self-image enabled you to cultivate a web of devoted family and intimate friends, to bond with the future even when it was merely a shimmer of possibility. Thereby you gained a hold on a meaningful life.

Hedgehog and the fox. The quotation that follows was found, circa 670 BCE, in a fragment of writing of the Greek philosopher Archilochus:

The fox knows many things,
But the hedgehog knows one great thing.

For me, this idea provides an insight into our nation's money managers. We have an army of sly foxes who survive and prosper by knowing many things about complex markets and sophisticated marketing. The hedgehogs in the field know only one great thing: that investment success is based on simplicity — plain service and honest stewardship. (Alas, the hedgehogs in the field are few.) Do I need to tell you in which category I cast Vanguard's lot?

Impartial spectator. The words that follow, written by Adam Smith in *The Theory of Moral Sentiments* (1759), need no embellishment:

> *What is it which prompts the generous to sacrifice their own interests to the greater interests of others? It is the impartial spectator who calls to us, with a voice capable of astonishing the most presumptuous of our passions, that we are but one of the multitude, in no respect better than any other in it; and that when we prefer ourselves so shamefully and so blindly to others, we become the proper objects of resentment, abhorrence, and execration.*

> *It is from him only that we learn the real littleness of ourselves. It is this impartial spectator . . . who shows us the propriety of generosity and the deformity of injustice; the propriety of reining the greatest interests of our own, for the yet greater interests of others . . . in order to obtain the greatest benefit to ourselves.*

> *It is not the love of our neighbor, it is not the love of mankind, which upon many occasions prompts us to the practice of those divine virtues. It is a stronger love, a more powerful affection, the love of what is honourable and noble, the grandeur, and dignity, and superiority of our own characters.*

Now, please read those passages once more. Maybe twice.

Investment Company Institute. From 1969 to 1974, I served on the board of the ICI. That era was a central part of my career. There I found two great mentors, ICI President Robert Augenblick and Chairman D. George Sullivan, then-executive vice president of Fidelity. They were consummate leaders, and they showed me the way.

Today's ICI leadership mystifies me. It is quick to spring to the defense of the investment management companies that control our nation's mutual funds, often at the expense of mutual fund shareholders. Shouldn't its name be changed to the "Investment Managers Institute" (IMI) to reflect its true function?

The fund industry calls out for reform. Are advisory fees too high? Has aggressive marketing gotten out of hand? Are fund directors truly independent? Why do index fund returns outpace the returns of the vast majority of actively managed funds? Are brokerage commissions being used to serve the interests of shareholders or the interests of managers?

This list only begins a long menu of subjects that I believe should have found their way onto the agenda of the ICI's annual General Membership Meeting (GMM). But none did. In the hope of finding at least a hint of introspection on those and other issues, I used to attend those meetings. Alas, each year I'd come back to Vanguard empty-handed.

ICI Chairman, 1969–1970

In the interest of full disclosure, I served for five years on ICI's Executive Committee. As ICI chairman from 1969 to 1970, I worked to develop the compromise passage of the Investment Company Amendments Act of 1970. (Not sure how proud I am of that!) I brought four subsequent ICI chairmen into the fund industry. I created the index mutual fund, which now represents nearly one-half of the equity mutual fund assets of its members. And I founded the ICI's largest member – and largest dues-payer. Even those credentials, however, were insufficient to merit an invitation to speak at the ICI's 2017 GMM, as suggested by a 2017 article about me in *The Times* of London. Go figure!

"Jo." Josephine Hipkins Bogle. My mother, Jo (1896–1952), was a saint. Yes, beautiful, utterly charming, vivacious, a joy to everyone who was lucky enough to know her.

To this day, I don't know how, given an uneasy marriage and constant financial strain, she held herself together. Her firstborns were twin daughters who did not survive their birth. Yet I never saw my mother wince or weep or complain about the challenges that she faced.

She devoted her life to her three boys, doing her best to have us grow up with solid friends (a home run) and to make sure that we got the best education imaginable (a grand slam).

For all three sons, "Hello, Blair Academy!" For her youngest son, "Hello, Princeton University!" Providentially, she lived to see me graduate, and snapped a photo of me (I still have it) on her little Hawkeye camera as I strode across the stage and received my diploma, *Magna Cum Laude in Economia*. Eight months later she was gone. But not gone from my eternal love and memory. Never.

Lake Placid. Ever since 1958, Eve and I have enjoyed our family retreat in New York on Placid Lake, where our children and grandchildren and great-grandchildren now come and go all through the summer. We love our ancient place, its expansive old boathouse, especially our electric boat (*Blue Heaven*), and our lake. I've memorialized the lake with this prayer.

For the beauty of our Earth
For the glory of our skies
For our mountains ever there
For the Placid Lake we prize.

Lord of all, to thee we raise
This our hymn of grateful praise.
Amen.

Life. In his 1938 play, *Our Town*, Thornton Wilder tells us the story of a few ordinary people in Grover's Corners, New Hampshire. The central character is a young woman named Emily Webb. She gets married, but dies after giving birth to her second child. Years later, the spirits of the cemetery allow her to leave her grave for a day to revisit her family in Grover's Corners. She is pained by what she observes—how little the living appreciate the joy of everyday life—and returns early to her grave. To paraphrase the character Emily's dialog:

Goodbye mama. Goodbye papa. Goodbye world. . . .
I didn't realize it goes so fast. All that was going on
in life and we never noticed. Oh earth, you're too
wonderful for anybody to realize you. Do any human
beings ever realize life while they live it . . . every,
every minute? . . . That's all human beings are. Just
blind people.

Mentors, protégés, and friends. This subject could take a whole chapter, but I've condensed it, and mention names only where necessary.

My first great mentor was James P. Harrington, Princeton (BSE Class of 1947; PhD Class of 1950), and manager of the Princeton Athletic Association student ticket office. Jim, who held an engineering degree, set standards that I would do my best to honor for the rest of my life: responsibility, reliability, timeliness, diligence, and punctilious accuracy. We (with his wife Anne) worked together for two years as I served as assistant manager and then manager. We remained close friends until time and distance took their toll.

In 1951, I graduated from Princeton and joined Wellington Management Company. Founder Walter L. Morgan, Princeton Class of 1920, was my mentor. But he was not alone. Executive vice president Joseph E. Welch, sales vice president A.J. Wilkins, and general counsel Andrew B. Young, Esq., all seemed eager to share with me the knowledge that they had accumulated during their long careers. Could they have seen something in me that was worth mentoring? They must have. At his death at age 100, I had known Walter Morgan for 50 years. I later learned that he considered me "the son he never had."

Proteges

During nearly all my career, I've relied on a series of "assistants to the president," usually fairly young men with undergraduate degrees, and often graduate degrees as well. I've worked with a dozen of these protégés over the years, and their career outcomes have been remarkably diverse. Some have earned considerable business success; others less so. Some remain friends today; some, doubtless busy, have made no connections with me for two or more decades. Indeed, I have come to conclude that, as a broad generalization, it is unwise to assume that today's protégés will remain tomorrow's friends. (I'm not suggesting that gratitude for one's mentor, while it might be nice, should necessarily be eternal.) As a group, my assistants have lit up my life.

Other Friends

Today's list of my best friends is quite extensive enough . . . and surely diverse enough: One of the nation's most respected leaders of a giant firm focused on alternative investment strategies. Two distinguished professors of finance. My classmates of Princeton, Class of 1951 (we're vanishing fast!), and another Princetonian, Class of 1949, who served as Chairman of the Federal Reserve Board. The couple that led Blair Academy for 24 years.

Plus a special friend I grew up with whom I've now known for 75 years. A former CEO of a major mutual fund complex. A U.S. senator from the Midwest. A money manager in a family office who was kind enough to charter a Cessna Citation to fly Eve and me and a few of our children to Omaha for the Berkshire Hathaway Annual Meeting in 2017. The managers of two of the nation's largest university endowment funds. Three editors, one directing a major regional newspaper, one a brilliant observer of interest rates, and another the former managing editor of *Time* magazine.

★★★

Finally, two closing, "shout-outs," one for Erica and Loretta, my pals in the Vanguard Galley who serve our crew so ably, day after day, and one for Bob and Billy and their colleagues who drove me on my commutes and trips, arriving timely and safely.

Friendship, it turns out, is where you find it. Paraphrasing a song from the musical *South Pacific,*

Once you have found friends, never let them go.

National Constitution Center.   In 1998, a fine opportunity for me to serve our nation arose. It was then that my tenure as chairman of the National Constitution Center began. When my predecessor, Philadelphia mayor Ed Rendell, was named to lead the Democratic National Committee, he felt he should leave the board. With then-president Joe Torsella, he asked me to serve as the new chairman. I declined: "You have a lot of candidates on the board who would be far more effective than I to lead the board. Anyway, I can't spare the time to do it!"

"A Real Chairman?"

But they pushed, and, with time of the essence, I agreed . . . "but only until you can find a real chairman." Seven years later, in 2005, I stepped down as chairman, succeeded by one former president of the United States (William Jefferson Clinton) and then by another (George H. W. Bush). My seven years flew by like a whirlwind: leading the board, fund raising, planning, testifying before Congress, helping this great undertaking move from idea to reality. Please be clear. Joe did the lion's share of the heavy lifting. (See my comment about a chairman's role in "Blair Academy," earlier in this chapter.)

Our National Constitution Center museum now stands proudly at the north end of Philadelphia's Independence Mall, with Independence Hall anchoring the south end. At our ground-breaking ceremony in 2000, I spoke right before President Clinton's inspired address on "what it means to be a citizen of the United States of America." Our grand opening took place on July 4, 2003.

I was thrilled to contribute to a great American mission: to bring the Constitution into the lives of our citizens. Working with president Torsella, a Rhodes

Scholar, was a delightful experience. In 2016, he was elected Treasurer of the Commonwealth of Pennsylvania. Joe was a wonderful (senior) partner during an era in which I could follow my passion of devotion to our nation, her values, and her institutions.

Presidents. In 1969, at the New York World's Fair, I had just completed my trip on a moving walkway past Michelangelo's *Pieta*. There, I recognized a familiar face, seemingly standing alone and without bodyguards. It was Harry S Truman, and I shook the hand of a U.S. president for the first time.

My second handshake took place in the White House on May 27, 1970. After a sharp drop in the stock market, I was invited to a dinner called by the White House with 35 other CEOs and officers of Wall Street firms. The gathering was designed to calm the nerves of investors. (You can't make this stuff up.)

"Mr. President . . ."

When President Richard M. Nixon called for questions, no one else stood up, so I did. "Mr. President, in view of your campaign pledge to bring us all together, what are you doing about the growing gaps between our generations and our races?" He was clearly thrown off-balance by a question like that from a typically friendly Wall

Street audience, and responded uneasily. As we exited the State Dining Room, we met face-to-face and shook hands. He didn't seem amused.

I later met Lyndon Johnson at a dinner of about 30 people in New York City. He signed a photograph of himself for me and one for my youngest son, Andrew. I framed it and presented it to him.

Two More Presidents

Serving as chairman of the Constitution Center also gave me the opportunity to work with my first two successors: William Jefferson Clinton and George H. W. Bush. I came to know President Clinton fairly well; he wrote a lovely foreword to the second edition of my book *Enough: True Measures of Money, Business, and Life*, published in 2010.

I observed many characteristics that these men seemed to have in common: presence, intelligence, speaking skills. But each had his own idiosyncrasies. President Truman was terse. When we met, President Nixon seemed nervous. (I can't imagine why.) President Johnson, self-confident, almost to the point of arrogance. President Clinton, with an extraordinary charisma that showed through at a one-on-one meeting as clearly as in a State of the Union speech. (He graciously signed copies of

Enough – as the author of the foreword – for each of my 12 grandchildren.) President George H. W. Bush, who seemed more to the manor born in Connecticut than the hard-bitten Texan he sought to become.

Press on, regardless. This biblical motto goes all the way back to St. Paul's admonition, "press on." It was introduced as a family motto by my uncle Clifton Armstrong Hipkins, long-time commodore of the Greenwich (Connecticut) Yacht Club. He named his boat *Press On, Regardless*, an inspiring challenge. But don't forget this: The motto means not only "press on" when times are tough, but also "press on" when times are easy. That's what "regardless" means.

Princeton.   *Stranger, you have reached the noblest home on earth.*

More than two millennia after Sophocles wrote these words (they come from *Oedipus at Colonus*), they were etched on a plaque on Goheen Walk on the Princeton campus. The inscription resonates with me today as the best summary of the role played by Princeton University in my life. As an undergraduate, as I noted earlier, I was awarded generous scholarships, worked diligently on my studies, and, as a freshman, worked as a waiter in the university's magnificent dining halls.

Picked Out of Obscurity

In my sophomore year, I was picked out of obscurity (as I like to say) as a waiter in our dining halls and named by the manager of the Athletic Association student ticket office, Jim Harrington (see "Mentors, protégés, and friends," earlier in this chapter), to serve as his assistant manager; I became his manager a year later. The work involved enormous responsibility and long and hard hours, especially during the Tigers' 1950 football season, when we earned the Ivy League championship. I watched every kickoff, but never saw a game. (There was work to be done.) Basketball season was less demanding; baseball season was, in terms of tickets sold, a laugher.

From D+ to A+

I loved the work and sought for ever more responsibility. But the duties were time-consuming, and during a terrible first semester in 1948, my grades tumbled to the danger point. But they got better. Semester by semester, my 3s (Cs) and a 4+(D+), rose to 2s and finally to 1s (Bs and As), capped by a 1+ on my senior thesis, another example of my early determination to stay the course.

During my college years, it was pretty much "all work and no play." But I made some great friends, and regularly attend our annual class reunions. I proudly march in the colorful P-rade each year, and also still participate in periodic Princeton seminars, often on the subject of "Ethics and Finance."

Scholarships and Fellowships

I've also spent much time with the fine young men and women who have held Bogle Brothers Scholarships, so far 160 students and counting. I also remain involved as a sponsor of the Pace Center for Civic Engagement. In 2016, thanks to a generous gift to Princeton from my son, John C. Bogle Jr., and his wife Lynn, the John C. Bogle Fellowships in Civic Service program was established. In 2017, 28 freshman members of the Class of 2022 were awarded fellowships that funded their summer internships in civic projects. What a joy it is to help these young people along the road of life!

This son of Princeton has been honored beyond measure by his beloved alma mater: the Woodrow Wilson Award for Distinguished Achievement in the Nation's Service (1999), an Honorary Doctor of Laws Degree (2005), and "One of the 25 Most Influential Princetonians of All Time" (2008).

From the university's alma mater, 1951 version.

In praise of old Nassau, my boys,
Hurrah, Hurrah, Hurrah.
Her sons will give, while they shall live
Three cheers for old Nassau!

Quakers. While I was baptized as an Episcopalian and attend a Presbyterian church (a tad irregularly) with my family, I have come to believe that, deep down, I'm truly a Quaker. I do my best to honor those stern Quaker values personally. In retrospect, I see that my life and my design for Vanguard reflect many of the basic Quaker values that William Penn fostered – simplicity, economy, thrift, efficiency, service to others, and the conviction, in the words of Quaker founder George Fox, that "the truth is the way." (I confess that I'm not so strong on some of the other Quaker values; in particular, consensus, patience, silence, and humility.)

Staff. Where would I be without my veteran assistants Emily Snyder (33 years at Vanguard) and Michael Nolan (17), and our associate Kathy Younker (16)? Nowhere! Could this book about Vanguard and the index revolution – written by the founder of both – have been published without their enthusiastic participation and infinite patience? Maybe. But it would have been less of a book – far more arduous – have taken far longer, and been far less fun.

Teaching and learning. When I'm asked what is the secret of a life well-lived, I often answer, "First rule: get out of bed in the morning. If you don't do that, not much will happen. Then, every day, teach something and learn something. Along the way, give an enthusiastic compliment to a deserving soul whom you may have never before met. Then you've earned a great night's sleep. You'll get it. When you awaken the next day, repeat these rules."

Tennyson. The closing words of Alfred Lord Tennyson's poem "Ulysses" (1842) begin as the oarsmen of his launch sweep Ulysses out to his flagship for one last voyage:

... Come, my friends
'Tis not too late to seek a newer world.
Push off, and sitting well in order smite
The sounding furrows; for my purpose holds
To sail beyond the sunset,
until I die. ...
Though much is taken, much abides; and though
We are not now that strength which in old days
Moved earth and heaven, that which we are, we are –
One equal temper of heroic hearts,
Made weak by time and fate, but strong in will
To strive, to seek, to find, and not to yield.

T. Rowe Price. This is a firm that I've always admired – right up there with Dodge and Cox and Dimensional Fund Advisers – for professional conduct, low-key marketing (or none), and good people. When my one-time assistant, then-executive vice president of Vanguard, James S. (Jim) Riepe, left Vanguard for T. Rowe Price in 1980, I was crestfallen at the loss of my heir-apparent. But I was confident he had found the perfect home. (I was right!)

But T. Rowe Price has put me into an awkward position. Back in 1994, in order to collect current information about Vanguard's peers, I made a token investment in the stock of T. Rowe Price, Incorporated, the publicly held investment adviser to the Price mutual funds. I bought 100 shares at $42 per share, a total cost of $4,200.

A Great Investment

I've received the firm's glossy but interesting annual reports ever since, but paid little attention to the stock price. But, my goodness, I made a great investment. Those 100 shares have split five times, and I now hold 3,200 shares. At Price's market price of $121 per share in mid-2018, my casual investment of $4,200 in 1994 is now worth $384,000. My annual dividend of $8,960 is more than double that of my initial investment. Is it really a good idea for me to have so much invested in one of our major competitors? That's the "awkward" part.

As founder of a mutual company in which the lion's share of profits are returned to fund shareholders rather than to management company owners, I marvel at the enormous profitability of T. Rowe Price and our peers in the mutual fund business, generated in part by management and marketing, but largely by the soaring prices of stocks in the great bull market and the staggering economies of scale available in managing mutual funds. But the lion's share of those economies of scale have been arrogated by the managers to themselves, and barely shared with the mutual fund clients whom the officers and directors of mutual funds are duty-bound to serve.

Work. I've been working since I was nine years old, beginning as a newspaper deliverer, store clerk, postal worker, and waiter. I worked my way through school and college waiting on tables (and also worked during summer vacations and holiday breaks). After college, I worked to build my career in the mutual fund business.

In all my working career, however, I've had only a single job that I could call real "work": when I was a pin-setter in the bowling alley of the Sea Girt (New Jersey) fire department. Other than that, all of my work has been fun, productive, and deeply fulfilling, even with a spiritual element.

The joy of work was beautifully expressed by Thomas Carlyle:

Blessed is he who has found his work; let him ask no other blessedness. . . . There is a perennial nobleness and even sacredness in work.

Lin-Manuel Miranda described Alexander Hamilton's standards for getting ahead in one's work in his hit Broadway musical *Hamilton*. To paraphrase:

The founding father with no father,

Got farther, by working harder,

by being smarter, and by being a self-starter.

Mr. Miranda described Hamilton this way to NPR, "All in the strength of his writing, he embodies the word's ability to make a difference."[2]

Hamilton would, I think, endorse the spirit of Carlyle's words, reflected, even enhanced, by the words of this familiar hymn:

Work, for the night is coming,

Under the sunset skies;

While their bright tints are glowing,

Work, for the daylight flies.

Work till the last beam fadeth,

Fadeth to shine no more;

Work, while the night is darkening,

When man's work is o'er.

---

[2]www.npr.org/2017/12/26/572622911/lin-manuel-miranda-on-disney-mixtapes-and-why-he-wont-try-to-top-hamilton.

You . . . and me . . . and the universe. My final reflection starts with an existential issue that applies to you, dear reader, and to me, and to every other human being who exists on the face of our planet Earth.

We may think of ourselves as small, merely a single one of Earth's seven billion (plus or minus) human beings. Yes, we enjoy the beauty of living. But we live for only a brief moment in time and space, and then we move on. But we're far *less* important than that.

Our Earth is but a single planet in the solar system, which in turn is part of the Milky Way galaxy, our huge galaxy 100,000 or so light-years in diameter. Our galaxy, in turn, is but one of at least 200 billion galaxies in our universe, each galaxy with more than 100 billion stars. If you want to measure the relative importance of a single human being, just do the math!

And yet . . . and yet to dwell on our own insignificance in the grand scheme of things doesn't seem particularly useful. There's work to be done here on Earth, and we'd best get on with it. We might begin by acting, before it's too late, to save our own planet. Beyond that, our task is to live productive lives, to raise our families, to contribute to our communities, and to serve to our nation and our global society.

Each of us human beings must be the best that we can be, helping others – especially those less privileged –

along the road of life. We must leave everything that we touch better than it was when we found it. Yes, we are here for only a short while, but isn't it our obligation to make the most of every moment of it?

We must remind ourselves each day that "even one person can make a difference." (Remember to apply that axiom to one's self!) That's the way that I've strived to live my own imperfect life, maybe even why I've survived for so long. Looking back from the vantage point of my 90th year on Earth, I can easily imagine that my mission of serving investors and the values I've established for Vanguard, the firm that I founded in 1974, will endure.

Stay the Course

I've usually used the phrase "stay the course" as one of the great rules of investment success. Ignore the day-to-day fluctuations in the stock market and focus on the long-term growth of the U.S. economy. But as I complete this memoir, "stay the course" is also a splendid rule for fighting our way through the inevitable ups and downs of the short spans of our existence on this Earth, and for enjoying a productive and honorable life well lived.

John C. Bogle's Afterword to *Enough*

A Personal Note about My Career

Back in 2007, I was invited to give a talk at a CEO Leadership Summit sponsored by Yale University. Since I was bound to be the old warhorse among the group, I settled on a subject that I thought would be both retrospective and prospective: "Why Do I Bother to Battle?" It happened that the television writers were on strike at the time, so on the theory that the summit participants might be suffering from an absence of late-night humor, I decided to frame my talk as one of those inverse "Top Ten" lists from the *Late Show with David Letterman*.

As comedy, my list might be wanting. (Remember, I was an economics major!) But as a summation of what has pushed me on during my entire life and what continues to push me on today, it's right on the mark.

10. Damned if I know why I bother to battle. I just do it, and I don't know how to stop.

9. Because, in all the nearly nine decades of my life I've never done anything *but* battle—as a boy delivering newspapers; then as a young man working as a waiter (in many venues), ticket seller, mail clerk, cub reporter, runner for a brokerage firm, even a pinsetter in a bowling alley (as I wrote earlier, a Sisyphean battle!); and as a man, fighting the battle for personal advancement, for attention, for innovation, for progress, for service to society, and yes, even for power and the hope of being remembered. (Might as well admit it!) That's one reason why I write books, including this one.

8. Because the great battlers of history have always been my heroes. Think Alexander Hamilton. Think Teddy Roosevelt. Think Woodrow Wilson. Heck, think Philadelphia's own Rocky Balboa.

7. Because all those battlers, finally, lost their battles. I battle to be the exception.

6. Because, in the mutual fund field, no one else in the system is battling to bring back our traditional values of trusteeship and our high promise of service to investors. Someone's got to do it. By the process of elimination, I got the job.

5. Because when the battler stands pretty much alone, he draws a lot more attention to the mission. If you have a large ego (I do), that's a nice extra dividend, especially because those who are *outside* the system—our "man in the street" investors, exemplified by the Bogleheads of the Internet—give me the strength to carry on.

4. Because, sad to say, I no longer play squash, and playing golf on grown-up courses is now something of a stretch. So what else can I do but transfer the spirit of those old battles on the fields of athletic combat onto the fields of combat to improve our society at large?

3. Because what I'm battling for—building our nation's financial system anew, in order to give our citizen/investors a fair shake—is *right*. Mathematically right. Philosophically right. Ethically right. Call it idealism, and it's as strong today as—maybe even stronger than—it was when I wrote that idealistic Princeton thesis 57 years ago. How could an idealist fail to fight such a battle?

2. Because, even as I battle, I love the give-and-take, the competition, the intellectual challenge of my field, the burning desire to leave everything that I touch better than I found it. Using Robert Frost's formulation, my battle is "a lover's quarrel" with our financial world.

1. Simply because I'm a battler by nature—born, bred, and raised to make my own way in life. Such a life demands the kind of passion evoked by the words of the great sculptor of Mount Rushmore, Gutzon Borglum: "Life is a kind of campaign. People have no idea what strength comes to one's soul and spirit through a good fight."

While I simply can't imagine that my own soul and spirit will ever fade, I know deep down that time is not on my side. So I'll continue to fight the battle until my mind and strength at last begin to dull. Only then, I hope many moons from now, will I take time to revel in the memories of all the wonderful battles I've fought during my long life. After all, paraphrasing Sophocles:

One must wait until the evening
To appreciate the splendor of the day.

Author's
Acknowledgments

This book was inspired by the short poem written by Kurt Vonnegut that appeared in the *New Yorker* in 2005. That poem inspired the commencement address I delivered at Georgetown University two years later, which in turn inspired me to think that the idea of "Enough" could be expanded to encompass reflections not only about money (the focus of the poem) but also about business and about life. (I should make it clear that the strong opinions I express on these issues do not necessarily reflect the views of Vanguard's present management.)

As I was considering the idea of the book, I quickly realized that I had been trancing on these ideas in a sort of uncoordinated way for at least several decades, indeed, in some sense back to my long-past youth. Indeed, many of the speeches I've delivered over the years seemed ready-made to fit into the organizing pattern that I developed for the book. Most had never been published, so putting the ideas—some old, some new, all relevant to the subject of *Enough*—into book form would give them an endurance possible in no other way.

I confess, however, that in perhaps a half-dozen cases, some of my words in the book and some of the quotations I've cited have appeared in my previously published works. Much as I was hesitant to do so, I concluded that if I had got it right the first time—and it amplified my theme this time—it would be foolish not to stay with the original version.

I want to thank Howard Means for helping me to pull all this material together. I also want to thank three readers of the manuscript for their helpful commentary: William J. Bernstein, neurologist, investment adviser, and prolific author, most recently of *A Splendid Exchange*; Andrew S. Clarke, a Vanguard principal who worked with me on *Common Sense on Mutual Funds* a decade ago; and Elliot McGuckin, PhD, of Pepperdine University, whose course "The Hero's Journey in Artistic Entrepreneurship and Technology" is an inspiring tribute to the relevance of classical ideals in our modern lives.

Without the help of my staff at Vanguard's Bogle Financial Markets Research Center, bringing the simple idea expressed in a short poem to its flowering into a book would have been virtually impossible. So I extend special thanks to Emily Snyder and Sara Hoffman for their efforts—always under the pressure of time—to fight their way through my inscrutable handwriting and to type and edit endlessly. I also salute Kevin P. Laughlin, my staff assistant for the past nine years, for his admirable performance, producing research on demand, checking accuracy, and making constructive editorial suggestions that made this a better book. Best of all, each of these wonderful souls did their work with infinite patience, good cheer, and professional excellence.

Speaking of patience and good cheer, I also thank Eve, my wonderful wife of 52 years, for her caring and loving support through all those years and through good times and times that were not so good, even as she wonders about my commitment to keep on battling, speaking, and writing books. Of course she's right to do so!

J. C. B.

Notes

The Great Seduction

p. xli   Reprinted from the *New York Times,* June 10, 2008. © 2008 The New York Times (www.nytimes .com). All rights reserved. Used by permission and protected by the Copyright Laws of the United States. The printing, copying, redistribution, or retransmission of the Material without express written permission is prohibited.

Introduction

p. 2   *According to the International Monetary Fund,*   John Cassidy, "Loan Rangers," *New Yorker,* July 28, 2008, 23.

p. 24   *I honor and love you:*   Plato, *The Apology* available at www.bartleby.com/2/1/1.html.

Chapter 1   Too Much Cost, Not Enough Value

p. 29   *Some men wrest a living*   I have been unable to locate the exact source for this epigram. I have taken the liberty of adding "and with their hands" to the original wording.

p. 31   *Most money-making activity*   Charles T. Munger, speech before the Foundation Financial Officers Group, Santa Monica, CA, October 14, 1998.

p. 36   *Mr. Prince was paid $138 million*   Compensation amounts taken from http://oversight.house.gov/documents/20080306165144.pdf.

p. 36   *Yet Mr. O'Neal's compensation*   Compensation amounts taken from http://oversight.house.gov/documents/20080306164458.pdf.

p. 37   *James E. Cayne . . . was paid*   Landon Thomas, "Down $900 Million or More, the Chairman of Bear Sells," *New York Times*, March 28, 2008, C1, and Andrew Ross Sorkin, "JP Morgan Pays $2 a Share for Bear Stearns," *New York Times*, March 17, 2008.

p. 38   *In 2007 alone, the 50 highest-paid hedge fund managers*   Jenny Anderson, "Wall Street Winners Get Billion-Dollar Paydays," *New York Times*, April 16, 2008, A1.

p. 40   *The number of Chartered Financial Analysts*   Alan Abelson, "Swarm of Analysts," *Barron's*, May 28, 2007, 5.

p. 41   *Over the past 50 years,*   Long-term stock returns are from author's calculations.

p. 44   *In 2007, the direct costs*   Investment intermediation costs data are from Bogle Financial Markets

Research Center estimates based on data from the Securities Industry and Financial Markets Association, Lipper Analytical Services, and Empirical Research Associates. I recognize the fragility of these data and continue to urge a thorough and independent economic analysis of the costs and benefits of our financial system.

p. 48   *There are questions so important*   Glen Weyl, Princeton University valedictory address, June 5, 2007, quoting Nobel laureate Robert Lucas.

Chapter 2   Too Much Speculation, Not Enough Investment

p. 50   *Keynes defined*   John Maynard Keynes, *The General Theory of Employment, Interest and Money* (New York: Harcourt, Brace & Company, 1936). Also available at www.marxists.org/reference/subject/economics/ keynes/general-theory/.

p. 51   *Listen to Warren Buffett,*   Quoted in Chairman's Letter, Berkshire Hathaway 1996 Annual Report, February 28, 1997. Also available at www .berkshirehathaway.com/letters/1996.html.

p. 51   *Benjamin Graham once pointed out,*   Benjamin Graham, *The Intelligent Investor* (orig. pub. 1949; New York: HarperCollins, 2005).

p. 53   *History tells us,*   Stock market returns are from author's calculations.

p. 56   *the annual rate of turnover*   Kenneth R. French, "The Cost of Active Investing," *Journal of Finance* (2008, forthcoming).

p. 57   *By the beginning of 2008,*   Futures and options totals are from the Chicago Board of Trade and Chicago Board Options Exchange.

p. 61   *Financial markets will not only respond*   Hyman P. Minsky, "The Modeling of Financial Instability: An Introduction," *Modelling and Simulation* 5 (1974).

p. 63   *In investing, tortoises,*   Peter L. Bernstein, "The 60/40 Solution," *Bloomberg Personal Finance,* January/February 2002.

p. 64   *Bernstein changed his mind.*   Peter L. Bernstein, "Are Policy Portfolios Obsolete?" *Economics & Portfolio Strategy*, March 1, 2003.

p. 69   *Trust is the cornerstone*   Henry Kaufman, *On Money and Markets: A Wall Street Memoir* (New York: McGraw-Hill Trade, 2001).

Chapter 3   Too Much Complexity, Not Enough Simplicity

p. 75   *The notional principal value of all derivatives*   Bank for International Settlements, *Quarterly Review,* June 2008.

p. 75 *$66 trillion gross domestic product (GDP)* CIA, *The 2008 World Factbook*.

p. 79 *As Benjamin Graham pointed out* "A Conversation with Benjamin Graham," *Financial Analysts Journal* 32 (5) (September/October 1976).

p. 81 *Let's compare* Investor returns are from author's calculations.

p. 84 *Paul Samuelson called the first index mutual fund* From author correspondence with Paul Samuelson.

p. 86 *What the wise man* Lisa Sandler, "Mania to Buy Back Stock Is Going Too Far, Some Say," *Wall Street Journal*, September 18, 1987.

p. 86 *There are three i's* Brian M. Carney, "The Credit Crisis Is Going to Get Worse (Interview with Theodore J. Forstmann)," *Wall Street Journal*, July 5, 2008, A9.

p. 89 *It's hardly surprising,* Fund flows data from Strategic Insight.

p. 90 *In fact it is clear that fund investors* Jonathan Shieber, "Read's Exit Is a Boost for Clean Tech—Calpers Head Aims to Start Own Fund Focusing on Sector," *Wall Street Journal,* April 29, 2008, C11.

p. 93 *The fundamental market failure* David Swensen, *Unconventional Success* (New York: Free Press, 2005).

Chapter 4　Too Much Counting, Not Enough Trust

p. 98　*Not everything that counts*　Alice Calaprice, ed., *Dear Professor Einstein: Albert Einstein's Letters to and from Children* (Amherst, NY: Prometheus Books, 2002).

p. 106　*On average, the projections*　Earnings predictions data from Morgan Stanley 1981–2001, author's estimate thereafter.

p. 107　*The aggregate profits*　Profits and GDP rates from author's calculations using data from the Bureau of Economic Analysis.

p. 111　*serial acquirers*　Jeffrey Sonnenfeld, "Expanding without Managing," *New York Times*, June 12, 2002, A29.

p. 111　*in 1946, Warren Avis had an idea.*　Michael Kinsley, "We Try Harder (but What's the Point?)," *New York Times*, May 16, 2007, A19.

p. 115　*It is true that Nelson*　From the Bishop of London's sermon commemorating the 200th anniversary of the Battle of Trafalgar, October 24, 2005. Available at www.stpauls.co.uk/page .aspx?theLang=001lngdef&pointerid=754804RF A3tsB3ydyNHKhPcNWK0U8O8J.

p. 117 *We are . . . living at an age* David Boyle, "The Tyranny of Numbers" (lecture to the Royal Society of Arts at Gateshead, U.K., October 18, 2001).

p. 117 *Trust is everything,* Bill George, *True North* (San Francisco: Jossey-Bass, 2007).

p. 118 *The first step is to measure* Daniel Yankelovich, quoted in Adam Smith (George J. W. Goodman), *Supermoney* (New York: Random House, 1972).

Chapter 5 Too Much Business Conduct, Not Enough Professional Conduct

p. 121 *The article in* Daedalus *defined a profession* Howard Gardner and Lee S. Shulman, "The Professions in America Today: Crucial but Fragile," *Daedalus* 134 (3) (Summer 2005).

p. 126 *"Calvinist rectitude"* Roger Lowenstein, "The Purist," *New York Times Magazine*, December 28, 2003, 44.

p. 129 *Managers of other people's money* Adam Smith, *The Wealth of Nations*, 1776, available online at www .adamsmith.org/smith/won-intro.htm.

p. 130 *In 1980, the compensation* John Bogle, *The Battle for the Soul of Capitalism* (New Haven, CT: Yale University Press, 2005).

p. 131   *CEO compensation . . . at truly awesome levels,*
Updated CEO compensation figures from a
study by ERI Economic Research and the *Wall
Street Journal* and data from the Bureau of Labor
Statistics, quoted at www.aflcio.org/corporatewatch/
paywatch/pay/index.cfm.

p. 132   *Benjamin Graham got this issue exactly right.*
Benjamin Graham, *The Intelligent Investor* (orig.
pub. 1949; New York: HarperCollins, 2005).

p. 140   *I am an American*   Felix Rohatyn, "Free, Wealthy and
Fair," *Wall Street Journal*, November 11, 2003, A18.

Chapter 6   Too Much Salesmanship, Not Enough Stewardship

p. 142   *In 1951, mutual fund assets*   Mutual fund sta-
tistics from Wiesenberger *Investment Company
Yearbook*, the Investment Company Institute,
Morningstar, and Strategic Insight.

p. 143   *In 1951, the average fund investor*   Turnover
rates from the New York Stock Exchange and
Morningstar.

p. 146   *During the 1950s, and 1960s*   Fund formation statistics from author's calculations and
Morningstar.

Chapter 7   Too Much Management, Not Enough Leadership

p. 159   *There is a profound difference*   Warren Bennis and Joan Goldsmith, *Learning to Lead* (New York: Perseus, 1997).

p. 168   *It is the merest pretense*   John Maynard Keynes, *The General Theory of Employment, Interest and Money* (New York: Harcourt, Brace & Company, 1936).

p. 175   *What distinguishes a superior company from*   Robert Greenleaf, *Servant Leadership: A Journey into the Nature of Legitimate Power and Greatness* (Mahwah, NJ: Paulist Press, 1991).

p. 176   *Value profit chain*   James L. Heskett, W. Earl Sasser, and Leonard A. Schlesinger, *The Value Profit Chain: Treat Employees Like Customers and Customers Like Employees* (New York: Free Press, 2002).

p. 178   *When you've built an institution*   Jim Collins, "The Secret of Enduring Greatness," *Fortune*, May 5, 2008.

Chapter 8   Too Much Focus on Things, Not Enough Focus on Commitment

p. 187   *Are you in earnest?*   Apparently from a loose translation of Goethe's *Faust*. See www.goethesociety.org/pages/quotescom.html.

p. 187   *Until one is committed,*   W. H. Murray, *The Scottish Himalayan Expedition* (London: J. M. Dent & Sons, 1951).

Chapter 9   Too Many Twenty-First-Century Values, Not Enough Eighteenth-Century Values

p. 200   *Had Franklin possessed the soul of a true capitalist,* H. W. Brands, *Benjamin Franklin—The First American* (New York: Doubleday, 2000), 166.

p. 202   *Every individual intends only his own security;*   Adam Smith, *The Wealth of Nations*, 1776, available online at www.adamsmith.org/smith/won-intro.htm.

p. 203   *[The impartial spectator] calls to us,*   Adam Smith, *The Theory of Moral Sentiments*, 1759. Available online at www.adamsmith.org/smith/tms/tms-index.htm.

p. 207   *Authentic leaders genuinely desire*   Bill George, *Authentic Leadership: Rediscovering the Secrets to Creating Lasting Value* (San Francisco: Jossey-Bass, 2003).

p. 208   *The real test*   Tamar Frankel, *Trust and Honesty: America's Business Culture at a Crossroads* (New York: Oxford University Press, 2006).

p. 210   *In reality, there is, perhaps, no one of our natural passions* Benjamin Franklin, *The Autobiography of Benjamin*

Franklin. Available online at www.ushistory.org/ franklin/autobiography/singlehtml.htm.

Chapter 10   Too Much "Success," Not Enough Character

p. 211   *I said to the dog,*   Fred B. Craddock, *The Cherry Log Sermons* (Louisville, KY: Westminster John Knox Press, 2001).

p. 220   *I long to accomplish*   Attributed to Helen Keller in Charles L. Wallis, *The Treasure Chest* (San Francisco: HarperSanFrancisco, 1983).

p. 220   *The treasury of America*   Woodrow Wilson and Ronald J. Pestritto, *Woodrow Wilson: The Essential Political Writings* (Lanham, MD: Lexington Books, 2005).

p. 221   *Highly educated young people are*   David Brooks, "'Moral Suicide,' à la Wolfe," *New York Times*, November 16, 2004, A27.

What's Enough For Me? For You? For America?

p. 230   *According to an authoritative article in* American Psychologist *magazine,*   Richard M. Ryan and Edward L. Deci, "Self-Determination Theory and the Facilitation of Intrinsic Motivation,

Social Development, and Well-Being," *American Psychologist*, January 2000.

p. 239 *"Do Americans have enough?"* Steve Landsburg, "A Lot More Than a Penny Earned," *Wall Street Journal*, June 5, 2008, A19. Review of *Whatever Happened to Thrift?* by Ronald T. Wilcox (New Haven, CT: Yale University Press, 2008).

p. 240 *the wealthiest 5 percent* Sam Roberts, "New York's Gap between Rich and Poor Is Nation's Widest, Census Says," *New York Times*, August 29, 2007, B3.

p. 241 *this stark financial polarization.* David Brooks, "The Great Seduction," *New York Times*, June 10, 2008, A23.

p. 244 *True story, Word of Honor:* Kurt Vonnegut, "Joe Heller," *New Yorker*, May 16, 2008, 38. Reprinted with permission. Copyright © Donald C. Farber, Trustee of trust under the will of Kurt Vonnegut, Jr.

p. 246 *I cannot rest from travel*: Alfred, Lord Tennyson, *Poems* (London: Penguin, 1985).

Index

345

Praise for *Enough*

"Jack Bogle's passionate cry of *Enough.* contains a thought-provoking litany of life lessons regarding our individual roles in commerce and society. Employing a seamless mix of personal anecdotes, hard evidence, and all-too-often-underrated subjective admonitions, Bogle challenges each of us to aspire to become better members of our families, our professions, and our communities. Rarely do so few pages provoke so much thought. *Read this book*."

—David F. Swensen
Chief Investment Officer
Yale University

"*Enough.* gives new meaning to the words 'commitment,' 'accountability,' and 'stewardship.' Bogle writes with clarity and passion, and his standards make him a role model for all of us. *Enough.* is must reading for millions of U.S. investors disenchanted by today's culture of greed, accounting distortions, corporate malfeasance, and oversight failure."

—Arthur Levitt
Former Chairman
U.S. Securities and Exchange Commission

"Jack Bogle's wonderful, thoughtful, helpful, and fun-filled little book inspired me to create my own title: *Never Enough of Jack Bogle!*"

—The late Peter L. Bernstein
Author of *Capital Ideas Evolving* and *Against the Gods*

"Jack Bogle, the 'conscience of Wall Street,' single-handedly founded the Vanguard Group—still the nation's only *mutual* mutual fund organization—and then grew it into the gentle giant that funds the retirements, educations, and philanthropic goals of millions of Americans. Now, in *Enough.,* he distills his half-century of observations on the capital markets, and on life in general, into a few hundred entertaining pages—required reading for those concerned about their own future, their family's future, and the nation's future."

—William J. Bernstein
Author of *A Splendid Exchange* and
The Four Pillars of Investing

"This is an impressive message from a distinguished businessman. It will challenge all decision makers to consider the sufficiency and direction of their lives and work. What do we mean by *Enough? Enough* of what? *Enough* for what purpose? Feast here and reflect."

—Robert F. Bruner
Dean and Charles C. Abbott Professor of Business Administration,
Darden Graduate School of Business, University of Virginia

"From one 'battler' to another: Thank you for putting in one little book the premise for an active, long life. A primer for those who will abjure complacency and just wanting more, who'd rather focus on the joy of trying to move some ball downfield."

—Ira Millstein
Senior Partner, Weil Gotshal & Manges LLP

"What went wrong? What can, and should, go right? The great Jack Bogle has the answers. *Enough.* will leave you hungry for more."

—James Grant
Editor of *Grant's Interest Rate Observer*

"The balances one must create in investing, in running a business, and in life more generally are simply and clearly stated in Jack's most recent book, *Enough.* Unfortunately there are not enough Jack Bogles around in today's world of instant gratification. *Enough.* should be must reading for business students and corporate board members."

—David L. Sokol
Chairman, MidAmerican Energy Holdings Company

"One Jack Bogle has more horse sense than the entire Wall Street herd. If you open this book, you'll be hooked after the first paragraph, as I was. But keep on reading. This small book pays huge dividends."

—Alan S. Blinder
Co-Director, Princeton University Center for
Economic Policy Studies, and Former Vice Chairman,
Board of Governors of the Federal Reserve System

"Although *Enough.* is presented in a small volume, John Bogle's wisdom is writ large and profound. The messages are particularly meaningful as we all reel from the moral, economic, and financial meltdown that confronts us today."

—William H. Donaldson
Former Chairman, U.S. Securities and Exchange Commission

"This is the book that all current Bogle enthusiasts have awaited and one that will inspire countless future Bogle enthusiasts. It offers both mesmerizingly candid autobiographical insight from one of the nation's most pioneering financiers and a wise handbook of life perspectives and savvy investment. These personal reflections eschew technical financial jargon and provide the path to escape the desperate chase for 'more' regardless of 'meaning.' Terms like *trust, value, success, satisfaction, stewardship, character*, and *contribution* are woven together into a life tapestry that reminds experienced readers how they can master the treadmill of their lives and guides young readers in how to control their destiny from the start of their careers. When Jack Bogle speaks, CEOs, scholars, and the rest of us all listen . . . or *should* listen."

—Professor Jeffrey Sonnenfeld
Senior Associate Dean, Yale School of Management